Chicanas of 18th Street

Chicanas of 18th Street

Narratives of a Movement from Latino Chicago

LEONARD G. RAMÍREZ

with

YENELLI FLORES

MARÍA GAMBOA

ISAURA GONZÁLEZ

VICTORIA PÉREZ

MAGDA RAMÍREZ-CASTAÑEDA

CRISTINA VITAL

UNIVERSITY OF ILLINOIS PRESS

Urbana, Chicago, and Springfield

Library of Congress Cataloging-in-Publication Data
Chicanas of 18th Street : narratives of a movement from Latino
Chicago / Leonard G. Ramírez ; with Yenelli Flores ... [et al.].
    p.   cm.—(Latinos in Chicago and the Midwest)
Includes bibliographical references and index.
ISBN 978-0-252-03618-7 (hardcover : alk. paper)
ISBN 978-0-252-07812-5 (pbk. : alk. paper)
1. Mexican American women—Illinois—Chicago—Biography.
2. Community activists—Illinois—Chicago—Biography.
3. Mexican Americans—Illinois—Chicago—Social conditions—
20th century. 4. Chicano movement—Illinois—Chicago.
5. Pilsen (Chicago, Ill.)—Social conditions—20th century.
6. Chicago (Ill.)—Social conditions—20th century.
I. Ramírez, Leonard G. II. Title: Chicanas of Eighteenth Street.
F548.9.M5C55   2011
305.8968'72073077311—dc23   2011022668

Dedicamos este libro a la memoria de
Isaura González y María Saucedo
y a todas aquellas mujeres que han
luchado por justicia social

In memory of
Isaura González and María Saucedo
and to all those women who have
fought for social justice

Contents

Illustrations

Preface

At the end of the 1990s, a social gathering unexpectedly set me on a journey that was to last more than a decade. That night, a group of six women asked that I help them document the experiences that contributed to their activism and eventual involvement in a political network based in Chicago's Pilsen community. The project was unique for several reasons. Little had been written about Chicago's Mexicano/Chicano Movement in the 1970s. Even less was known about the participation of radical Chicanas during the days of the Movimiento in Chicago. Only those who participated in the activist 1960s and 1970s might be aware of the importance of independent radical Mexicano/Chicano political networks and the militant leadership of Mexicanas/Chicanas during those lively days of Chicago's Movimiento. The initiative was also unusual in that it was to be, as much as possible, a collaborative endeavor.

The women decided early on to highlight their individual accounts rather than concentrate on lengthy analysis. Their belief was that focusing on their personal reflections might reach a broader audience, particularly new generations of social justice activists. The expectation was that the issues, community campaigns, and people included in the women's testimonials might provoke the interest of others. The narratives would then provide a starting point for activists and researchers who wished to further explore the events and themes of that period.

The centrality of the women's narratives is reflected in the structure of the work. The introductory essay provides a brief historical framework and a rough sketch of the political influences and context that helped to shape

Mexicano/Chicano activism in Pilsen. The chapter "Homecoming, 1997" introduces the women. The next six chapters are taken directly from the 1998 interviews with the six activists, although follow-up discussions occurred through 2009. Historical notes, explanations, comments, and academic references that surfaced within the core chapters are relegated to footnotes. The final chapter is a reflection on the nature of these women's political activism and some brief closing remarks on their complex relationship to feminism, the character of the Comité, and the problems that it encountered that are still relevant today.

Both individual and group interviews were conducted with the six women throughout the entire project. Collective sessions reviewed themes related to the events and politics of the period or focused on specific aspects of the undertaking itself. There was an attempt to have at least one other woman present during the personal interviews. This was done to create a more supportive environment, and the participation of another female activist was expected to assist in the recollection of important details from the period. Interviews and administrative meetings lasted about two hours, most of which were recorded.

The project encountered many roadblocks. The group nearly decided to abandon the venture on several occasions due to feelings stirred by revisiting old and sometimes painful memories from that period of intense mobilization. The attack on the Twin Towers on September 11, 2001, raised questions about how a book about 1970s radicalism would be received given the blinding patriotism that overwhelmed the nation and a jingoistic media that did little to diminish the thunder of the war chorus. George W. Bush administration's manipulation of the crisis to launch an unprovoked war against the Iraqi people led some of us to consider abandoning the project altogether or possibly delaying it until a return to a more sober time. The confounding of radicalism with extremism and terrorism by conservatives and others in the wake of 9-11 seemed to offer yet another reason why the project should not go forward. In each instance, we decided that sharing these recollections with those with an interest and passion for social justice was more important than our personal misgivings or succumbing to the temptation to seek temporary refuge from the tremors of current events.

The biographical fragments of these women's lives are divided into three sections: early home and school life, the road that led the women to Pilsen and the Comité, and the collapse of the vision that brought them together into a collective political process. Although the intent was to privilege the voices of those involved, the women's words are edited, passed through various filters, and represented by me. Although I attempted to minimize my presence in the core chapters, this does not deny that my participation and knowledge of those times inform these accounts both directly and indirectly. I am an insider who lived through a portion of their herstories. I was an active participant in the Comité and shared its values and general political orientation. Yet, I have my own sense of that time and have arrived at an interpretation of it that does not totally coincide with all of those who were involved. I have tried to reserve much of my overt evaluation and sense of that period to the introduction and conclusion and at the edges of the document in the form of footnotes.

The vignette that introduces each chapter describes one of the major political events of that period and was written collaboratively or was a memory that I drafted and later developed with the assistance of one of the other contributors. The collective voice of the group is present in the epilogue and is largely woven from the six individual interviews. A Chicago time line, which includes a selection of national events that influenced local politics, is provided, although it is a developing reference, incomplete and in need of further elaboration and verification.

References to political conflicts are intended to promote reflection of these issues. Veterans of that period from every political tendency made valuable contributions. Yet, historically rich experiences contain many lessons and challenging questions. At the onset of the Movement, there was greater unity. Even when differences arose, it was often necessary to work in alliance with others in order to make progress. There was a moment when the powerful effects of racism and class marginalization created strong bonds of solidarity. Initially, the them-against-us perspective tied activists to one another despite political differences, personalities, and organizational allegiances. Issues related to the fundamental sources of local community division are among the historical artifacts that have yet to be recovered, examined, and catalogued. There has certainly been no thorough overview of the 1970s in Chicago or even an initial assessment of the relative merits and limitations of political perspectives or organizational strategies. Perhaps, this book might motivate such work.

Understanding the nature of the divisions that arose during the 1960s and 1970s is important for contemporary political mobilization. Massive protests in support of immigrant rights in the first decade of the twenty-first century and the subsequent differences and rivalries that surfaced within the ranks of the immigrant-rights leadership are reminders of the continuous need to identify, clarify, and understand the roots of tension among leaders and not merely assume that it is solely a question of personalities, ambitions, or a general tendency for all social movements to splinter and disintegrate over time. Alternative strategies to advance community agendas continue to stifle Mexican political empowerment. The testimonies of the six women may help to shed some light on these issues.

Public figures and others that we thought appropriate to make part of the historical record are identified by first and last names. In some instances, the usage of first names only or the avoidance of names altogether was done to shield identities when information might be seen as sensitive or unflattering. Five of the women agreed to use their legal names for this book. *Yenelli Flores* is a pseudonym. I have followed the 1970s Chicago convention of using the bifurcated *Mexicano/Chicano* to refer to those claiming either a Mexican or a Chicano identity. In the 1970s, identity was a contentious issue among some activists, and this formulation was used to bridge the gap. When using *Mexican, Mexicano,* or *Chicano* independently, the referent should be understood in context. *Anglo* or *Euroamerican* is used to denote non-Latino Whites. The use of the upper case in *Movement* or *Movimiento* is used when referring to Mexicano/Chicano political activism. The use of the lower case *m* refers to the broader political "movement" of that era, which would include among others the civil rights, antiwar, and women's movements.

We thank many people for their assistance. First and foremost is Héctor Gamboa, a Comité leader who selflessly volunteered to help in every aspect of this endeavor. His willingness to share his memory, energy, and time is only second in importance to his political wisdom. Claudio Gaete helped in all areas related to inclusion of artifacts from the time: photographs, leaflets, and other images. Alicia Amador, Nancy (Rusty) Barcelo, Juan Calixto, Susan Carmona, Father John Harrington, Carlos Heredia, Omar López, María Ovalle, Santos Rivera, Diana Solís, Patricia Wright, and Antonio Zavala contributed to the development of the time line and provided valuable details that are particularly important given the scarcity of written records and the fallibility of human memory. Theresa Christenson and Mitzi Ramos, two University of Illinois at Chicago (UIC) doctoral students, provided editing assistance and served as technical guides. Steve Tozer, Bernardo Gallegos, and Jonell Smith read sections of the manuscript and made suggestions. Gerardo DeAnda, Elizabeth Gomez, Rebecca Piñeda, Adrian Ramírez, Tlaloc Rodríguez, Enrique Rojas, and Nikki Valentine provided additional student assistance. I also thank Areli Castañeda and Rosa Ortiz along with the entire LARES staff at UIC who lent their support throughout the project. Special thanks go to Lorenzo Duran, Margaret Kleist, Elizabeth Ortiz, Jose Perales,

Harold Roth, Kim Sanborn, Andrew Sund, Mary Kay Vaughan, and the late Marguerite Ortega, who served as sources of inspiration and encouragement. I also wish to acknowledge the support of the Ramirez family that has always been unconditional and fundamental. I also thank Joan Catapano, Daniel Nasset, and Jennifer Reichlin at the University of Illinois Press and copy editor Mary Lou Kowaleski for their guidance and patience. This collaborative experiment was not a linear process, and many missteps happened along the way. All those mentioned helped to make this a better book. Although the six women were involved in most aspects of this project, I take full responsibility for the inaccuracies and errors that have undoubtedly occurred in this fledgling attempt to add to the discussion of the 1970s Mexicana/o / Chicana/o left in Chicago.

Leonard G. Ramírez

Abbreviations, Organizations, and Programs

Acronyms

APO	Asociación Pro–Derechos Obreros (Association for Workers Rights)
ATM	August Twenty-Ninth Movement
BPP	Black Panther Party
CAMI/CAMY	Comité Anti-Militarización (Anti-Militarization Committee)/Committee Against the Militarization of Youth
CAR	Committee Against Racism
CASA-HGT	Centro de Acción Social Autónoma—Hermandad General de Trabajadores (Center for Autonomous Social Action—General Brotherhood of Workers)
CBSU	Chicano-Boricua Student Union
CCHE	Coordinating Council for Higher Education
CMSU	Chicano-Mexicano Student Union
CP/CPUSA	Communist Party / Communist Party USA
CPS	Chicago Public Schools
CSC	Community Safety Committee (María Saucedo Safety Committee)
CSFS	Committee in Support of the Farah Strikers
CTA	Chicago Transit Authority
CTM	Confederación de Trabajadores Mexicanos (Confederation of Mexican Workers)

Cuadro	El Cuadro Latinoamericano (Latin American Group)
El Comité–MINP	El Comité—Movimiento de Izquierda Nacional Puertorriqueño (The Committee—Puerto Rican National Left Movement)
FALN	Fuerzas Armadas de Liberación Nacional (Armed Forces of National Liberation)
FLOC	Farm Labor Organizing Committee
FPCC	Fair Play for Cuba Committee
FUSP	Federación Universitaria Socialista Puertorriqueña (Puerto Rican Socialist Federation of the University)
InCAR	International Committee Against Racism
IRC	Independent Radical Caucus (WSA-SDS)
JOC	Juventud Obrera Católica (Young Catholic Worker)
LADO	Latin American Defense Organization
LARES	Latin American Recruitment and Educational Services
LARP	Latin American Recruitment Program (now LARES)
LAST	Latin American Studies (now LALS, Latin American and Latino Studies program at UIC)
LASU	Latin American Student Union
LRUP	La Raza Unida Party (in Illinois, El Partido de La Raza Unida)
LULAC	League of United Latin American Citizens
LYHS	Latino Youth High School
MACE	Mexican American Council on Education
MEChA	Movimiento Estudiantil Chicano de Aztlán (Chicano Student Movement of Aztlán)
MeSA	Mexican Students of Aztlán
MSC	María Saucedo Committee (Comité María Saucedo)
MTO	Mexican Teachers Organization
NACCS	National Association of Chicano and Chicana Studies (previously National Association of Chicano Studies)
NEIU	Northeastern Illinois University
NLF	National Liberation Front (Vietnam)
NOW	National Organization of Women
OLAS	Organization of Latin American Students
OTEP	Organización de Teatros del Pueblo (Organization of People's Theaters)
PLM	Partido Liberal Mexicano (Mexican Liberal Party)
PNCC	Pilsen Neighbors Community Council

PLP/PL	Progressive Labor Party / Progressive Labor
PSP	Puerto Rican Socialist Party
RCOCC	Rafael Cintron-Ortiz Cultural Center / Rafael Cintron-Ortiz Latino Cultural Center, University of Illinois at Chicago
RCP	Revolutionary Communist Party (previously RU)
RU	Revolutionary Union
RYM I	Revolutionary Youth Movement I (Weatherman)
RYM II	Revolutionary Youth Movement II
SDS	Students for a Democratic Society
SELA	Sociedad Estudiantil Latinoamericana (Society of Latin American Students)
SMC	Student Mobilization Committee
SNCC	Student Nonviolent Coordinating Committee
SWP	Socialist Workers Party
TFWU	Texas Farm Workers Union
UFAI	United Front Against Imperialism
UFW	United Farm Workers
UIC	University of Illinois at Chicago
UICC	University of Illinois at Chicago Circle
UIMC	University of Illinois Medical Center
UIUC	University of Illinois Urbana-Champaign
U-M	University of Michigan
UNO	United Neighborhood Organization
UPRS	Union for Puerto Rican Students
YIP	Youth International Party (Yippie)
YLO	Young Lords Organization (Chicago)
YLP	Young Lords Party (New York)
YPO	Young Patriots Organization
YSA	Young Socialist Alliance (SWP youth group)
WCYC	With Chicanos You Can (Radio Arte)
WSA	Worker Student Alliance
WUO	Weather Underground Organization (previously Weatherman)

Other Groups, Organizations, and Programs

La Alianza Federal de Pueblos Libres (Federal Alliance of Independent Communities)

Brown Berets
Casa Aztlán
El Centro de la Causa (Latin American Youth Center)
Chicano Mental Health Clinic
Chispa (Spark)
Círculo de Obreros Católicos (Circle of Catholic Workers)
Comité, The (Chicago Pilsen activist network)
Kalpulli (Community)
Mujeres Latinas en Acción (Latina Women in Action)
National Teacher Corps
Pana Pa' Ti (Partner for You)
Pilsen Community Planning Council
Right to Read program
Spanish Action Committee of Chicago
Teatro de los Barrios or Teatro del Barrio (community theater, people's theater)
United Slaves
Young Men's Christian Association

Chicago Movement
Time Line

1965
SEPTEMBER 8   First UFW nationwide grape boycott lasts five years

1966
JUNE 12–15   Division Street Riots, anger erupts over police brutality against Puerto Ricans
JUNE   SACC formed by the Catholic Church through the Cardinal's Committee as a response to the riots
SEPTEMBER   LADO formed and headed by Obed López-Zacarias to advocate for Puerto Rican families in Humboldt Park

1967
FLOC founded in Toledo, Ohio, by Baldemar Velásquez

1968
APRIL   OLAS founded by Carlos Heredia, Guillermina Heredia, Ada López, Omar López, and Nora Villarreal at Loop Junior College, Chicago
First Chicano generation mural in Chicago, *Metafísica,* also called *Peace,* an antiwar mural painted by Mario Castillo, located outside the Halsted Urban Progress Center at Halsted and Cullerton Streets (Adrian Lozano painted first Mexican-style mural at Hull-House in 1940)
OLAS demonstration at Mexican Consulate condemning the October 2, 1968, Tlatelolco Massacre at the Plaza de las Tres Culturas in Mexico City
Young Lords gang reorganized as Young Lords Organization under the leadership of Jose "Cha Cha" Jimenez and Ralph Rivera

1969

MARCH 27–31 First National Chicano Youth Liberation Conference, hosted by Crusade for Justice, Denver, Colorado; Chicago OLAS members participate

JUNE SDS National Convention, Chicago Coliseum; split produces various factions, including RYM I and RYM II and WSA led by PLP

APO founded by Pablo Torres, Saul Medina, and Reverend James Colleran, pastor of Saint Vitus Catholic Church

Benito Juárez Free People's Clinic opens at Howell House

Harrison High School student walkout demanding Mexican American teachers and counselors

Historic peace truce of 18th Street gangs: Ambrose, Latin Counts, Morgan Street Duces, Rampants, and the North Side gang the Latin Kings in order to travel together and participate in the National Chicano Youth Liberation Conference in Denver, Colorado

LADO opens Centro Pedro Albizu Campos Health Clinic, Para la Salud del Pueblo

YLO opens its Ramón Emeterio Betances Free Health Clinic

1970

MARCH 25–29 Second National Chicano Youth Liberation Conference, hosted by Crusade for Justice, Denver, Colorado

MAY 24 Elgin Watch ad appearing in Chicago Tribune suggests that Emiliano Zapata "Would kill to obtain an Elgin watch"

JUNE 7 Five thousand march to Chicago Tribune Tower to protest racial stereotype of Emiliano Zapata as bandit; Dr. Javier Prieto is spokesperson

JUNE 13–15 Midwest Chicano Committee on Mass Media, Northwestern University; Arthur Carrillo, Benny Quiroz, and Magda Ramírez-Castañeda elected as officers

AUGUST 29 First National Chicano Moratorium against the Vietnam War, protesting the disproportionate number of Chicano casualties, the largest Chicano antiwar demonstration of the Vietnam era; Los Angeles, California, journalist Rubén Salazar killed

SEPTEMBER 7 Report on First National Chicano Moratorium provided by Froben Lozada, chairman, Chicano Studies at Merritt College, Oakland, California, hosted by Casa Aztlán, LASU (UICC), and OLAS

APRIL La Raza Unida Party wins majority of the city council seats in Crystal City, Texas

Casa Aztlán murals painted by Ray Patlan

Howell House renamed Casa Aztlán; community members named to the board; Martin Cabrera becomes director; Aztlán operates with an all-volunteer staff and becomes the center for the Chicano Movement in Chicago

Latin American Student Union formed at UICC by Gilbert De Leon and Magda Ramírez-Castañeda

Teatro de la Raza formed by OLAS with students from Harrison High School: María Aguilar (Gamboa), Héctor Gamboa, Victor Heredia, and others, including Martha Gómez, Guillermina Heredia, Benny Pintor, and Magda Ramírez (Castañeda), with assistance and direction from Jesus "Chuy" Negrete; practices held at El Centro de la Causa

1971

SUMMER El Teatro Campesino performs at St. Joseph's (El Centro de la Causa)

FALL Latin American Youth Center (El Centro de la Causa) opens as a community agency

El Cuadro Latinoamericano at UICC formed by students entering from Loop College and area high schools

Harrison High School Bilingual Program, with the support of teacher Dolores Guerrero and her assistant Ricarda Sainz, becomes a base for Chicano Movement initiatives (such as Teatro de la Raza and People of the Sun newsletter)

National Teacher Corps, with a community committee, enrolls thirty Chicano students to be the first generation of bilingual education–trained teachers from UICC; ASPIRA (aspire) of Illinois recruits thirty Puerto Rican students for the program

1972

MAY 4 Farah workers, mostly Mexicana/Chicana women, strike in New Mexico and Texas; CSFS begins shortly thereafter; Comité sponsors regular Saturday picket lines at Carson Pirie Scott and Wieboldt's stores; Farah pants damaged at one weekend protest

JUNE 30 Twelve people arrested in blockade of buses at 18th Street and Blue Island; demonstration, led by APO, is first of three demonstrations against the CTA

SEPTEMBER 1–4 Eighteen Illinois delegates, including Magda Ramírez-Castañeda (Illinois chairperson) and Cristina Vital (Illinois delegate), attend the First Raza Unida Party Convention in El Paso, Texas

SEPTEMBER 25 Seven hundred to one thousand individuals attend peaceful, APO-sponsored demonstration at 18th Street and Ashland; melee ensues after police harassment; CTA buses taken over, seven buses and police cars damaged, thirty-two people jailed, one hospitalized, and four policemen injured

NOVEMBER 20 Discussions held with Dr. Lee, District 19 superintendent, with the Chicago Board of Education on process to request a new school; five-year struggle begins

DECEMBER 20 Petition for a new school with three thousand names delivered to Dr. Lee's office

DECEMBER Librería Nuestro Continente opens

Concerned residents and PNCC undertake feasibility study to build a new school in the neighborhood

National farmworkers' lettuce boycott

Puerto Rican community representatives meet with UICC to discuss the need to establish a program for Latino recruitment and support

Six hundred students walk out of Harrison High School to protest the war in Vietnam; U.S. flag taken down and Mexican flag raised; Tu Raza Club focuses on Chicano identity and acts as a counter to the conservative Spanish Club

1973

JANUARY 22 Sit-in by sixty people at Superintendent Dr. Lee's office protesting delays in building a high school in Pilsen

FEBRUARY 24 APO benefit dance for Rutila Rico Mendoza, a young girl injured in APO demonstration

MARCH 29 Eight hundred people rally to demand a new school for the Pilsen community

APRIL Chicano Conference, Reflexiones de la Raza (reflections of a people), Chicano/Indian American House, University of Iowa

MAY César Chávez leads hunger strike and national lettuce boycott

SPRING Froebel Uprising, organized by college students from University of Iowa's Chicano and Indian Cultural Center and Pilsen community leaders (not civic organizations) to demand a new school for the Pilsen community, twelve arrested; three days of rallies and protest follow

JUNE 9 Latina Women's Conference, La Mujer Despierta, cosponsored by National Education Task Force de La Raza and Centro de la Causa, held at El Centro de la Causa in Chicago

JUNE 13 Chicago Board of Education votes to build a new high school in Pilsen; community demands role in site selection and urges board to hire a Latino architect; Adrian Lozano eventually selected

SEPTEMBER 27   At UICC, thirty-nine people arrested while protesting the vandalization of Latino-recruitment office and inadequate institutional support

NOVEMBER 7   UICC student demonstrations continue over inadequate recruitment and enrollment of Latino students on campus

FALL   UFW Caravan, César Chávez speaks at El Centro de la Causa and at UICC and is housed at Providence of God in Pilsen

Angel Moreno from El Partido de La Raza Unida runs as an independent in the Seventh Congressional District in Illinois

APO post-office struggle for fair testing and the hiring of Latinos

Chicago 21 Plan unveiled by Chicago Central Area Committee; community sees it as a gentrification plan that will uproot working-class Mexicans

CA. 1973   Margarito Resendo Padilla shot; APO leads campaign against INS

PCPC is formed under the leadership of Juan Velásquez (also referred to as John Velásquez or Mama John) of El Centro de la Causa, Juan Morales of PNCC, and Dorothy Cutler of Casa Aztlán in response to the Chicago 21 Plan

Statewide Latina conference leads to formation of Mujeres Latinas en Acción

1974

MARCH 9   Chicago International Women's Day Demonstration in Chicago; Farah contingent organized by the Comité

MARCH   Compañia Trucha formed with ex-members of Teatro de La Raza with a collective, nontraditional, multiple director, and antihierarchical model of leadership; María Gamboa becomes a key director

NOVEMBER   Librería Nuestro Continente closes

FALL   PNCC organizes Chicago boycott of nine community schools to protest lack of timetable for school completion

Comité network discusses reorganization into a collective; "party building" phase of Comité begins

Farah strike settled with the Amalgamated Clothing Workers of America; Farah operations moved outside the United States in 1976

Latino Institute formed, initially a community project and the result of a citywide effort of activists to develop health and education plans as well as a research agenda

Latino Youth High School founded by UICC activists including individuals from CASA and the Comité

1975

APRIL 18th Street Farm Workers Support Committee, fundraiser held at Saint Vitus Church

JULY 21 Union strike against Grede Plastics, Maywood, Illinois; partly a response to company campaign to decertify union; various community groups involved

SEPTEMBER 16 Contingente del Pueblo (people's contingent), participation in Mexican Independence Day Parade of those involved in community, labor, high school, and immigration struggles as well as UICC cultural-center campaign

MAY Five hundred march on Chicago Board of Education offices to protest inaction on building of the new high school in Pilsen

AUGUST Texas Farm Workers Union formed by Antonio Orendain

SUMMER Brach's wildcat strike

Chicago 21 Community Alternative Plan for Pilsen under the auspices and fiscal sponsorship of PNCC

Community-wide meeting and subsequent demonstration at Chicago Board of Education; organized by PNCC; forces vow to take up the issue of bilingual education

LARP at UIC restructured and renamed LARES

OTEP Festival held in South Chicago, participants include Bread and Roses, Compañia Trucha, Teatro del Barrio, and Teatro Desengaño del Pueblo (Indiana)

Yenelli Flores begins organizing with parents for bilingual education and a new Komensky (grammar) School

1976

FEBRUARY 29 PNCC's First Annual Convention, community members raise questions about the alternative plan and cooptation by Chicago Central Area Committee of PNCC

MARCH 24 Sit-in and "take over" of Rush Presbyterian Saint Luke's Medical Center organized by Chicano leadership at Casa Aztlán with support from APO

APRIL 4–7 Valentín Campa, Mexican Communist Party leader and former candidate for president of Mexico, visits UICC; sponsored by CASA and Latin American Studies

AUGUST 12 Twenty-three people arrested at Rush Presbyterian Saint Luke's Medical Center sit-in demonstration; trial lasts a year ending with a hung jury and acquittal, four of the twenty-three defend themselves

SEPTEMBER   UICC Latino Cultural Center inaugurated (RCOCC)

All Pilsen churches sign document declaring themselves sanctuaries against the migra INS (Immigration and Naturalization Service)

MTO formed by Mexican teachers in the public schools

Pilsen residents form a citywide Coalition Against Plan 21 with other community residents in West Town, Cabrini Green, and Uptown to fight gentrification; Rudy Lozano and Art Vasquez are the Pilsen representatives in the coalition

1977

JUNE 4   Humboldt Park "Puerto Rican Riots," two people killed by police

FEBRUARY   Chilili reestablishes self-government (Pueblo/Consejo) in New Mexico; Chicago Contingent under ATM's direction travels to Chilili; members of Compañia Trucha and Teatro del Barrio from South Chicago go in support of the people of Chilili

SEPTEMBER   Benito Juárez High School opens; at dedication ceremony, a banner reads, "La escuela fue construída por el pueblo, no por los políticos—que vayan mucho al diablo" (This school was created by the community, not by the politicians—who should go to the devil)

1978

SEPTEMBER 26   Boycott of Komensky School in support of bilingual program, reinstatement of Yenelli Flores, and removal of teacher who assaulted her

NOVEMBER 18–20   Congreso Del Pueblo, social-justice student conference sponsored by SELA at UICC

CA. 1978   APO campaign for jobs: Chicago Fire Department, U.S. Post Office, Greyhound, Jewel, People's Gas, and Rush Presbyterian Saint Luke's Medical Center

Chispa music group formed

1979

JANUARY 16   Iranian Revolution, Shah and Empress leave the country

JULY 19   Nicaraguan Revolution, overthrow of Anastasio Somoza Debayle, son of Anastasio Somoza García

1980

Kalpulli formed as an art and indigenous cultural center

1981

NOVEMBER 12   María Saucedo dies in a suspicious home fire; motivates campaign for adequate fire services

María Saucedo Committee (Comité María Saucedo) formed

1982

MARCH 27   Comité María Saucedo organizes a bus envoy to Washington, D.C., against U.S. intervention in the war in El Salvador

CA. 1982   Trust endowment ($100,000) divided and transferred to Boards of Casa Aztlán and El Hogar del Niño with the help of Juan Velásquez and Humberto "Beto" Salinas

1983

JUNE 8   Rudy Lozano assassinated

MARCH   First North Side Latino education organization formed, Lakeview Latinos Allied for Better Education

FLOC six-hundred-mile march from Ohio to New Jersey

1984

Candlelight procession passes Roberto Clemente High School with empty casket to dramatize high dropout rates of Latinos

1989

SEPTEMBER 7   Rudy Lozano Library opens after twelve-year struggle to replace inadequate Chicago Public Library facilities in Pilsen

Chicanas of 18th Street

INTRODUCTION

Second City Mexicans

LEONARD G. RAMÍREZ

At the 1969 National Chicano Youth Liberation Conference in Denver, Chicano poet Alurista was surprised to learn that Mexicans had arrived
from such exotic places as Kansas City and Chicago (Alurista, conversation,
April 29, 2009).[1] From the vantage point of the twenty-first century, this
narrowly focused vision on the Southwest may be difficult to comprehend
when the Mexican population in the Chicago metropolitan region in 2006
was second in the United States only to Los Angeles.[2] In 1970, however, only
eighty-two thousand to perhaps one hundred thousand Mexicans resided
in Chicago (Alejo, 2008; Kerr, 1975/2000, 1976).[3] The largest concentration
of Mexicans continued to be in California and Texas. Today, the presence
of Mexicans outside the Southwest may no longer be surprising, yet their
historical absence continues to be reflected in our limited knowledge of
Mexicans in Chicago. The appearance of recent works signals an increased
interest in the area.[4] Nevertheless, despite continued settlement of the Mexican population outside the Southwest, research has not kept pace with the
growing importance of Chicago and other areas to our understanding of
Mexican experience in the United States.

The modest number of Mexicans that initially migrated to the Chicago area
contributed to the group's marginal historical status. According to the 1900
census, less than two hundred people in Illinois were identified as Mexican
(J. R. Garcia, 1996). The stream of itinerant laborers following the agricultural cycle into the Midwest eventually added to the Mexican population of
Chicago (Arredondo, 2008b; J. R. García, 1996). The labor needs of railroads
also brought increased numbers of Mexicans to the Midwestern region (J. R.

García, 1996; Valdes, 1991, 2000). Contractors often traveled deep within Mexico to obtain cheap labor, especially during the war years when labor was scarce. Mexicans were recruited to Chicago in large numbers, such as when they were used to break the 1919 steel strike or were brought into the Stockyards district to replace packinghouse workers in 1921 (J. R. García, 1996; Valdes, 2000).

The use of Mexicans, unaware of the local situation, as a wedge against labor was not always successful. Mexicans often sympathized with the plight of other workers. At times, they refused to act as strikebreakers. They demonstrated an interest in unions and a willingness to become involved in labor activities (J. R. García, 1996; Kerr, 1975/2000, 1976). Mexicans became labor representatives in both industrial and agricultural settings. Yet their manipulation by employers led many union leaders to assume that Mexicans could not be organized and only served to undermine the efforts of organized labor. White workers commonly saw Mexicans as a threat to their interests (J. R. Garcia, 1996; Valdes, 1991). Mexican-White divisions were institutionalized through segregated housing and differential treatment that occurred in agricultural labor camps as well as in industrial communities. The relative privilege of White workers fanned the flames of competition and ignited racial rivalries (Kerr 1976; Valdes, 2000).

Immigrants initially came mostly from the central and north-central states of Mexico including Guanajuato, Michoacan, Jalisco, Zacatecas, Chihuahua, Coahuila, and Nuevo Leon (A. E. Jones, 1928; Valdes, 2000). Mexicans did not always travel a direct route from a point of origin across the border to a final destination place in the States such as Chicago. Many migrated from areas of the Southwest, especially Texas. Some followed the agricultural migrant stream and spread across the Midwest. Those fortunate to find jobs that offered stability and better pay sank roots and raised families in towns and cities (Arredondo, 2008b; J. R. García 1996).

Migrants were generally young and male. Mexican women constituted only one quarter of the twenty-five thousand Mexicans in Chicago in 1930 (Arredondo, 2008b). Migration affected women in distinct ways and was understood by them differently depending on their economic situations, sense of the roles women should play, and exposure to different geographical and cultural contexts as well as varying legal and social structures that shifted the conditions under which they lived (Arredondo, 2008a). Women were generally paid poorly and earned less than their male counterparts and were the primary caretakers of children. New possibilities became open to women in places like Chicago, where laws and cultural expectations varied from those in Mexico. Expansion of women's participation, however, often came at a cost. The greater availability and use of divorce led to increased abandonment of families by males. This was a particular concern for religious groups and social workers in the 1920s that worried about the "morality" of immigrants and their "Americanization" (A. E. Jones, 1928; Kerr, 1976). Yet, while the departure of males added to the burden of women, it also could lead to greater independence, which at least some women may have seen as advantageous (Arredondo, 2008a).

In the 1920s, Mexicans began to be a more significant ethnic population (J. R. Garcia, 1996).[5] Early witnesses to Chicago's Mexican population growth traced this development through local employment rolls of railroad and packing-house industries at the turn of the twentieth century (Taylor, 1930a, October, 1930b). The development in the United States of the railroad and steel industries drew Mexicans north in search of jobs. Numerical growth was also a consequence of social upheaval in Mexico and the increasing availability of cheap transportation that could take immigrants across the border to work (Arredondo, 2008b). A diversity of employment sources such as slaughterhouses, meatpacking, and manufacturing created favorable economic conditions for Mexican settlement in Chicago (Kerr, 1976). The push-pull factors commonly offered to explain Mexican migration, however, occurred within a larger economic context. "A transnational mode of economic colonialism" was working to subjugate Mexico to foreign domination. United States' investment in Mexican railroads, mineral extraction, and agriculture were all components of an externally determined modernization process (González & Fernandez, 2003).

The Colonies

When they arrived in Chicago, Mexicans settled in three major areas (Arredondo, 2008b; Kerr, 1976).[6] At the beginning of the twentieth century, they began to appear in the South Chicago working-class, steel-mill district. They settled in the Packinghouse vicinity to be near the stockyards. By the 1920s, the largest Mexican enclave was located on the Near West Side, adjacent to the city's downtown, central business district, circled by an elevated train and often referred to as the "Loop."

Like South Chicago and Back of the Yards, the Near West Side was home to a number of ethnic neighborhoods. At various times, Greeks, Germans, Jews, Italians, Puerto Ricans, and Blacks had entered the Near West Side. In the first half of the twentieth century, Mexicans never constituted a majority in any of the areas where they settled, including the Near West Side. As was the case of South Chicago and Back of the Yards, Mexicans on the Near West Side lived among other ethnic groups. Pockets of Mexicans tended to develop where housing was least expensive and where Whites allowed them to reside (Kerr, 1976). Many newly arrived Mexican immigrants worked on the railroads and in the stockyards, but Mexicans were employed in manufacturing as well. A significant number of *betabeleros* (beet workers) attracted by cheap housing entered the Near West Side (J. R. Garcia, 1996). Different from the other *colonias* (residential neighborhoods), no one particular industry employing Mexicans predominated on the Near West Side (Arredondo, 2008b; Kerr, 1976).[7]

Mexican workers received lower wages than other ethnic groups for similar work (Kerr, 1976). In Chicago, they typically occupied the worst housing or even lived in labor camps or boxcar communities (Arredondo, 2008b; Kerr, 1996). On the Near West Side, they generally resided in poor and crowded living conditions, in basements, and in rat-infested, dilapidated buildings (Arredondo, 2008b; Jones, 1928; Kerr, 1976). Some Mexicans in South Chicago lived in more "comfortable quarters," and others even lived in more "desirable" neighborhoods, such as, the small group that settled in an enclave within the triangle of Clybourn Avenue, Fullerton Avenue, and Halsted Street (Jones, 1928).

No matter where Mexicans resided, their lives were made difficult, given that they occupied the lowest social and economic rungs of society and were disparaged as a racialized group. Only the situation of Blacks was worse than the marginalization of Mexicans. This was particularly apparent with respect to housing. White ethnics typically rented only the worst apartments to Mexicans. They charged higher rents to them and relegated Mexicans to the least desirable tracks within neighborhoods. However, Whites refused to rent at all to Blacks. Citizenship was color coded and not merely a product of longevity in the country or residency status.

Still, the conditions for Mexicans varied. Their dispersal within three settlement areas shaped their experiences. Distinct characteristics and patterns developed that conditioned their existence. Racial animosities shifted in intensity depending on the area of the city and specific time period. Racial antagonisms between Polish and Mexican immigrants in South Chicago and Back of the Yards were particularly explosive. Mexicans in Back of the Yards arrived in groups to public baths for protection. Poles refused to share public space with Mexicans and identified certain days when Mexicans would be allowed to use the facilities without being harassed. Mexicans in the Yards were reluctant to attend public events for fear of confrontation with other groups. They were less inclined to use neighborhood social services because of poor interracial relations. In the 1920s and 1930s, Poles identified certain streets that formed boundaries that Mexicans were not to cross. Mexican movement within neighborhoods was restricted by informal curfews that operated during particular times of the day (Arredondo, 2008b; Kerr, 1976).

Racial tensions existed in South Chicago, as they did elsewhere. South Chicago, however, developed community resources that made life for Mexicans somewhat more convenient. South Chicago was the location of the first Mexican Catholic church in the city. Our Lady of Guadalupe began to minister to Mexicans in 1923. Mexican Catholics in other areas celebrated Mass in storefronts because they were discouraged by priests and congregants from entering sacred ethnic spaces. Saint Francis of Assisi on the Near West Side originally served the German community. Once the Germans moved west, the church's population shifted, and Saint Francis became the Mexican church on the Near West Side. It was not until the 1940s that Mexicans in the Stockyards district obtained their own church.

Settlement houses in the Back of the Yards and Near West Side offered services and recreation, education, and training opportunities. The University of Chicago Settlement House located in the Packinghouse area established small branches in South Chicago. However, Mexicans in Back of the Yards limited their contact with community services in order to avoid racial conflict. Hull-House on the Near West Side was a community center founded in 1889 by Jane Addams and Ellen Gates Starr. Its mission was to serve the needs of newly arrived immigrants to the city (McCree-Bryan & Davis, 1990; Elshtain, 2002). Many Mexicans saw Hull-House as a place for other ethnic groups but gradually found a home there as well (Kerr, 1976; Ganz & Strobel, 2004).

Beginnings of Community

Mexicans created their own businesses and organizations to meet their own needs (Parra, 2004). South Chicago in the 1920s had more Mexican businesses than the Near West Side. The Back of the Yards trailed behind the other two Mexican settlement areas with respect to commercial services and civic groups. In the 1920s, South Chicago had the only Mexican-owned pharmacy in the city. Pool halls, tailors, bakeries, and meat markets were among the small Mexican businesses that sprung up in local neighborhoods. Mexicans traveled across the city to take advantage of resources in other areas. Sometimes those resources came to them, such as, the priests from Saint Francis that traveled to Back of the Yards to say Mass in storefronts (Arredondo, 2008b; Kerr, 1976).

South Chicago had more ethnic organizations. Of the twelve Mexican civic organizations listed for Chicago in the 1930s, five were in South Chicago (Arredondo, 2008b; Kerr, 1976). Mutual-aid societies were among some of the first organizations to be developed among Mexicans. These cooperatives offered emergency financial aid for burials or for the temporary support of widows and children. Although they provided critical assistance, these self-help organizations were often short lived.

Settlement houses offered recreational opportunities for children and adults. A Mexican mothers' club existed at Hull-House. It was most likely an outgrowth of the nursery school attended by Mexican children (Kerr, 1976). Young men's clubs often met at the settlement houses. Clubs sponsored music groups and offered classes. In the 1930s, Hull-House provided English instruction. In the 1940s, Centro Social Mexicano also offered English classes that attracted Mexicans (Kerr, 1976).

Ethnic Consciousness and Differentiation

The Great Depression continued the process of racialization and the development of Mexican ethnic consciousness. Anti-Mexican attitudes present since the Mexicans' arrival in Chicago were inflamed under the strains of economic collapse. Anger and frustration fueled anti-immigrant sentiments nationwide. The situation of Mexicans deteriorated. They were denied services, deported, or encouraged to leave the United States. Some assistance came from the Immigrant Protection League. The league pressured the Mexican government to help returning immigrants left at the border to return to their hometowns.

The colonias underwent significant changes during this time. The numbers of Mexicans fell from about twenty thousand to sixteen thousand in 1930 (Arredondo, 2008b, Kerr, 1976). The Near West Side experienced a 30 percent reduction in the number of Mexicans but still contained the largest number in the city. With the curtailment of immigration and return of immigrants to Mexico, the character of the population shifted. There were fewer single men, more women and children, and more families headed by married couples (Arredondo, 2008b; Kerr, 1976).

Louise Kerr (1976) suggests that historical moments of population stability created possibilities for greater Mexican integration with less strife. However, war and the increased need for labor yielded new programs and less-stringent immigration policies. An agreement between the United States and Mexico reversed the cycle, which led to the return of Mexican immigrants. The guest-worker program commonly known as the Bracero Program was established in 1942. It brought workers into the United States under contract. The expectation was that they would return to Mexico once their service period was over. However, the desire for cheap labor led to large numbers of Mexicans entering the country as undocumented workers. Changes in immigration policies in the 1950s and 1960s excluded Mexicans from quotas and expanded opportunities for relatives of immigrants to enter the United States. Demands for cheap labor and relaxed immigration policies may have closed out whatever possibilities existed for Mexicans to be more easily incorporated into U.S. life (Kerr, 1976).

The formation of Mexicans into a distinct community was influenced by their tenuous attachment to the United States as well as their racialization. Mexicans often entered the country with the desire to return to their homeland and, more specifically, their hometowns. They initially resisted citizenship because they saw this as an act of disloyalty. Developments sweeping Mexico also affected them. The reframing of Mexican identity using the symbols of the Mexican Revolution and indigenous folklore provided a basis for a popular reconceptualization of national identity. A reinvigorated nationalism served to reinforce and strengthen the connection between immigrants and their homeland. The marginalization that Mexicans encountered across the border in the United States made a mental and spiritual return to a familiar and welcoming culture more appealing.

The benefits of U.S. citizenship were not always apparent. Mexicans regardless of their status lived in poor housing and received inferior wages. The prejudice and differential treatment they received from other ethnic groups and social institutions stemmed from their identity as non-Whites. Acquiring a degraded citizenship that did not even prevent immigrants from deportation, as Mexicans learned during the Depression, hardly made citizenship seem worthwhile. Mexicans reasonably understood social benefits to be largely a function of race. Perhaps the most visible sign of this reality was the condition of Blacks, who occupied the bottom rung of the racial hierarchy despite their long-term and formal status as citizens (Arredondo, 2008b).

Racism contributed to the development of a Mexican ethnic consciousness in the United States. However, the development of ethnic consciousness as an "other" did not produce one single unifying identity but a fragmented array of identities that were elaborated and informed by race, geography, politics, gender, and immigrant generation (Acuña, 2007; Arredondo, 2008b; Kerr, 1976; Menchaca, 2001). Lighter-skinned Mexicans were tempted to pass for Whites. The impulse to create a more acceptable racial identity was formalized in other parts of the country such as New Mexico and Texas where communities of Mexicans claimed an exclusively "Spanish" ethnicity or staked a claim to a micro "citizenship" on the basis of a historic attachment to a specific state. Both strategies provided distance from Mexico, the first via a claim to Whiteness while the other through loyalty to a regional identity that distanced them from an association to a non-White nation.

Gabriela Arredondo refers to the many variants of Mexican identity as "striations" (2008b). Mexicans not only began to differentiate themselves racially but in other ways as well. Some sought greater legitimacy by virtue of their earlier migration, which at times reflected a more stable economic situation. One reaction to racial tensions and pressures to assimilate was to return to "traditional" Mexican culture, which did not always bode well for women if their greater independence was seen as adopting American ways and straying from Mexican cultural preferences.

Symptomatic of these fractured Mexican identities were the multiple responses to the infamous California Zoot Suit Riots of the 1940s. White military personnel roamed the streets of Los Angeles and attacked mainly Mexican youth, shaving their heads and stripping them of their flamboyant garments. However, this attack did not act to unify Mexicans. The antipathy by some Mexicans to *pachucos*,[8] popularly seen as marginal and rebellious Chicano youth, reflected the deep ideological, class, and generational divisions within the Mexican community. Despite the difficult circumstances that Mexicans found themselves in in the United States, they were not able to escape intra-ethnic conflict that might facilitate their ability to address the conditions of their existence (Kerr, 1976).

Left Politics in Mexican Chicago

A major challenge for Mexicans in the United States has been attaining some threshold of unity that might serve to advance their collective interests. Ethnic groups in Chicago have a long history of using group solidarity to progress as a community and gain some control or influence over institutions. Using neighborhood networks, the Irish and Italians each vied for control of city hall and jobs associated with urban government. Patronage has been the vehicle that provided White ethnics entre into public service employment and access to other city benefits. African Americans achieved a similar degree of political coherence and community spirit in the 1950s and 1960s that allowed them to gain civil rights. A similar level of African American group loyalty and cooperation was essential for Harold Washington in 1983 to become Chicago's first Black mayor. However, achieving a level of ethnic or racial cohesion capable of promoting political unity has been difficult for Mexicans to obtain. This has been the historic challenge of those who possess a collective vision for social change, specifically, the Mexican left in the City of Chicago.

The existence of leftist politics may have arrived with the first workers to Chicago. The Partido Liberal Mexicano (Mexican Liberal Party), founded at the start of the twentieth century to oppose Porfirio Díaz's dictatorship, encouraged the formation of small nuclei of supporters among Mexican immigrants. The Flores Magón brothers, creators and leaders of the party, were influenced by anarcho-syndicalism. Later, with the rise of the Confederación de Trabajadores Mexicanos (CTM, Confederation of Mexican Workers) and its leader Vicente Lombardo Toledano and Mexican President Lázaro Cárdenas, radical ideas began to be broadly diffused within the trade-union movement in Mexico and among Mexican workers in the United States. The cooperation among Cárdenista nationalists, labor, and the Communist Party of Mexico during the period of the popular front furthered the dissemination of left ideas within the nation's schools (Vaughan, 1997).

The formation of popular-front organizations was promoted by communists in the 1930s. The popular-front strategy sought to build coalitions between center parties and the left in order to combat the rise of fascism. The Communist Party in Mexico and Toledano were enthusiastic supporters of Cárdenas and his nationalist politics. In Chicago, Frank Paz, a leftist Mexican leader and community representative on the Near West Side, was a participant in popular-front activities. Ramón Martinez, a labor leader, was also a supporter of popular-front politics. Both of these leaders maintained contact with labor and political organizations on both sides of the border.

Labor and socialist organizing was not solely or perhaps even in the main a product of political socialization in Mexico. Mexicans had created their own mutual-aid societies and other self-help organizations in Chicago. The Great Depression was an impetus to mobilization among the working classes. Mexicans also participated in initiatives aimed at organizing the unemployed. In the 1930s, unions became more open to Mexicans. This occurred during a time when union membership was on the rise and organizing efforts were increasing (Kerr, 1976; Vargas, 2005). Left currents often developed in tandem with events and political influences coming from both the United States and Mexico.

Simultaneous with the rise during the 1930s of the left was the fear of conservatives, including some religious leaders worried by the growth of left political movements worldwide. In response to the increase of radicalism, the Catholic Church hierarchy invested resources in the creation of alternative integrative structures meant to match the initiatives of the labor movement. The churched created the Círculo de Obreros Católicos (Circle of Catholic Workers) and Juventud Obrera Católica (Young Catholic Workers), among other organizations, in its attempts to capture working-class support. These alternatives were meant to curtail the involvement of Catholics in the labor movement. In Chicago, the voice of conservative Mexican Catholicism was embodied in the perspective of *El Ideal,* the local Spanish-language newspaper. The conservative church and the Mexican left occasionally clashed openly, such as when Father de Prada closed a talk by exclaiming, "Long live Spain, Franco's Spain." This was quickly condemned by Frank Paz, who opposed the Spanish dictator.

While the Catholic Church attempted to create religious parallel structures to siphon Catholics away from labor radicalism, Saul Alinsky developed a technical approach to civic non-socialist action. His politically circumscribed perspective focused on local issues that targeted winnable demands (Alinksy, 1946/1969). The Back of the Yards Community Council was based on the Alinsky model. It seems to have met with some success in reducing racial antagonisms within the Packinghouse community (Kerr, 1976). An organizing approach that emphasized technique over ideology and unity around a limited set of goals over a long-term agenda had obvious appeal. This organizing approach became popular with activists in various Chicago neighborhoods.

By the 1940s, Mexicans on the Near West Side were able to create their own community center. The Centro Social Mexicano was established in 1945. However, the growth of the Mexican population and its organizations increased internal differentiation and multiplied its representative voices (Kerr, 1976). Internal dissension often became public, as it did when radio host Jorge Chapa questioned the right of the Mexican American Council to speak for the Mexican community on the occasion of the 1954 armed attack of Puerto Rican nationalists on the U.S. Congress (Fernández, 2005). Dissension in some respects signaled the development of the Mexican population. However, it also demonstrated the challenges that needed to be addressed by Mexican spokespersons in order to achieve a level of consensus that would allow them to become effective advocates for change.

The Mexicano/Chicano Left of the 1970s

Urban renewal changed the configuration of the Near West Side. Several neighborhoods were upended in order to accommodate an expressway interchange and establish a permanent site for the Chicago campus of the University of Illinois.[9] The evisceration of the Near West Side Mexican community prompted many Mexicans to settle in Pilsen, another traditional immigrant port of entry, just south of the Hull-House area. In the 1960s, Pilsen became the first predominantly Mexican community in the city (Kerr, 1976). Concentration of the Mexican population facilitated Mexican community development.

The changing character of Pilsen allowed Mexicans to have some impact on local community institutions. Churches began to adjust to the influx of Mexicans. Masses were offered in Spanish, special outreach programs were developed for Mexican families, and churches became vibrant community centers that involved entire families. Although Mexicans certainly influenced the local schools, the relationship between the Mexican community and the Chicago Public Schools was problematic. Issues such as bilingual education, the hiring of Mexican teachers, inadequate facilities, and the general poor quality of education became points of tension and eventually open opposition. Mexicans were soon able to exert their influence through the neighborhood civic organizations. Pilsen Neighbors Community Council, originally serving a Bohemian population, eventually became a vehicle for Mexican civic action. Developed as an Alinsky initiative, Pilsen Neighbors became a center for community grassroots leadership.

In the 1960s, economic and political systems were being challenged at every turn. Across the Third World, those nations conquered and exploited by Europe and the United States, such as Vietnam, were demanding independence. Popular forces in developing countries were rebelling against neocolonial exploitation (Galeano, 1973). Armed rebellion against authoritarian regimes linked to foreign interests was commonplace. The Cuban Revolution proceeded on a left trajectory and defeated the United States at the Bay of Pigs. Revolution was in the air, and it was reaching the United States (Elbaum, 2006; Gitlin, 1993; Pulido, 2006).

In the United States, Blacks tired of economic, political, and educational marginalization and gradualist remedies that amounted to little progress entered a community process to secure civil rights that soon transitioned into a call by some for Black power and fundamental structural change. The Black civil rights struggle and the antiwar movement ignited other campaigns for social justice, including women's and gay rights movements. Subordinated groups that historically had been exploited and relegated to the bottom of the social and gender hierarchies joined the appeal to democratize the nation, seeking full citizenship rights either within the constraints of the current political system or as a product of the reconfiguration of another.

Mexicans had a long history of resistance in the face of adversity. Political strategies such as those advocated by the League of Latin American Citizens and the GI Forum, organizations that had developed in the face of great adversity in the 1920s and 1940s, attempted to exchange patriotic loyalty and military service for the prerogatives of full citizenship. However, segments of the Vietnam generation tired of this strategy that seemed to yield few results. Despite being loyal constituents of the Democratic Party, the needs of Mexicans continued to be ignored (G. Mariscal, 2005; Navarro, 2000; Oropeza, 2005).

The turbulent political climate of the 1960s generated a new style of leaders, organizations, and political strategies to mobilize Mexicans for social change. César Chávez's farmworkers' struggle provided an iconic figure that captured the imagination of Mexicans, particularly youth.[10] Chávez symbolized the impoverished and oppressed Mexican masses and gave Mexicans across the nation a sense of being part of one community. The Chicano Movement redefined what it meant to be Mexican American, locating identity on a migrant trail that started in the Southwest (Aztlán) and moved south through Mexico only to be reconstituted again across the Rio Grande (Acuña, 1972, 2007; Menchaca, 2001). The new Chicano identity was not only geographic but also political. It rejected the politics of accommodation for more-aggressive direct-action tactics (I. M. García, 1997; Gómez-Quiñones, 1990, 1994).

The national political changes had their expression in Chicago. One of the more important sites for leadership and mobilization in the city was Loop Junior College. Those few Mexicans who entered college typically began their educational careers in two-year institutions. It was at Loop where the Organization of Latin American Students (OLAS) was founded. OLAS quickly established a community site at Saint Joseph's Church in Pilsen and spread to several other area colleges. Through its work in secondary schools, it ignited yet another center for leadership and action. Especially important was its presence at Harrison High School, attended by Pilsen youth. Once OLAS members transferred to four-year institutions, they began new organizations and provided leadership to more students. Another important initiative was the National Teacher Corps training project at UICC, where Mexicans and Puerto Ricans came together to be trained to serve Spanish-speaking students. Community agencies constituted yet another training ground for Mexican leaders. It was there that many people became knowledgeable about issues and met others of similar mind. Antipoverty programs became places where those individuals involved in community issues obtained skills and learned to navigate official bureaucracies. Community agencies were often energy centers where concerned people learned to become activists (Fernández, 2005; Padilla, 1985).

Another source of Latino leadership in Chicago came from Students for a Democratic Society (SDS), an organization that had become increasingly militant and socialist in character. SDS was eager to extend its work with students to other constituent groups.[11] However, ideological divisions and internal rivalries led to its splintering into various factions in 1969.[12] A small but significant number of Latino students in Chicago were members or sympathizers of the organization. Latinos were present in all SDS factions. Latinos also participated in other left student groups, such as, the Young Socialist Alliance (YSA) and its affiliate the Student Mobilization Committee (SMC). By 1972, the Worker Student Alliance (WSA) faction of SDS at UICC included a small cadre of Latinos who were expelled by the Progressive Labor Party (PLP) for their support of the National Liberation Front (NLF) of Vietnam and their sympathy for the Cuban Revolution, which ran counter to PLP's brand of Marxist politics. Later, other Mexicans that passed through a PLP experience left the organization and became community organizers. These Mexicans from the antiwar, anti-imperialist student left brought their talents and experience to the developing political movement in Pilsen.

The Pilsen network of activists that came to be known as the Comité had various names including the Committee in Support of the Farah Strikers and, later, the María Saucedo Committee. It developed gradually sometime between 1972 and 1973 as an informal network of friends and activists. By 1973, it began to meet regularly and had established a loose leadership structure. It brought together OLAS members, community artists, and high school and college students including Mexicanos/Chicanos who had been active in various SDS and other left student groups. The Comité network grew to include agency staff members and volunteers. Some of the Chicanos that found a home at Casa Aztlán were associated or became involved in Comité campaigns. The Comité held meetings and programs at the Librería Nuestro Continente bookstore during the two years of the center's existence.

The central membership circle comprised twenty to thirty activists, with additional allies in the outer rings of the organization. The Comité was actually a constellation of small groups with a greater mobilizing capacity. There was a desire to join together with other groups, particularly the August Twenty-Ninth Movement based in California, but this attempt was short lived. Because the Comité remained a local group, it was not known outside of Chicago. The group was unique in many ways. It had a loose organizational and leadership structure. It was fiercely independent, resisting various attempts of Latino and non-Latino groups to integrate it into a larger structure. Participation of members in all facets of the group was encouraged, and the

organization was generally resistant to excessive hierarchy. Although it valued its political independence, it attempted to build alliances with other left
groups in and out of Pilsen. The Comité also had strong female members
that constituted much of its leadership core.

Perhaps the majority of Pilsen activists never formally affiliated with either of
the two major Third World left organizations in Pilsen defined by Laura Pulido
(2006) as "revolutionary nationalist, Marxist, Leninist, or Maoist" with at least
half of its members being people of color.[13] The short-lived Raza Unida Party
included future members of both the Comité and the Center for Autonomous
Social Action (CASA-HGT) or CASA. These members were criticized for their
Marxist politics and blamed for the problems within the organization and the
party's eventual demise in Chicago (Navarro, 2000; Badillo, 2004).

In the beginning, there was a great deal of collaboration between individuals in CASA and the Comité. Both were critical to the Movement and helped
advance the struggles of the Mexicano/Chicano community. Community
activists often attended events sponsored by both groups. However, issues
related to the priority of goals, the balance between nationalism and working-class politics, and divergent strategies on how to promote a Mexicano/
Chicano agenda eventually created deep rifts in the Movimiento in Pilsen.

More is known about CASA because it existed in several states including
California (García & Montgomery, 1994; A. García, 2002, July–August; Gómez-
Quiñones, 1990; Mariscal, 2002, July–August). It was also allied nationally
and worked locally with the Puerto Rican independence movement, specifically the Puerto Rican Socialist Party, which played a significant role in Latino
revolutionary politics in the 1970s. CASA members later became involved in
electoral politics, which further elevated its visibility in the city (*Rudy Lozano,*
n.d.). Less is known about the Comité or the women that provided much of its
energy. This volume serves to introduce these women and the local networks
of activists who played such a pivotal role in the Movimiento in Chicago.[14]

Notes

1. Muñoz (1989) credits Alberto Baltazar Urista Heredia (Alurista) and Luis Valdez
for being the cultural architects of Chicanismo.

2. Chicago's moniker as the Second City was in relation to it being the second most
populated urban center in the United States by 1900 (J. R. Garcia, 1996). Los Angeles
eventually replaced Chicago as the second most populated city.

3. According to Kerr (1976), the actual number of Mexicans is widely believed to
be 250,000 because of undercounting.

4. Newly available works on Chicago explore complexities surrounding class, gen-

der, ethnic consciousness, and pan-Latino collaboration (Arredondo, 2008a, 2008b; Fernández, 2005). I am aware of dissertations in development on Chicago Mexicano/ Chicano activism and identity development in Chicago: immigrant rights activism from the late 1960s, and another on transnational political movements from 1920 to 1954. José González's recently published (2010) biography provides information on the contribution of a Chicano artist whose politics orbited around cultural nationalism rather than the more-left currents in the Movement in Pilsen such as the one to which the women in this work belong. The women seem to assume at least three tendencies in the Movimiento: cultural reformist and revolutionary nationalists, with the third being left groupings that blended socialist and nationalist politics including the Comité and CASA.

5. Anita Jones (1928) provides Mexican immigration figures to the United States from 1820 to 1927 and to Illinois from 1909 to 1927.

6. They also settled in nearby Gary and East Chicago, Indiana.

7. *Colonias* is a term Mexicans initially used to refer to the areas where they settled, but they have a past and present connotation. In the past, this also hinted at the poor or struggling nature of these settlement areas while current use, especially in the Southwest or border areas, also speaks to the poor or limited services, meager resources, and marginal existence of the inhabitants, for example, the Texas border colonias. The term today is used more for these border communities.

8. *Pachucos* has no real direct translation, but they were the Mexican American "homeboys" of that time whose roots developed in the 1920s and 1930s.

9. Created to accommodate military veterans, Navy Pier was a temporary site of the urban campus of the University of Illinois. The University of Illinois at Chicago Circle (UICC) on the Near West Side was inaugurated in 1965. Although initially City Hall contributed to the impression that the impetus for redevelopment rested elsewhere, it became clear that Mayor Richard J. Daley was behind the plan to transform the New West Side. Many years later, according to community activists, history repeated itself with Mayor Richard M. Daley suspected of being the architect for the South Campus Expansion Project that upended the Roosevelt Road corridor lying just north of the Pilsen community. A needed university expansion was the official justification for the construction of private townhouses, condominiums, and an upscale business district, along with a few student residences. In 1982, the unification of the UICC and the University of Illinois at the Medical Center (UIMC) resulted in the formation of the University of Illinois at Chicago (UIC). See Eastwood (2002) and Beuttler, Holli, & Remini (2000).

10. Ironically, Chávez may never have considered himself a Chicano or strayed outside the Democratic Party, although he became a symbol of the Chicano Movement (Munoz, 1989).

11. Muñoz (1989) mentions several Latinos, such as, Elizabeth Martinez, Luis Valdez, and María Varela, who came out of SDS and the antiwar left and subsequently played an important role in the development of the Chicano Movement.

12. A number of SDS histories have been written from different perspectives. See Adelson (1972), Berger (2006), H. Jacobs (1970), R. Jacobs (1977), Moore (2001), and Sale (1973).

13. Comité members were Mexicano/Chicano, although other Latinos and non-Latinos attended events and supported its politics.

14. Latin American testimonial literature has been one way to recover the history of revolutionary women (Beverley, 1989, Spring). For examples, see Chungara (1978) and Menchú (1983). A growing number of radical memoirs of the 1960s have begun to be published. For examples, see Alpert (1981), Ayers (2001), Avakian (2005), Brown (1992), Dunbar-Ortiz (2001), Hillard & Cole (1993), Oglesby (2008), Pardun (2001), Rudd (2009), and Sherman (2007). There are far fewer Mexicano/Chicano memoirs. For examples, see Buss (1993), García & Montgomery (1994), Gutiérrez (1998), Tijerina (2000), and Treviño (2001).

Homecoming, 1997

LEONARD G. RAMÍREZ

I look down from my window hoping to see Isaura's blue two-door sedan pull in front of the arched doorway of my six-flat. Only a faint seam of daylight remains at the edge of the clouds. The vehicles pass quickly through the glow of the streetlights. The car that had momentarily caught my attention moves down the avenue without pause. The one at the corner continues north past my street.

Chicago is in the midst of a transformation. Miniature white cyclones swirl outside my living room windows. Naked tree branches reach in all directions up to the sky. Swaying limbs extend upwards like the pleading hands of a devout congregation. A woman moves briskly down the street, her head sunk turtle deep inside the lifted collar of a winter coat. A young man caught unexpectedly by the abrupt change in weather digs his hands deep into his thin jacket. He pushes forward, head bent, attempting to shield his face from the icy wind shards hurling off Lake Michigan from only a block away.

Tonight's holiday gathering will welcome Yenelli Flores and her husband, Matin, back to the city. In the late 1970s, Yenelli, a community organizer, left Chicago with her family for a small Midwestern college town where Matin was able to secure a position as a college professor. It is difficult to reconcile the vision of the fiery activist from those early years with the pastoral images of a faculty wife attending department socials, school picnics, and church peace vigils.

I think back to Richard M. Nixon's visit to Chicago in 1972 when he walked onto a stage to the tune of *Hail to the Chief* only to have the evening's proceedings interrupted by Yenelli racing down the aisle shouting antiwar slogans.

Caught momentarily off guard, the Secret Service was slow to respond. Just before she reached the stage, Yenelli was lifted high off her feet, whisked out of the ballroom, and unceremoniously deposited outside the auditorium. Behind her a room full of conservatives clamored for "Four more years!" However, Yenelli had managed to pierce the self-congratulatory bubble of well-being that Republican America was trying so hard to project. After more than a decade, Yenelli had returned to the Chicago area.

Tonight would also be an informal minireunion of a 1970s independent community-activist network, a local expression of the national Chicano Movement.[1] Comité women were known to be among the most outspoken militants of Chicago's Movimiento. In the late 1960s, Pilsen became the heart of the city's Mexican community as well as the center of the Mexicano/Chicano Movement in Chicago. The bifurcated name acknowledges the participation of ethnically identified Mexicans and those who framed their identity at the intersection of two cultures and national experiences.[2]

María Gamboa, a Comité member, was an ardent proponent of Chicano nationalism as were other members of Compañia Trucha, the theater group to which she belonged.[3] Trucha members saw themselves not only as entertainers but, perhaps more important, as popular educators whose theatrical performances used everyday experience to draw critical life lessons. Trucha worked closely with other cultural groups including Teatro de los Barrios (barrio theater group), a South Chicago troupe.[4] Before the collapse of the steel industry, South Chicago was a bustling community. Activists from South Chicago like those from other parts of the city were attracted to the cultural and political renaissance that was occurring in Pilsen. Politically conscious youth were particularly drawn to a social-service center and an activist hub called Casa Aztlán. Aztlán housed adult-education programs, art studios, and a health clinic and served as a community meeting place. Before acquiring its own space, Compañia Trucha operated out of Casa Aztlán and often performed at the various functions that took place there.

When not performing, María remained disciplined and serious, so I was somewhat surprised the day she invited members of the Comité to attend a house party in South Chicago. On a sweltering summer evening in the mid-1970s, a group of us piled into a car and headed to an apartment near the steel mills. After an extended time on the dance floor, a line of perspiring dancers made its way to the back porch for a bit of evening breeze and a breath of fresh air. We stepped out on the porch and were immediately overtaken by crimson and purple-green–colored gasses bursting intermittently from flamethrowers sunk deep within the bowels of a steel fortress.

It deceptively appeared to be only a few yards away. Colored rockets flared brightly as they rose and then blackened into a smoky sky. Those of us who were witnessing this for the very first time stared open mouthed, surprised to find ourselves at the portal of a shadowy volcanic world, a channel into the throbbing heart of an industrial community.

In the 1970s, South Chicago was one of the two original Mexican settlement areas that still survived. The other was the Back of the Yards. Some of those associated with the Comité had family members that lived near or worked at the stockyards. It was sometimes possible to find the Back of the Yards by following the stench of freshly butchered animals. The putrid smells of bloody carcasses traveled the farthest during the summer. They drifted downwind seeping into communities far removed from the slaughterhouses.

Traveling on the expressway, our family car was more than once overtaken by foul odors that reached out from the butchering factories like a greasy cellophane glove. On those occasions we rolled up our windows fast, even though the car didn't have air conditioning, which was still a luxury. However, it was preferable to suffer the blistering heat than inhale the rotten smells that threatened to curdle into explosive balls deep within the pits of our stomachs.

Until the 1960s, the Near West Side, an area west of the Chicago River and adjacent to the city's downtown business district, was considered to be the cultural and civic center of Chicago's Mexican community. It was where the largest number of Mexicans resided until they were displaced by urban renewal. Even if they did not live in the area, many Mexican families had some tie to the Near West Side. This was true for most of the women affiliated with the Comité. Isaura's family had lived and worked in the Madison Street skid-row corridor, just north of Hull-House. Magda Ramírez-Castañeda's family had initially settled in the Near West Side when they first arrived to Chicago in the 1950s. Yenelli's parents were social workers at Hull-House. But perhaps it is Victoria Pérez, another Comité member, who has the clearest memories of the Near West Side, where her parents often took her in the 1940s.

Victoria's aunt Guadalupe Pérez Marshall Gallardo had been encouraged by Ellen Gates Starr, one of the founders of Hull-House, to attend a workers' strike as an observer. Many years later, Victoria unexpectedly saw her aunt walking among the dead and wounded in a film about the 1937 Republic Steel Massacre. Guadalupe continued to fight for the rights of labor in the United States until the 1950s, when because of her political beliefs, she was forced to leave the country where she had resided for many years. Victoria's own colorful childhood memories of the Near West Side are, however, mostly of the enticing sights and smells of ethnic grocery stores, pastry shops, and restaurants. Later, as an adolescent, the Centro Social Mexicano, which was west of Halsted Street on Roosevelt Road, began to occupy more of her attention. The community center was the site of social and cultural events for Mexicans of all ages.

Like several of her sisters, Victoria became active in the United Farm Workers (UFW) campaign to extend labor rights to agricultural workers. UFW picketing and leafleting often took place in Pilsen as did so many other mobilizing efforts. Though she lived on the north side of the city, Victoria was attracted to the Mexicano/Chicano mobilizations that were taking place elsewhere. Victoria eventually became a member of the 18th Street community in the early 1970s. She joined Compañia Trucha and worked to improve the conditions of Latino workers.[5]

In the 1960s and 1970s, the world was spinning left on its political axis with African, Asian, and Latin America nations—or what is often referred to as the Third World—waging wars of national liberation.[6] The Vietnam War was at the forefront. It was a virtual David fighting the world's military Goliath. Its record of success in the face of such odds offered a valiant and inspirational example of resistance for others to follow.

Che Guevara, the revolutionary that had helped overthrow Batista, the Cuban dictator, embodied the revolutionary spirit of the era. He challenged people of conscience to join in the fight to destroy the international apparatus of racism and class oppression and dedicate themselves to the struggle for social justice and liberation.[7] Che issued a call to "Create two, three, many Vietnams" that signaled a worldwide campaign to topple the corporate giants and local elites willing to bargain off the national patrimony in order to secure a privileged perch at the imperialist banquet (Deutschmann, 1987). Che's message resonated especially with youth, the so-called children of Che, who responded and became the vanguard of the world revolutionary movement. In Latin America, guerillas sought to overthrow dictators and authoritarian regimes masquerading in democratic mufti, students revolted against tyranny, peasants expropriated land, workers demanded livable wages and union rights, and a popular democratic upsurge led to the growth of leftist political parties and oppositional electoral alliances that challenged the established order. The response of the multinational corporate, political, and military elites was repression, torture, and death. Among the many examples were Mexico in 1968, Chile in 1973, and Argentina in an extended "dirty war" that did not end until the 1980s.[8] The result of the suppression of civil, political, and human rights was a flow of exiles to other countries. Some Latin American activists joined organizing efforts at schools and in communities in the United States.

* * *

The headlights of the car below blink on and off. I shut the apartment lights off and move quickly down the hallway steps. The snow falls faster and thicker. It has begun to accumulate on the ground. In the open air, the sting of winter is painfully invigorating, but I welcome the comforting warmth of Isaura's car. I direct her off the side streets. We move on to Sheridan Road en route to the northern suburbs. Isaura, a small and unassuming woman, has had the most contact with Yenelli during her absence from Chicago. She has kept all of us connected throughout the years. She fills me in on details of our friends' lives and the situation of her own family, some of whom live in Illinois and others in various parts of Texas. Tonight, however, her words are mostly lost amidst my private reveries of the days when many of us shared a common vision.

I met Isaura at the University of Illinois at Chicago Circle (UICC) in 1971 when the campus antiwar movement had already begun to enter into an extended identity crisis, and students searched to find more-fertile organizing environments than colleges with their constantly shifting populations and institutional instability. Isaura became my bridge to community-based organizing. She moved easily from the campus to neighborhoods. She had been active in antiwar as well as Latino organizations such as El Cuadro.[9] Isaura and I worked with the local Worker Student Alliance (WSA) faction of Students for a Democratic Society (SDS) until the former's demise in the early 1970s.[10] We then helped to found the Sociedad Estudiantil Latinoamericana (SELA), which directed the campaign to establish the Rafael Cintron-Ortiz Cultural Center (RCOCC) at UICC.[11]

We turn down a cul-de-sac. One remaining parking spot is at the end of the block. From across the street, we can barely see the gathering through the frost that covers much of the living room window. The muffled sounds of festive chatter become slightly clearer as we approach.

"Come in." Yenelli greets each of us with a hug as we enter her home. The volume of party noise rises, and the conversation becomes more distinct. From somewhere inside the house, the familiar voices of old friends can be heard above the din of conversation. The hallway is littered with boots, high heels, and men's shoes. They serve as a notice for us to remove our own wet things. A conga line of people snakes through the corridor kicking aside the footwear below them as they make their way to various destinations.

The banister going to the second floor is draped with layers of coats. To our surprise, we find two hangers in the hallway closet and manage with only one collective shoulder push to squeeze our coats into it. Isaura disappears into the traffic moving from the hallway to the kitchen. The line is intersected by another group seeking to join the queue outside the bathroom.

I make my way to the dining area, then to a more expansive family room. It is a generous space. A television and a treadmill have been pushed into opposite corners of the room. Under a glassless window looking into the kitchen is a table with liters of soda, bottles of wine, plastic cups, and a bucket of ice cubes, along with bowls of salty snacks. I wave to Magda, who is in the living room involved in conversation. I pour a glass of wine and find a wall at the back to lean against.

From this vantage point, I watch people as they pass. I recognize a few, others are only vaguely familiar. I eavesdrop on conversations taking place around me. Matin is across the room. Laughter rises from deep within his belly. He slaps a raised knee to emphasize some point. He glances in my direction as if I have been privy to his conversation all along and naturally agree with him. He arches an eyebrow, a salutatory gesture, before returning to the mathematician whom I remember as a leader of the Iranian Student Association (ISA).[12] The party is a mixture of ethnicities and races, a United Nations of languages and cultures.

My early encounters with Yenelli were at similar gatherings many years ago. Her apartment near UICC was a social meeting place. At those smoke-filled parties, international music often played in one room while contemporary rock, blues, or folk played in another. An interesting array of guests walked in and out of her apartment, alternative-lifestyle youth, Black Panthers, student radicals, and community activists. The kitchen was generally the center of serious political debate. Several heated conversations typically raged simultaneously.

A goateed Peruvian acting rather formally introduces himself to me. We make casual conversation, and eventually he begins to tell me about the book of poems he is writing. The Peruvian drifts away when a couple I had not seen in years approaches and enters the conversation. The evening continues this way with polite exchanges of smiles from unknown people as they pass and an occasional meeting with individuals that I seem to remember crossing paths with over the years. After yet another glass of wine, I lose track of time.

Eventually the party begins to wane. The crowd thins out considerably although it is not quite midnight. Guests offer the usual excuses for an "early" departure. The Latino ritual of prolonged good-byes seems endless.

"What are you doing here all by yourself? Are you being antisocial?" Magda approaches with a newly filled glass of wine in her hand.

"No, I was just thinking about how long it has been." The first time I saw Magda, she was on a raised dais in front of a microphone at a Vietnam war protest. On a late Saturday afternoon, her booming voice ricocheted forcefully across a downtown city square to a gathering of a few thousand people. Magda is at her best when she is on a platform. That day she spoke with impressive clarity and resolve. I was proud to see a Mexicana leader who refused "to go forward in life on bended knee," as my grandmother used to say. I decided to introduce myself, but before I could make my way to the speaker's platform, she was quickly surrounded by several Anglo women trying to make a connection after her speech. By the time my eyes searched the stage area again, she was gone. I caught a parting glimpse of her as she entered a car at the far end of the downtown plaza.

"Did you try some of the tamales? They're good." As a member of the Asociación Pro–Derechos Obreros (APO, Association for Workers Rights), Magda was involved in the demonstrations against the Chicago Transit Authority in the 1970s. She and Yenelli were among those who commandeered buses to protest CTA's discrimination against Latinos.

"I'll wait until later," I say to her as she moves off in the direction of the kitchen, perhaps in search of more tamales. Magda's high school classmate and college roommate is seated at a distance. Cristina Vital, a slender, angular woman with a long neck and a giraffe's aloof gaze, talks to someone on a couch across from her. During those times of constant mobilization, she and her partner at that time founded Librería Nuestro Continente, the first and only Chicano bookstore to ever exist in Chicago, which also served as a community center and home for the Comité.[13]

Customers wandered into the Librería throughout the day, mostly neighborhood activists and students and occasionally visitors from other states who heard about the bookstore and came to Chicago to meet its proprietors. During the week, the back-store area became a classroom. Immigrant workers arrived after leaving their jobs to learn English as part of the Right to Read outreach program.[14] They sometimes purchased books, pamphlets, and a sampling of movement newspapers. Neighborhood residents were invited to attend special events, view educational films, listen to speakers, and participate in discussions. Controversial topics such as the 1968 student massacre in Mexico drew standing-room-only audiences.

The Librería provided a forum for people to cultivate a leadership voice. It was not until years later that I fully appreciated the importance of those sessions. On many evenings, barely literate men and women gathered the courage to speak. But there were also times when there was no reluctance on the part of workers to express their views, sometimes forcefully challenging the evening's speaker and the Comité.

María and her husband, Héctor, nod in my direction. They move from the table filled with wine and soft drinks back through the dining area and into the adjacent living room. María was one of the younger members of the Comité and a proponent of Chicanismo despite the controversy over the use of that term in Chicago. In the 1960s and 1970s, Mexicans in Chicago often rejected the word *Chicano,* viewing it as a crude way to refer to recent Mexican immigrants, one that characterized them as unsophisticated or even as criminals (Acuña, 2007). In the Southwest, where the Movimiento was defined and led by those born in the United States or primarily socialized north of the border, the term was more readily accepted, especially by those activists who wanted to distance themselves from what they saw as the political conformity of past generations.[15]

In Chicago, where the numbers of second-generation Chicanos were fewer and the steady stream of immigrants predominated, activists sometimes reacted with mixed feelings. Although they questioned the need for a new identity, politically left-leaning Mexicanos eventually came to accept Chicanismo, though they often preferred to emphasize its politics rather than its claims to a unique cultural identity. As an early participant in the activities at Casa Aztlán, María had the opportunity to interact with Chicano cultural nationalists, artists, and members of the Brown Berets who called Casa Aztlán their home.[16] In an era of multiple political influences, María, like many others, underwent many changes, eventually moving away from a strictly Chicano nationalist perspective to one that came to encompass issues of social class.

I enter the kitchen, where Yenelli and Isaura are busy washing dishes. Most of the guests have left except for Comité stalwarts and a few others. The house has grown eerily quiet. The soft voice of Silvio Rodríguez can barely be heard in the background.[17] I volunteer to help straighten up.

"Can you pick up the rest of the things from the other rooms?" Yenelli asks. Much has already been cleared off the dining room table, but there are still some remnants, half-filled bowls of tortilla chips, a platter of tamales under a stack of empty corn husks, a dish of refried beans and yellow cheese. I scan the assortment of leftovers that have been picked at, gone through, spilled, or crushed on the table or broken into crumbs on the rug below. I return to the kitchen with an armful of glassware.

The evening is settling down to a meeting of some of the old gang. Magda's and Yenelli's teenage daughters anticipating a political revival quickly move upstairs, away from "adult" conversation. They seem so young, still almost little girls, yet some of us were about their age when we became politically involved. I do not blame them for wanting to retreat from what must seem to ·

them to be an endless recording, a conversation caught in a continuous loop, repeated every time a few of the activists from the old days find themselves in the same room with a glass of wine in their hands. They have heard it all anyway, the reminiscences, humorous stories, the old issues, the occasional arguments, the what-ifs. We return to the past not only to relive it and be buoyed by the victories but also to attempt to make sense of those times and understanding what affect it has had on our lives.

"Hey, guys. Why don't you come and join us?" Magda's demanding voice coming from the living room startles us. Yenelli, Isaura, and I glance at each other. A mischievous grin begins to spread across Yenelli's face. Isaura responds with a look of sweet and already forgiving amusement while I am beginning to feel a growing sense of dread. It is that time of the evening. I wonder if this will be a game of charades or worst. Maybe, we will be urged to reveal the most embarrassing moment in our lives, or sing a song, or recite a poem. In any case, these end-of-the-evening amusements are often dominated by Magda and Yenelli, who are ready at a drop of a hat to take center stage and perform.

"Come on, hurry up. When was the last time we were together? We didn't come here to watch you do dishes." Isaura hangs a wet cloth on the refrigerator door handle. I find my glass of wine that I am sure I will need to get through this part of the evening. Yenelli is already on her way to join the others. We all move into the living room. Some sit on the backs of couches. Chairs are being brought in from the dining area.

"We need to write a book."

"About what?" Cristina asks dryly and with more than a tinge of sarcasm.

"It will be about us, those still in touch, the women from the Comité. Héctor can help us remember, and Leonard can be responsible for the writing. I think we need to tell our stories. I think we need to let others, especially the youth, know what we did and why we did it."

Cristina remains skeptical, as is her nature. But there is growing interest. Yenelli has quickly taken up the project and chimes in. She and Magda have assumed their usual roles as co-conspirators. I look around at the women and remember the life we once shared. Despite my own misgivings, I pull my chair closer. I sense an important beginning.

Notes

1. The term *the Comité* is used throughout to distinguish this Chicago group from El Comité, a primarily Puerto Rican organization based on the East Coast and active around the same time. The Comité is the general name used here to represent the

activist network to which the six women of this book belonged. The network was actually referred to by many names, including the Committee to Support the Farah Workers (or the Farah Support Committee) and the María Saucedo Committee.

2. The term *Chicano/a* became popular in the 1960s and was used by those associated with radical organizing and/or those who identified with a dual Mexican- and U.S.-based cultural orientation that combined into a new synthesis. The term *Chicano* was rescued from its more negative connotations and brandished with a new found sense of pride, similar to the word *Black,* a once-disparaging term that replaced the obsequious connotations associated with *negro.*

3. *Ponte trucha* was a slang expression used by Chicanos in the 1960s meaning "wise up" or "watch out." "Heads up Theater" is another rough translation for Compañia Trucha. In 2008, Trucha reorganized with a cast of new cultural activists under the name Compañia Trucha Reloaded. Their first performance took place on May 31, 2008, at a CAMI/CAMY fundraiser, "A Night of Justice for Juan Torres and Blanca Luna," the story of two Latino youths killed under mysterious circumstances while serving in the military.

4. The troupe is also called Teatro del Barrio.

5. Pilsen is often referred to by the major street that runs through the community, 18th Street. The major intersection is 18th Street and Blue Island Avenue.

6. The left refers to those countries exploited by the developed nations as the *Third World.* The Third World, which fueled the development of the first world, was trapped in unequal relationships that continued its underdevelopment.

7. Ernesto (Che) Guevara was an Argentine revolutionary (1928–67).

8. Argentina's *guerra sucia* (dirty war) was a state-sponsored campaign of terror aimed at intimidation and elimination of left-wing students, labor leaders, militants, and armed rebel groups.

9. El Cuadro Latino Americano (ca. 1971) was primarily, although not exclusively, a Mexican organization. It successfully lobbied for the creation of a Latin American Studies program at UICC, now the Latin American and Latino Studies program.

10. SDS became synonymous with student radicalism of the 1960s (Sale, 1973). The organization formally divided at the 1969 Chicago convention. In the early 1970s, control of the Worker Student Alliance faction of SDS in Chicago slipped away from the Progressive Labor Party (PLP or PL) and its sympathizers to a group of independently minded activists. In Chicago, the short-lived Independent Radical Caucus, in opposition to PL, passed resolutions supporting national liberation struggles, including the National Liberation Front of Vietnam, and one in support of Cuba. Sometime between 1972 and 1973, the PLP-led minority faction expelled the Independent Radical Caucus. Across the country, including New York City, Pittsburgh, Seattle, and Columbus, Ohio, WSA-SDS chapters were either expelled or voluntarily left the organization. Shortly thereafter, PLP disbanded WSA-SDS and created at UICC the Committee against Racism (CAR). The group became an affiliate of the International Committee against Racism (InCAR) when PLP developed a multi-

campus structure for the organization, thus absorbing the remnants of WSA-SDS. Members of the Independent Radical Caucus (IRC) went on to found the United Front against Imperialism (UFAI) at UICC. Several United Front members became active in the 18th Street Comité.

11. The other organization that was involved in the effort to create a Latino cultural center at UICC was the Union for Puerto Rican Students (UPRS), which until about 1975 was unaligned to any citywide political organization. Several UPRS members had belonged in the early 1970s to Pana Pa' Ti (roughly translated, partner for you), a social cultural mentorship group that had been criticized by some Latino activists for being "apolitical" or "uninvolved" or even an obstacle in the creation of Latin American Recruitment Program (LARP, now LARES). By the late 1970s, with contentious issues resolved, UPRS joined with other forces to promote independence for Puerto Rico. Several former UPRS members were later arrested for allegedly being members of the Fuerzas Armadas de Liberación Nacional (FALN). Sociedad Estudiantil Latinoamericana (SELA) was probably the last attempt on the UICC campus to create one unified Latino student organization. Earlier, the Chicano-Boricua Student Union (CBSU, ca. 1973 to 1974) tried to unite the two major Latino ethnic groups present in Chicago. After the establishment of the Rafael Cintron-Ortiz Cultural Center (RCOCC), the Mexicano-Chicano Student Union was formed. It maintained close relationships and even overlapping memberships with SELA. Over time, several members of the Mexicano-Chicano Student Union became affiliated in the community with CASA.

12. Mohammad Rezā Shāh Pahlavi ruled Iran from 1941 to 1979. The Iranian Student Association (ISA) played an important role in bringing down the Shah and the Iranian monarchy. ISA was informally divided into three major factions. The "red faction," as it was informally referred to, often collaborated with the Revolutionary Union (RU) while the "white faction" developed close relationships with the October League (OL). Both RU and OL were Maoist groups with roots in SDS. The third ISA faction (Mujahedeen) was a Muslim group with a left orientation.

13. The bookstore included English- and Spanish-speaking works and news items that primarily focused on Latin America and Latinos in the United States. The materials, including the literary works, were mainly left oriented, while the atmosphere of the store with its posters, Mexican artifacts, and leaflet-laden bulletin boards identified the enterprise as a Movement site. Nuestro Continente possessed a Chicano perspective of the world in that Mexicanos/Chicanos were seen as indigenous to America and not viewed as alien or immigrant to it despite what side of any border they happened to be born because the border was not seen as a natural barrier but as a social construction. Chicanos with a long history in the United States or whose family was rooted in the Southwest popularized the slogan "We did not cross the border, the border crossed us."

14. Right to Read was a federally funded program targeted at youth and aimed at increasing community literacy. In Chicago, it was based at Centro de la Causa and directed by Yenelli Flores.

15. Since the 1960s and 1970s, scholars, including many of those who participated in the Movimiento Chicano, have reconsidered their initial assessment of earlier Mexican generations as simply political conformists and cultural assimilationists. Some came to view the history of Mexicans in the United States not as a break with conformity but as an arc of continuous struggle that included the Mexican American generation and the Chicano generation.

16. Casa Aztlán located on South Racine Avenue near 18th Street was once a Bohemian social settlement house. One or two of Casa Aztlán's original murals can still be seen today. Several murals paid tribute to the spirit of the Mexicano/Chicano generation, which can be seen at http://www.neiu.edu/~casaaztl/index.htm. Interestingly, the image of María Saucedo, a Comité militant tragically killed in a fire, was once included among the pantheon of activist dignitaries and heroes on the outside front mural of the building. The inside mural with her image no longer exists. María Saucedo's face on the façade outside was at some point erased. It is believed by some Comité members that it was intentionally painted over by those sympathetic to other left political tendencies in the community.

17. Silvio Rodríguez is a well-known Cuban singer and major figure in the Nueva Trova cultural movement, a politically left–inspired folk and popular music tradition that began in the 1960s in Latin America.

A Legacy of Struggle

YENELLI FLORES

A Parade, 1973

Just north of Chicago's downtown shopping area, elaborate floats, decorated automobiles, and dancers in ornate costumes attempt to form some semblance of order.[1] Organizers scramble to take care of last-minute details. High school youths dressed in red uniforms with brass instruments at their sides search for fellow band members. Groups prepare to move in unison at the first sign of the parade marshal's signal. A float is out of order, causing a great deal of confusion. An official shouts directions to a frustrated driver. The flatbed truck is trying to pull out of formation but must wait for further directions to maneuver into the correct position somewhere down the line. The portly official flips up her sunglasses, wipes the sweat above her lip, and nervously checks her clipboard, leafing through forms and bits of paper held firmly by a metal clasp.

The Pilsen contingent lines up behind the Casa Aztlán float. Plumed Aztec warriors stand defiantly in front of a white, red, and green tissue backdrop. Atop a cactus, an eagle with a snake held firmly in its mouth completes the insignia of the Mexican flag. Members of various political groups fall behind street-size banners: "Justice for the Farah Strikers," "Sin Fronteras" (No borders), "Que Onde Sola" (Let it fly alone).[2] More people join the Chicano contingent that is already nearly one hundred strong, comprising agency workers, high school and college students, teachers, professors, artists, and poets.

The demonstration is in solidarity with the Puerto Rican independence movement that marches just up ahead but is also a community gathering. There are always reunions at these events. People greet each other with warm hugs and kisses. They talk animatedly in groups and exchange telephone numbers. Friends reestablish contact after falling out of touch. Some have returned from extended stays in Mexico or newly adopted cities in the Southwest.

Puerto Rican parade officials from business and civic organizations patrol the edges of the gathering. They hurry past the Pilsen and Boricua protest contingents, frowning with displeasure.[3] But like their counterparts in the Mexican community, they are well aware of the cost of a public confrontation and do not attempt to exclude activists from these ethnic celebrations, today the annual Puerto Rican Day Parade. The line finally begins to move forward.

Those along the street nervously watch rows of majorettes in colorful sequined outfits toss batons high above their heads. The anxious eyes of onlookers follow the spinning wands upwards, waiting to see if the rows of young women will be able to snare them on their descent. Miniature paper flags twirl around the antennas of cars as the vehicles cruise by decorated in the island's tricolors. On both sides of State Street, onlookers admire waving princesses crowned with jeweled tiaras and squeezed tightly inside sparkling gowns. The sound of timbales traveling down the long State Street corridor excites the crowds up ahead long before the popular musical groups can actually be seen.[4] Men, women, and children clap and dance in rhythm to the salsa and merengue bands playing from the backs of slowly promenading trucks.

The Boricua contingent leads the protest since it is the occasion of their holiday. "¡Fuego! ¡Fuego! ¡Fuego! ¡Los Yanquis Quieren Fuego! ¡Si Los Yanquis No Se Van, En Borinquen Morirán! ¡Jíbaro Sí! ¡Yanqui No! ¡Jíbaro Sí! ¡Yanqui No!" ("Fire! Fire! Fire! The Yankees want fire! If the Yankees do not leave, in Puerto Rico they will die! Puerto Rican yes! Yankee no!"). Marchers in the Pilsen contingent carry Mexican, Puerto Rican, and red flags in solidarity with the struggle of the island republic. Surprised looks are on many of the faces on the sidelines. Most seem too confused to react. But as the contingent passes an increasing number of onlookers begin to clap. Brigades of youth waving Puerto Rican flags rush to the front of the crowds. A woman drapes herself in a banner while a young girl unfurls a large flag, waving it energetically in the air. Smiles begin to appear across a scattering of faces in the crowd. A few fists slowly begin to rise in the air from those who have reconnected to stagnant memories. Others shake their heads "no" or remain frozen faced and silent. The growing if tentative volume of cheers and applause begins to add another dimension to the patriotic and cultural assembly along the parade route. A ribbon of defiance ripples through the crowd as the marchers proceed down the broad avenue.

After about an hour, the protest contingent arrives at the southern edge of the Loop. Toward the end of the parade route, the number of onlookers begins to thin.

Yenelli carries a red flag with a single white star in the corner bounded by an arc of stars. It is the flag of the *independentistas* of the Puerto Rican Socialist Party. Many of the Pilsen activists are already beginning to disband while others continue to amble down the middle of State Street. Yenelli talks incessantly to those around her as music continues to rise like colored balloons into a Caribbean ocean of sky. She is oblivious to the person barreling toward her at high speed. Several demonstrators point in the direction of the fast-approaching woman. Yenelli finally turns to see the lady headed directly at her. She rolls her eyes and quickly hands her red flag to another marcher as the woman pulls Yenelli out of the demonstration. Yenelli turns back and shouts, "Can you believe it? I'm twenty-five years old, and my mother is still doing this to me!"

Home, Family, and School

BORN ON THE SIDE OF JUSTICE

When I was a child, I constantly heard stories about my father. I remember my mother writing letters to the *Sun-Times* about the Spanish Civil War and the rights of Mexican farm workers.[5] My parents were very supportive of the Spanish Republicans and were anti-Franco, antifascist. My father, who was born in 1909, was a strong supporter of the Cuban Revolution. He was active in the Fair Play for Cuba Committee.[6] I had a deep awareness of social justice, and advocating for the oppressed was always on my mind. I had a positive image of Fidel Castro from my parents.

My mother never told me, but I think my dad was a CPer (member of the Communist Party) or sympathizer. He was the Mexican spokesman for many White leftist groups. He was an organizer and involved in all kinds of campaigns. I have pictures of various events that took place around Jane Addams Hull-House, like of Primero de Mayo (the first of May).[7] I remember a sign that said, "Railroad workers support Primero de Mayo." It was a May Day march or rally. A lot of political activities started off at Hull-House.

My parents lived on Halsted Street. They married during the Depression, but initially my father lived with his parents on Roosevelt Boulevard, and my mother lived with her family on Newport Avenue. Their first place together was at Hull-House sometime in the late 1940s, right before I was born. Hull-House had huge dormitories, and social workers lived in those places. Then my parents moved to the north side of the city on Broadway in Uptown.[8] Uptown was still an immigrant community back then. My parents got divorced when I was seven. So I don't have many memories. But I have a picture my aunt sent to my father. It was signed, "To comrade. . . ."

My mother was a strong person. She immersed herself in my father's life, like a lot of women did with their husbands at that time. But she worked while he got his bachelor's degree. She put him through school. He received a civil engineering degree from the University of Illinois at Urbana-Champaign back in the thirties, but I think he started his program at Lewis University.[9] My mother went to Wright Junior College after she was divorced. She always said that it was too hard for her to concentrate. I went to class with her all the time.

My mother worked at Newberry Avenue Center on the Near West Side. I was the only non-Black child in the preschool nursery program. For first grade, I went down the block to Saint Francis of Assisi, which was right across the street from the Birthing Center. Then my mother got a job as a clerk in the public schools. I went to McClaren, Jackson, and Jefferson schools, right by UICC because that was where the predominant Mexican community was at the time. My consciousness was always anchored in that neighborhood. Even when we lived in Uptown, I was going to school on the Near West Side.

I was frequently elected president of my class. In sixth grade, I had this imposing Irish Catholic woman as a teacher, she was a real tough type. She hated me and wanted me blue slipped. At that time in the public schools if someone thought there was something psychologically wrong with you or if they thought there was a behavior problem, you got blue slipped. My mother, who was the school clerk, had a fit. She told the principal she would not allow it, but the teacher said it was either she or I. I can't imagine what I did. I was president of the class. I was a top student. She claimed the students all listened to me and not her.

My mother didn't want me blue slipped because she thought it would follow me forever. So she transferred me from Jackson to Jefferson, a little farther south of Taylor Street almost by Roosevelt Road. The school was mostly African American, very few Mexicans. I was there for a year. It was all right, but I always wanted to go to a neighborhood school.[10] I didn't like traveling across the city. By eighth grade, my mother allowed me to go to school nearby. I enjoyed that experience and later attempted to go to Senn High School.[11] It would have been a nice school for me because it had a large immigrant population there, and I would have felt more at home, but my mother enrolled me in Sullivan High School. She thought she was doing the best thing for me.

A MEXICAN WITH A KNIFE

I went to high school from 1961 to 1965. I hated it. Uptown had been an immigrant community, which I liked, but that was before the city dumped a good number of halfway houses in one neighborhood. A lot of people from Appalachia were moving there. My mother perceived the neighborhood to be going down. She said we were moving to Rogers Park because it was Jewish, and she believed Jews loved education. But it was a horrible experience for me because it was a middle-class and upper-middle-class school. It was just a nightmare. I just couldn't relate.

The culture at Sullivan was so different from what I had been accustomed. The Mexican girls at my old school wore black sweaters with white Ship 'n Shore blouses and black tight skirts and black baseball shoes with white lipstick, the clear kind. Then all of a sudden, I go to this place, and they're wearing oxfords and bobby socks rolled down around their ankles. They looked so weird. I thought they looked like a bunch of babies. I couldn't believe it. The culture was different. I just couldn't relate to it. It was really horrible.[12]

One day in advisory group, kids were coming up to Laurie, this girl next to me, and said, "Oh congratulations!" "Oh how wonderful!" "Congratulations!" and I'm thinking, so what's going on here? She had made Heiresses, a club, which was like a sorority. The girls had to be voted in, and so she had made it. They were saying, "Isn't Laurie beautiful. I think she is so beautiful." Personally, I thought she was ugly. I just couldn't relate to the culture of that school. I wasn't a player at all until I was a senior.

I had my own little group of friends. We were the rough crowd. My best friend was Mexican. I was told not to hang around with her because she was going to ruin my reputation. She was an "outy." I was socially unacceptable but not as much as her. In my high school, the Christian kids, the Anglos, were mostly the lower-class kids. They lived on Clark Street above the stores. Their parents were laborers. The middle-class Jews lived in large apartments or houses.

I went out with a guy who later worked for Bill Clinton. He even asked me to the senior prom, but instead I went with his best friend. As I got older, I started hanging out with the intellectual Jewish kids. The others I just couldn't stand. When I was a senior, this guy from SNCC, an African American fellow, came to someone's house.[13] I don't know how I landed there, but I did. He came to organize us. We formed a SNCC chapter at my school. I didn't know what I was doing. It was just something that appealed to me.

Then, the mother of the guy I was going to senior prom with had a fit that he was going with a Mexican. She said, "Mexicans! They carry knives! She'll kill you!" That image has stuck with me all my life; the image of Mexicans and knives is really strong. I very much saw myself as Mexican even though my mother is Middle Eastern. When someone would ask about my nationality,

I would always say I was Mexican first because I was afraid of the reaction. I thought I'd get it out right away. I'd say it fast. "I am Mexican and Middle Eastern." I'd hold my breath and wait for the reaction. I was always scared that someone was going to dislike me.

In many ways, my mother was the one that pushed me toward being Mexican. She was the one in high school that made me go to Mexico to keep contact with my relatives. I had relatives in Chicago who my brother grew up with, but when my parents got divorced, we only saw them occasionally. I still see them every so often, but my brother grew up with them. They were very close. When I saw other Mexicans, I felt like I had lost out on something. It was always very emotional for me because I felt like a part of me was torn out. I missed it, and I loved it. They were me, and something was missing from me.

My mother was born in 1910. Imagine what a Middle Eastern girl who had a Mexican boyfriend went through at that time. My mother's family was much more accepting, probably because they were Christian and not Muslim. But my parents were both just different. My brother says we had such interesting, stimulating, intellectual parents. But sometimes, I wonder what life would have been like with normal, nonneurotic parents.

Getting Involved

FRED HAMPTON CHANGED MY LIFE

After Fred Hampton was killed, I went several times to the house where he was murdered.[14] The Panthers were giving public tours of the building where it all happened.[15] He changed my life a lot, Fred Hampton. When I first heard about the Black Panthers, I was so freaked out. I was scared to death of them. I thought, "Oh my goodness, they're militant." They wore these black leather jackets and carried guns. But I was curious nonetheless.

I had gone to something before that I could not relate to at all. It was an SDS rally.[16] It was at People's Church.[17] I hated it. I disliked the guy who was leading it. All these White kids were jumping up and down, waving flags, and chanting in support of the National Liberation Front of Vietnam.[18] I thought I was going to an informational talk, and all of a sudden, everybody is jumping up and shouting, "Ho! Ho! Ho Chi Minh! The NLF is gonna win!" I thought, "We're talking about the enemy! Oh my God, we're chanting for the enemy!" These weren't people I could identify with either. I just felt like they were all so weird, and, oh the guy who was leading the meeting . . . I didn't like him from the first day I met him. I was really scared. I felt very uncomfortable. I couldn't relate to these people even though I eventually came to believe, yes, Ho Chi Minh and the NLF are our allies, definitely. But at that time I couldn't relate to those people.

Then, I went to a Black Panther rally. It felt totally different even though initially I was very scared. When I heard Fred Hampton speak, he really touched me. He was such a beautiful charismatic leader; he spoke about poor people, about being for the oppressed. I thought he was great. I really related to everything he said. He ended his talk the way the Panthers often did, "Black power for Black people! Brown power for Brown people! Red power for Red people! White power for White people! Yellow power for Yellow people! All power to all people! More power to the people!" He was a great speaker, a great leader. I heard him speak at the church on Ashland Avenue and Jackson Boulevard. A lot of movement activities happened at that church, too. It was close to the row of union locals. I went just to listen, but Fred Hampton totally changed my opinion about the Black Panther Party, because before that, I was afraid. Hearing what Fred had to say made a lot more sense than what I was led to believe from the media's distorted perspective.

LOVING COLLEGE

I went to college and joined SDS. But I wanted to do work related to Latinos. SDS was very patronizing. They made me ad hoc chairperson of the grape-strike committee. So I would have programs and work at the information booth outside of one of UICC's cafeterias. It was sometime between 1965 and 1969. There were hardly any Latino students on campus, and it seemed like those that were there were mainly Cubans. They would go past my booth and yell at me, "¡Comunista! ¡Comunista!" (Communist! Communist!) They were very reactionary.

I really hated high school with a passion, but I loved college. I had a great time. I met many different types of people and really enjoyed it. The Chicano Movement began toward the end of my college years, around 1969. The Movimiento came a little later to the Midwest than the Southwest.

Initially, I started getting involved with the Young Lords Organization.[19] Omar López was one of the leaders even though he was Mexican. He lived on the North Side.[20] The Brown Berets weren't quite as active as the Young Lords Organization in Chicago.[21] I had been friendly with the Panthers, the Lords, and the Young Patriots, a group of radical Whites, many of whom had come from the South, but it was the Black Panthers and the Young Lords that were the most active.[22]

I was taking a film class at UICC when at the end of the period, this guy raised his hand and announced that he was going to a rock concert that afternoon on campus and would be raising money for the Black Panther Party. "I'm going to be taking a can around the rock concert. Would anyone like to go with me?" I raised my hand and said, "I'll go with you. I'll go and raise money for the Panthers," and I did, too. Just imagine, a White kid at the end of class saying, "I'm going to this rock concert to raise money for the Panthers." I mean we were living in a different era. It was really a different feeling. It was a great time to be alive.

As soon as I graduated college, I moved into the neighborhood around UICC. My boyfriend at that time was friendly to Weather politics.[23] Moving into that neighborhood started getting me a little more involved in community projects. I taught Head Start for a year in 1969 just south of UICC to mostly Mexican and Black kids.[24] I threw myself into that job.

The first thing I did was to take down the United States flag. Whenever we'd go to all-school assembly, all the other kids would know the Pledge of Allegiance except mine. Officer Friendly would also try to talk to my kids about how to behave and what values to have. But every time he came to my class, I would say, "We're just on our way out" or "We're going on a field trip," then I'd take the kids out of the building.

He finally caught up with me. My Black kids were the most militant. When Officer Friendly was in the room, I had to ask the children, "So what's the baton for?" They'd respond, "To beat the people on the head!" Then I had to ask, "What's the gun for?" They answered, "To shoot the people!" There was a little survey after the lesson to assess whether the kids gave more positive or negative responses to the questions they were asked. Of course, a positive answer was for them to say Officer Friendly's gun was to shoot the bad people or to protect the good people. You can imagine how my students scored.

GETTING OUR OWN THING GOING

My first involvement with 18th Street was when I was a patients' advocate for the Benito Juárez Free Clinic.[25] This was at Howell House, which later became Casa Aztlán. An ex-boyfriend from SDS helped me get involved in the clinic. I was minimally involved in setting it up. We offered a lot of health education. The main objective was to make people aware of their rights so that Mexicanos would not allow doctors to take advantage of them.[26]

The Young Lords met at Casa Aztlán for a while until one of the directors used a member of the Brown Berets to threaten people. That director did a lot of anticommunist red-baiting. He told a leader of the Brown Berets that the Lords were communist. He told them that they needed to get them out of Casa Aztlán. The Berets eventually drove the Young Lords out of the center.[27] Later, that director became affiliated with a Mexican socialist group.

A COLOR IN THE CHICANO RAINBOW

I don't know how it happened exactly, but I attended the 1969 Chicano Youth Liberation Conference in Denver sponsored by the Crusade for Justice.[28] The 1969 gathering was the first National Chicano Youth Liberation Conference.[29] I didn't have anyone to go with, but I really wanted to be there. I was pretty much on my own. A busload of people went from Chicago. The conference was a very positive experience for me because being half-Mexican and half–Middle Eastern and not having been raised with my father, I was always questioning my identity. Am I really Mexican? That kind of thing. I spoke Spanish, not necessarily very well, but my mother had pushed me to go to Mexico several summers, and my Spanish really developed there.

Attending the Chicano Youth Liberation Conference really paid off. At first, I questioned my role and whether I'd fit in. I happened to be the only person attending from Chicago by myself so I was placed in Corky Gonzáles's house. I stayed there during the conference. I was surprised that his daughters didn't even speak Spanish! These were the daughters of "Mr. Chicano," the head of the Movement. That actually helped me a lot. It made me feel better, like I really did belong. I realized that there are just different "shades" of Chicanos.

The conference was interesting for me, but I was mainly an observer. Many people were from the Southwest. It was different from Chicago. I liked the term *Chicano*. I used it because it meant not from Mexico not from the United States, something in-between the two experiences. It helped me to define my existence. But there was still something off balance, maybe because being Chicano was still associated with the Southwest. I felt a little bit funny. It was not until I got older that I said to myself, "What are we talking about? Mexican immigrants are coming here all the time." I did feel more of an affinity to Mexico initially than I did to the Southwest, although over time that changed.

At the conference there were all these rumors and whispers in the conference hall about a bunch of angry women who might be coming into the auditorium. I was waiting to see what was going to happen. Then, these militant Chicanas rushed in with Magda Ramírez (she was not yet married at the time) at the front.[30] I met Magda at the university before I saw her at the Chicano conference, but I really didn't know her. I had gone to a couple of OLAS meetings at El Centro de la Causa. Then in Denver she came storming into the room at the head of a group of very militant women. They were angry because they felt used by the men—"Women are not equal parts of this." Corky Gonzáles's wife was in the room. She stood up and tried to defend her husband. There was this two-line struggle. Actually, there were all kinds of points of view being expressed, and there was Magda very involved, raising issues. Later, we talked and from the beginning hit it off.

The experience was very positive. I wanted to live in that moment, see it for myself, and decide what I thought. It was good. Although I might have had different perceptions than the others, I could see myself being a part of this. It was good to see the multitude of different experiences represented there. You had Corky Gonzáles's daughters, whose father was the head of the Chicano Movement and who didn't speak Spanish. You had gangbangers, Latinos of all different stripes. I perceived the Movement as a rainbow, Chicanos as a rainbow. It was interesting. The conference was my introduction to the Chicano Movement.

PILSEN

I traveled for a year in Europe, North Africa, and the Middle East. When I came back, I was in a semi-crisis because I didn't know what I wanted to do with my life. I knew I wanted to be politically involved in the Latino community, but doing what I did not know. I knew Omar López, the Chicano leader of the Young Lords from the North Side. I felt like I could go there and work with them. But I really wanted to be on 18th Street, though it was going to be a little bit harder.

I got a job teaching on Taylor Street.[31] It was at a Catholic school, yet I got the job through the public school system. I didn't like it. So when you don't know what to do with your life, what do you do? I went back to college to try a little graduate work in linguistics. I met Matin (later Yenelli's husband) at a demonstration and saw him again at UICC. We started seeing each other. It was around that time that I met John Velásquez. He was hiring for a job with the Right to Read program. I did not have to interview. He just asked, "You want a job? You want to be director of this program?" I said, "Okay, why not?"

I went back to school and met Isaura González and Leonard Ramírez, who later became involved in community issues. They were somewhat friendly to one of the SDS groups. That's what attracted me to them. Knowing I needed to find staff for my program, I told them about the positions. I thought they liked these kinds of left ideas, too. I tried to find people I could relate to one way or the other. Silvia, who was in the Progressive Labor Party, had just graduated from UICC and was a friend of Isaura's.[32] Leonard was still at Circle.[33] Silvia became a full-time teacher, and Isaura and Leonard worked as part-time instructors.

I was living on Taylor Street with a Middle Eastern female student and a White woman married to this guy from the Middle East. I was living in my own apartment and teaching. One night, it was around three o'clock in the morning, the doorbell started ringing. "Who is it?" I asked half asleep before opening the door. "It's Magda, remember me?" She was coming in with some Argentine guy to spend the night at my house. I thought, "Oh, sure . . ." There were some Black Panthers and Weather People in the living room anyway. I said, "Come in and join the crowd."

Isaura moved in when one of my roommates moved out. That's when we decided to get a place with Magda. Isaura, Magda, and I got an apartment on Halsted Street in one of the buildings owned by the Podmajerskys.[34] That's when I started getting really involved in community issues. People used to call the building we lived in Raza Towers because a number of community activists and social-service people lived there. That was a fun period; it was really an enjoyable time. We were involved in so many activities. We participated in demonstrations against the Vietnam War. We marched in Chicano contingents in the Mexican and Puerto Rican parades. Our house became a little headquarters for so much activity. It was a very enjoyable and satisfying period of my life.

As an undergraduate, I was a sociology major because I really wanted to understand how society operated, what made people do what they did, but the curriculum was horrible. It was very unsatisfying. We learned about the dating patterns of fraternity guys and sorority girls, which meant nothing to me. I met Matin and became familiar with the student movement he belonged to from his country. He started introducing me to political theory, Marxism. It all began to make so much more sense to me. It still does to this day. That was really helpful to finally begin to understand society better, at least to some degree.

When we had come back from the Chicano Youth Liberation Conference, there was a lot of excitement among those who attended, and it quickly spread to others. Howell House became Casa Aztlán. The first thing they did after the Denver conference was to hang a big Mexican flag outside the window. One of the persons in charge of the center flipped out. He was so freaked. "What are you doing?" he asked, very flustered and upset. I think he sicced one of the Berets on all of us. He accused us of being ultraleft or something weird.[35] It was nothing, you know, just aspirations of people rising to the surface after the conference. I remember he was *always* struggling against us. He was scary.[36]

NO JOBS, NO MEXICANS, NO JUSTICE!

By the early 1970s, I had already started getting involved in the neighborhood more consistently. When you're young, you just land places. Now we do things so much more deliberately. I met Cristina Vital at the CTA demonstration on 18th Street when we were stopping buses.[37] APO and other groups led the campaign. I was curious about Cristina's relationship with Maximo. Were they friends or *compañeros*?[38]

We asked the mostly Latino passengers to get off the buses. We would say, "Vamos a tener un ocupación. Deben de salir. ¡Por favor, salganse, por favor! Bajanse de este autobús" (We are conducting an occupation. You should leave. Please, leave! Please get off the bus!) Oh God, we were so bold. I have this image of Magda and Pablo Torres being at the center of this.[39] People were actually pretty cooperative after we explained that we were not going to let the buses pass through the community because the CTA did not hire Mexicanos. It discriminated against us. At one of the protests, people starting sitting down in the middle of the intersection, in the middle of 18th Street and Blue Island. I don't know where I was when the police came, but somehow I avoided getting arrested.

My poor mom was always upset with me because she saw me getting too involved. She was worried about me. But we were having an effect on people. Isaura had a distinct lifestyle from Magda and me. She had always been so disciplined. She would go to bed early and get up at the crack of dawn. We changed her. We really corrupted her, poor thing.

Magda and I were different. Magda was working full-time for the Fair Employment Practices Commission downtown. Isaura was still in college and working for the Right to Read Program at Centro (El Centro de la Causa, Center for the Cause). Back then, there was more money for community programs compared to what there is today.

LATINO LIBERALS AND US

There were people at Centro who did nothing. Half of the time, they weren't even around, but I was the one that got fired. There was a struggle around that. It was at the end of the second year, and we had to write a proposal to get a grant renewed. I think the Right to Read Program was funded for two years. I had to write the proposal. I hated grant writing, but I worked really hard. It was like a final examination. I crammed all night to write the thing. Finally, I laid it on the boss's desk and said I'm going home because I hadn't slept all night.

I got to my apartment and crashed, but then I got a phone call from Phil and one of the other directors of El Centro. "Yenelli, we have to talk to you."

I said, "Can't it wait until tomorrow morning?" I was already in bed in my pajamas.

"We got to talk to you now. It's very important!" So I got dressed and went back. John, Phil, and Sandy, the center's administrators, were in one of the classrooms waiting for me. They all deny it now. They blame each other. They told me they were letting me go.

"What?" I said.

"We're going to let you go."

I was furious because they used me to do the proposal, and as soon as they had what they needed, they fired me. They said I was seen leafleting on the streets, organizing, and not running the program, doing politics on company time. A buddy of all of Centro's leadership at that time was on the board. He passes himself off as a progressive academic these days. He was John's *compadre*.[40] He backed them up. When the struggle occurred, I went straight to Father Harrington, who supported me.[41] I was reinstated.

POLITICAL DIFFERENCES

Most of us got involved in the Angel Moreno campaign that happened around 1973. He was running for U.S. Representative. It was after we came back from the Raza Unida Convention.[42] That whole year we worked on his campaign until election time. I remember I was fairly active in that campaign, although I always struggled with it. I didn't feel comfortable with electoral politics.[43] I thought it gave people the wrong idea. It just gave legitimacy to the system that was stacked against us. It's a waste of time. But there were no Mexican representatives, and people were excited about the possibilities of creating a Mexicano/Chicano electoral party. The alderman at the time was Vito Marzullo, a corrupt Twenty-Fifth-Ward politician who was part of the Daley machine. He growled at me once in a heavy ethnic accent, "Yah Mex-E-cans. . . . Yah don't even know how ta speak English." And he was supposedly the representative of the Mexicano/Chicano barrio.[44]

I went along and worked hard on the campaign. The director from Aztlán was involved, too. But Cardiss Collins won the election. Sometime after the campaign, the Raza Unida Party in Chicago split. Angel Moreno went into one group. I think Angel was originally from Texas, where the Raza Unida Party had originated and where it was the strongest. Angel told somebody that I was an Arab in Mexican disguise. But by that time, I was confident about who I was. I'm half Middle Eastern and half Mexican. I'm Mexican.

The head of the Texas Farm Workers Union (TFWU) in Chicago lived across the street from us. He was married to a White woman. She was an organizer, too, very nice progressive woman, but he had a wife and kids back in Mexico. I often overlooked these contradictions in Mexican men. We worked with him for a while on farmworker issues, but he wanted to be in charge, make all the decisions. He thought because he was the official union representative, this meant we were going to automatically fall in line behind him. But we felt we had no obligation to play a passive role, and so we organized our own pickets and decided what activities we were going to conduct in support of farmworkers.

We started the Farah Strike Support Committee in Chicago. Some Argentine syndicalists raised the idea at a few of our meetings.[45] We also later got involved with a woman who was a Farah unionist. Termudiz was from El Paso, and she came and stayed at our house. She was on a national tour. We had a big rally and a dance to raise money for the strikers. We always had dances, and many of them were quite successful.

Then the Revolutionary Communist Party started getting involved.[46] I never could relate to them. I liked their politics, but as people I never could relate to them. In the days of long hair, they had short-cropped hair to mimic workers. They dressed so conservatively. They tried to appear and act straight-laced, upholders of the nuclear family and all that. It was so weird to me. They looked totally different from my own perception of what working people were like.

A lot of things were going on, and the Comité was right in the middle of it. It was a different time. I don't think it was just because we were young. We didn't have kids. Of course, that makes a difference. But people weren't so bogged down in concepts of career or getting ahead. People were more open to different ideas and were less likely to let the media and politicians shape their minds. It was a freer time.

REJECTING MIDDLE-CLASS FEMINISM

Mexican men or Latino men in general are so oppressed that I didn't feel like the women's issue was the right issue for us at the time. That's how I felt. We're all so oppressed that these other distinctions seemed less important. I also didn't always interpret men's behavior as chauvinistic per se. I just interpreted it as someone's personality. Maybe I didn't see things as they were.

It was after I had children that women's issues had more of an effect on my personal life because I felt a lot of responsibility toward my kids. The kids themselves are what held me back as a woman because they became a priority. I felt like so many other women who took up the struggle. It was the women who were the activists whether they had our particular political orientation or a different one. It always seemed to be the women who were the most active. Cristina's and Magda's experiences were a little bit different. You know, a lot of women were more formally educated than the men. Maybe that was a factor.

Perhaps I encountered chauvinism in my own individual personal life but not in political organizations. In the beginning of the movement, we weren't able to make those distinctions because it was just a burgeoning movement. We rejected the White feminist model and had a lot of struggle against feminism. We felt it was a divisive thing. It was dividing men and women. We felt it was a White woman's thing because a lot of the argument was framed with a more middle-class spin on issues that we weren't really dealing with. It was Betty Friedan and Gloria Steinem, the woman who used to work for Playboy.[47] I remember thinking it was a personal and not a political thing.

Some of my students or mothers that I worked with at places like Komensky School had husbands who would exploit them.[48] I would try to deal with these things on a personal level, struggle with their husbands. A lot of husbands didn't particularly want their wives to hang out with me. But I saw this more as a personal thing. I dealt with this personally, not in a political way. I just couldn't figure out how to deal with it politically. If you are going to launch a campaign, women have to be as involved as they can be. You had to struggle with their partners. But what was the solution? They couldn't leave their husbands. Many of these women didn't have papers and were supported by their spouses.[49] What were they going to do?

We dealt with it on a personal level, not politically or in an open or public way. We really downplayed it because we felt that if a *trabajador Mexicano* (Mexican worker) was oppressing his wife, well, it was the same old thing: the system oppresses the husband, the husband oppresses the wife, the wife oppresses the kids, and the kids kick the dog. We downplayed the oppression and said he's not the enemy. He's alcoholic or he's beating his wife because of all the problems he is encountering in society. Not to condone it, but we didn't feel at the time that this was the central issue.

During the Farah strike, we brought up gender because most of the strikers were women.[50] We raised it and said that it was a women's movement, a struggle composed of and for women. So it wasn't like it was not mentioned at all. It was more like, yes, the man was an oppressor, but look how strong women can be, as opposed to saying that the Mexican working-class man is part of the problem or at least his chauvinism was part of the problem.

End of a Collective Vision

WHAT WAS GAINED

A lot of reforms occurred in the community that otherwise wouldn't have. I am not saying just because of us, our group, but because of all that occurred during that whole period of time. A lot of reforms were obtained. I think Latinos became more public in the U.S. scene. Before that, we were invisible to most people, especially to the powers that be. We gained more of a voice. Latinos were propelled onto the national stage at least to some degree, not as much as I think they should be, but at least they became players much more so than they were. We fought to establish Benito Juárez High School, the clinic at Aztlán, just a lot of reforms. Look at the college programs. We fought to have Latinos admitted to college. I hope many of our kids will have some degree of consciousness. Hopefully, they'll be able to take it up in their lives and do something with it. The six of us wanted to tell people that through the struggle, many goals were advanced. I sincerely believe that the squeaky wheel gets the grease. If you are quiet and passive, you don't get anything, whether it's reform or revolution, some change, or a new society. You have to fight for what's just and fair; otherwise, it's not going to happen.

On a personal level I really developed. At first, I couldn't even speak Spanish very well. Sometimes at meetings, somebody would say, "Well, we should try to speak in Spanish since we are in the Latino community." For a week, I would be terrified because there was this pressure to speak exclusively in Spanish. Then it would kind of subside, and you could start speaking English again. But because we were trying to get people from the community to become involved, and people from Pilsen would come and sit down at our meetings, we had to speak Spanish. Maximo generally chaired meetings, but as the years progressed, I came to the point where I actually could lead a meeting in Spanish.

Being involved helped me understand the world overall. Through social practice you begin to understand the complications and contradictions in politics and life much more easily. There was this seed from my childhood, always looking, being sympathetic to the underdog. I hate to use that term, *underdog*, but that was how my mom always saw it. Anyway, that seed just blossomed. Over time and through my involvement, I became satisfied. I'm very satisfied that I was part of the Movement and that I lived in Pilsen.

I would have liked to try to live there permanently, but then the gangs took over the neighborhood. I couldn't at that point. It was just too much. The only thing I couldn't handle was the gangs. The drive-by shootings every night, the fear that your kids walking home might get shot. That was too much. The gangs took up housekeeping on my block, and my son used to walk from Saint Pious School to Gads Hill.[51] There were drive-bys right on my block. There would always be gunshots . . . tish, tish, tish, tish. My neighbors and I literally started living in our kitchens. I was very naïve and innocent about drug dealing and crime. People could have a million dollars and not have a job, and it wouldn't even occur to me how they accomplished that. But now, I know.

LEAVING PILSEN

I don't feel you got to have an organized unified leadership to get anything done. We didn't have it. But I think a more formal organization could carry things even further. Yet, we lived in a historic moment. We were in the United States in relatively good times. Eventually, things went down hill, the struggles subsided nationwide, for whatever reason. I'm not sure why, but they did. What we were experiencing in our neighborhood was going on in the African American community and in colleges and throughout society. Our decline came a little bit later than some of the other 1960s struggles, but it kind of followed the approximate timeline.

It's hard to struggle. It saps your energy. It makes you tired. Bourgeois society, every society is pulling on you every which way. We activists needed more theory. We needed to know what we were doing and in what direction we needed to move. Our idea was that we were going to change the whole society, not just our particular neighborhood and not just for a few reforms. We wanted to change all of society. We had a lot of models. The Soviet Union failed as a model, but People's China was a model for a while. Cuba was important. Mexican politics were also important to us.

When it was time for me to get married, I said to myself, "I'm going to marry a Middle Easterner or a Latino." I never wanted to marry a White guy. I always thought my kids would go to Saint Ignatius High School, and I would live in the neighborhood.[52] I wanted to be a member of a community. I wanted to be struggling in that community. But when the gang thing started happening, it was just too much. I said, "Where are we going to go? I got to get out of here. I can't stand this drama. I can't stand the drive-by shootings." I felt like I was in Lebanon. I still get this knot in my stomach when I hear car wheels screeching. I was really traumatized by the entire thing. When I was dealing with the gangs, I was by myself. It wasn't in a collective. It was just my neighbors and I.

The last two years I lived in Pilsen were traumatic. Teresa was one of the heads of the Counts.[53] She was my neighbor from across the street. Mama

Count was after me because I was organizing the neighborhood. I didn't want them on our block. None of us did. We didn't want them because of our kids. You could handle the gangs when they were on the corner at a distance. You could cross the street so you don't have to walk past the drug dealers. But when they are driving by and shooting every other night, it's very difficult to live like that.

The day I moved, I cried my head off. All the neighbors who had been active were crying because I was very close to them. But I wasn't the first one to leave. Jesse, a Chicano and a great guy, lived two doors down from me. He was a real bulwark of our block.[54] He was the one who had the confrontation with Teresa when she started dealing drugs across the street from him. We used to have meetings at his house. I didn't fully appreciate the impact that the departure of a really strong figure has on a community until he left. Then they started renting his place. Before it was owner occupied. More people started saying they wanted to get out of there. It was really depressing. It was a good struggle, too, because people came forward. When we called the police, we asked them to please push the gangbangers off the street, to do something. But the police would point us out to the gangs. It was very scary.

I couldn't believe it. The Mexican head of the police district, the commander, was such a jerk. I remember him saying, "Oh, you people, I understand how you feel. I would get out of here as soon as I could. I know you all want to get out of here as soon as you possibly can."

I said, "What are you talking about? We're trying to make the neighborhood better. What are you saying?"

He said, "I got out as soon as I could." I thought, "What a total jerk. How is he going to try to protect us when he thinks the only way we can better ourselves is to leave the community?"

The police would basically tell the gangbangers, the kids, about us calling. They would say, "Are you the ones the lady called about? She said you kids were smoking reefer in front of her house." They would finger you so that the kids would know and get angry.

We had a meeting with the kids and told them, "You guys, if we see two of you hanging on the block, we're going to call the police."

They would get angry and say, "Oh, you can't do that, that's against the Constitution."

We said, "No, it isn't, and we feel really badly about it, but we're still going to do it because we're desperate. Because when two or three of you get together, the other gang comes and starts shooting. We don't want our kids to be shot at."

"Oh, man," they'd say.

We'd respond, "That's just how it is." And then we formed a telephone tree. It was mostly me initiating it. I said, "You know, there's three guys on the corner, and we told them what we were going to do." We'd call each other, and all the neighbors would go out on the street. We'd all stand there when the police came to send the message that we all called, and the cops couldn't single us out to the gang kids. It was very effective. It was great. I was very happy with my neighbors and the life we led. It was very disappointing when we moved.

My husband couldn't get any jobs in Chicago anyway. I wanted to try a small town, and it just kind of happened. I was sick of the violence. That was the only thing. You can always get around everything else but that. I learned a lot about drug dealing. I know that the government and the wealthy have no real will to win the war on drugs. That's a lie. They really are not working to end drug trafficking, just to control it and keep it in poor neighborhoods. In order to make our communities a little more tolerable, I support the legalization of drugs. That's the only way to make it safer. It's not a solution to the drug problem by any means, but it's a way to make the minority, oppressed communities safer. Take away the market. I feel that it's basically social-emotional reasons why kids are in gangs. But the reasons for the killings are more related to turfs, markets. The imperialists legally do a lot of atrocious things like conduct wars to maintain their profits and power worldwide, while the other market, the black market, or the illegal market, uses violence and corruption in another way. Living around the street drug scene in Pilsen changed me in a lot of ways. It's one of the harshest aspects of life in poor urban communities. I think it's the worst, almost.

A MESSAGE FOR YOUNG PEOPLE

Mexicans, Latinos, oppressed peoples, minorities have gotten as far as they have gotten because of the struggles that occurred. Granted, society itself has to incorporate people to some degree, or, otherwise, it's in trouble. But nothing really happens unless you struggle for it. Just trying to convince somebody might work on a very small scale. I suppose that can happen. But generally people respond to pressure. However you apply it. They respond to counter-power. I'm sorry to say, but that's how the world works. We had a lot of disagreements with Pilsen Neighbors, but the one thing they were doing that a lot of our allies weren't was organizing.[55] They were organizing in the schools.

The schools were a very good place to organize. Education is the one thing that people will always struggle around because people sense that they have no other way to advance themselves. What other way is there for them to be integrated into society? What other kind of investment in a future can they make? There is only education. There is no other route for people to chase the so-called American Dream or to fit in or to make their lives a little bit better for themselves. It is only through education. So a lot of the struggles I was involved in myself were related to education. Kids in the community with all their problems and poor skills see the world for what it is. They don't have illusions. Working people generally don't have illusions about life and society. At least, African American people and Latinos see things much more clearly. They see how things really are. Middle-class, Caucasian people have many more illusions about everything. People have to look to see where their gains have come from, and by far they have come through struggle.

I WOULD DO IT ALL OVER AGAIN

I have never been a career-oriented person. I have never seen myself working my way up some kind of ladder. I'm fifty years old, and sometimes I say to myself, "I don't have a career."[56] I wish I did, but it's no big deal. It's not a big thing. I'd rather have been more successful in the Movement and maybe have my family life be a little better. But I don't have any regrets.

I wish I could have stayed away from RCP. They were such a drain on my life. I liked their politics, yes, because of their connection with students from the Middle East. I played along with them for so long but never liked them as people. I almost liked the liberal left better. It was such a contradiction. I spent a lot of energy struggling with RCP, trying to reform them. I should just have done my own thing. My desire was always to try and get a unified left working in Pilsen. I was trying to get RCP and then ATM and then other people together with us.[57] It just didn't happen.

We all could have been more theoretical and obtained more guidance so we might know where we were going. But we were activists by nature. I certainly am more of an activist, a practitioner, than an academician. Maybe I would have tried to integrate my family life better, because I feel that I did throw myself so much into the Movement that I didn't pay much attention to being a wife and mother. Now that I'm fifty, it's easy to say, but I wish I had paid a little more attention to that.

I don't believe in God, but I believe in the expression, "There but for the grace of God go I." I really believe the more you have, the more you should give because it is just by luck that someone is born a *campesino* (agricultural laborer) in Central America or born to a middle-class family in Chicago. It's just luck. We owe it to each other, to *los de abajo* (the underdogs), to try to make a better society for everybody.[58] I felt like, hey, I happened to be born

Latina. I wanted to get to know my culture. I had a lot to offer, and I kind of felt like it was my obligation or duty to give back. People should try to do whatever they can to better society until we have the just and good society. It's a struggle. It's either a personal struggle or a political struggle, done in a more collective, communal way. That's certainly a better way, and you will benefit individually as well. You will reap the benefits of participating and giving.

Notes

1. This introductory vignette relies on Leonard Ramírez's memory of an event and was subsequently developed in collaboration with Yenelli Flores. The substance of this chapter comes from several interviews that occurred mainly in 1998 but that continued until 2008.

2. The latter slogan alludes to the call for only one flag to fly over Puerto Rico.

3. *Boricua* is a collective term for the inhabitants of Borinquen, the Taino name for the island of Puerto Rico.

4. A timbale is a set of compact drums, commonly used in Caribbean areas of Latin America.

5. The *Sun-Times* is one of two major Chicago newspapers. The struggle of Mexican farmworkers has a long history that extends at least back to the 1920s (Etulain, 2002; Griswald–Del Castillo & Garcia, 1995).

6. According to Saul Landau (1992), the Fair Play for Cuba Committee benefited from the enthusiastic participation of students who visited the island in the early years of the revolution. Dignitaries such as the French philosopher Jean-Paul Sartre and U.S. sociologist C. Wright Mills lent their support to the organization.

7. May First is celebrated internationally as a worker's holiday commemorating the battle for the eight-hour day.

8. By 1970, Chicago's Uptown community became known as a transient area populated by Appalachian Whites and Native Americans.

9. In a set of family papers Yenelli Flores provided is a profile of her father. Lewis Institute, where he received his civil engineering degree, merged with Armour Institute in 1940 to form the Illinois Institute of Technology. He received an economics degree from UIUC.

10. Yenelli is referring to the Uptown area where she lived.

11. In 2005, a wing of Nicholas Senn High School was converted into a naval academy despite protests by parents and students to not militarize the school.

12. A study by Pathey-Chávez (1993) provides an insightful example from Los Angeles of a school culture disconnected from Latino working-class student life.

13. The Student Nonviolent Coordinating Committee (SNCC, pronounced "snick") was one of the major Black civil-rights organizations. One of its projects was focused on voter registration (O'Malley, 1992).

14. Fred Hampton was deputy chairman of the Illinois Black Panther Party. Hamp-

ton was twenty-one at the time of his death in 1969. In his short life, he showed himself to be an impressive leader, organizing Black youth and brokering peace treaties among street gangs. He was an inspirational speaker and became a symbol of 1960s dynamic youth leadership. His assassination led activists to conclude that the movement had become the target of political repression. This was confirmed by the subsequent discovery of the FBI's COINTELPRO program (counterintelligence program).

15. The Black Panthers hosted tours highlighting the contradictions in the official police version of the raid that resulted in what the Panthers claimed was the intentional assassination of Fred Hampton and Mark Clark in 1969.

16. SDS was the most important activist student group of the 1960s. SDS became synonymous with 1960s radical youth. The organization split at its 1969 convention into rival factions including the Revolutionary Youth Movement, which subsequently divided into RYM I and RYM II and the Worker Student Alliance (WSA) led by the Progressive Labor Party (PLP). RYM I subsequently reorganized as Weatherman (also known as the Weathermen) and transformed into an armed underground organization (Berger, 2006; H. Jacobs, 1970; R. Jacobs, 1997; Moore, 2001; Sale, 1973; Varon, 2004).

17. People's Church on Armitage Avenue in the Lincoln Park community had been taken over by the largely Puerto Rican Young Lord's Organization in an action led by Jose "Cha Cha" Jimenez, the major spokesperson of the YLO. People's Church became a community center and for many years was the site of left activities in the city.

18. The National Liberation Front of Vietnam was also referred to derisively by the U.S. military as the Vietcong. The name was later used by U.S. radical students in a more positive and admiring way.

19. Jose "Cha Cha" Jimenez was said to have been impressed with Fred Hampton and the Panther's analysis of exploitation and later turned the Young Lords from a mostly Puerto Rican street gang to a political organization. For more about the Young Lords Organization, see the interview with Mervin Mendez at http://gangresearch. net/ChicagoGangs/latinkings/lkhistory.html (accessed March 31, 2007).

20. In the 1970s, Latino Chicago was often divided between the "Mexican" South Side and the Puerto Rican North Side, although Latinos from these groups could be found in both areas of the city.

21. The Brown Berets was a paramilitary organization that began in California but with loosely affiliated chapters in other parts of the country. Muñoz (1989) compares them to Ron Karenga's Black nationalist organization, the United Slaves, and not the more Marxist Black Panthers. However, the Brown Berets was difficult to categorize since the organization differed by region and chapter and contained varying political orientations even within each group. Interviews of ex-members of the Los Angeles Berets suggest rival tendencies within the Berets, a cultural nationalist and a more internationalist wing (Pulido, 2006).

22. The Young Patriots Organization began in Chicago and spread to several states. The alliance among this mainly Appalachian White youth group, the Black Panther

Party, and the Young Lords Organization has been referred to as the first rainbow coalition.

23. *Weather* refers to Weatherman, the Revolutionary Youth Movement I faction of SDS that formed after the 1969 SDS convention. Weatherman eventually came to advance an urban-guerilla-war strategy for the New Left. At the time referred to by Yenelli, Weatherman was still an above-ground organization.

24. Head Start was created in 1965 to address issues of health and educational achievement for low-income children and their parents. It is a program of the federal Department of Health and Human Services.

25. Benito Juárez, a Zapotec Indian, became one of Mexico's presidents. He is credited with heading the resistance against the French-imposed crown. The clinic, located at Casa Aztlán, was named after this Mexican patriotic leader.

26. The reference is to the practice of using Mexicans and other Latinos in medical experiments without their full consent.

27. There were often tensions between purely nationalist elements of the movement and the more politically radical tendencies, paralleling the conflict between Black cultural nationalist formations and the Black Panther Party in California, a division that the FBI is said to have exploited (Muñoz, 1989). Some members of the Brown Berets had once been in local gangs. A few Berets eventually adopted a friendly attitude toward socialist groups in the Movement.

28. It is not clear if Yenelli and Magda attended the 1969 or 1970 conference. But it seems as if they were present at the 1970 conference.

29. Crusade for Justice, based in Denver, Colorado, was led by Rodolfo "Corky" Gonzáles. It advocated for community control of institutions and was often associated with the more radical and even revolutionary nationalist wing of Chicanismo.

30. It is unclear whether this incident with Magda occurred at the first or second Denver conference.

31. Yenelli is referring to the Near West Side community in the vicinity of the Chicago campus of the University of Illinois.

32. PLP or PL provided leadership to the Worker Student Alliance faction of SDS.

33. The University of Illinois at Chicago Circle was also commonly referred to as Circle or Circle Campus.

34. John and Annelies Podmajersky were a husband-and-wife partnership of local developers who early on were involved in the gentrification of the Pilsen neighborhood. They attracted into the community White artists among others and, according to activists, raised rents beyond the reach of many poor and working-class Mexicans. "Raza Towers," as it was humorously referred to, was exceptional in that the majority of renters in that building were Mexican, mostly students and professionals. In 2011, Pilsen remained a contested area threatened by gentrification.

35. In movement circles, the phrase *to be ultraleft* was informally used in two ways: as a critique against those who quickly defaulted to confrontational tactics at mass rallies, protests, or other events or referred to an overly rigid adherence to

some set of idealized Marxist concepts that were removed from social context and practical realities. This ideological rigidity often led to individuals and groups being condemned for their deviation from some understanding of political orthodoxy.

36. The director that Yenelli is referring to later shifted among various political groups, at times supporting culturally nationalist positions or even affiliating with a socialist-oriented group in the community that he was eventually urged to leave. Yenelli and other Comité members saw him as an opportunist and obstructionist.

37. Latino activists accused the Chicago Transit Authority of discriminatory hiring practices.

38. The term *compañeros* (comrades) was also used by Movement people to refer to significant others.

39. Pablo Torres was a Mexican worker and founder of APO.

40. The term *compadre* can have a range of meanings from a close family friend to someone brought into an extended kin relationship who might serve as religious sponsor or as foster parent for children in the event that the biological parents are unable to care for their children.

41. Father John Harrington was the pastor of Providence of God, one of the major churches on the east side of Pilsen, where a number of events took place including community dances and fundraisers, such as for the Farah strikers.

42. For a discussion of this attempt to create a third-party Chicano alternative, see J. A. Gutiérrez (1998) and Navarro (2000).

43. El Partido de la Raza Unida in Illinois split and eventually dissolved. There are various versions as to why this occurred. Comité members mention the lack of a Mexican electoral concentration that could replicate successes in Texas. National divisions also may have come to play in the form of two left tendencies within the Mexicano/Chicano Movement represented nationally by José Angel Gutiérrez and the more outspoken leader Rodolfo "Corky" Gonzáles. However, Chicago also had a strong Marxist current. Magda Ramírez-Castañeda believes differences arose between those with a nationalist and primarily reformist agenda and those with a class-orientation and radical-transformative perspective.

44. Florence Scalla, the Italian community representative known for her efforts to stave off the gentrification of the Near West Side, discusses the negative role played by Marzullo, an ally of Richard J. Daley, in the campaign to locate UICC on the Near West Side (Eastwood, 2002).

45. These were members of the Sojourner Truth Organization (STO), a socialist group that advanced the idea that White-skinned privilege was a critical and divisive aspect of the U.S. class structure. Noel Ignatin (later Ignatiev), a leader of SDS and subsequently of STO, went on to edit the magazine *Race Traitor.*

46. RCP was an outgrowth of the Bay Area Revolutionary Union with roots in the Revolutionary Youth Movement II faction of SDS.

47. The criticism here is of White, middle-class feminism. Steinem worked as a Playboy bunny as part of research project on the treatment of women at Playboy.

48. Yenelli led a campaign to rid the school of mobile units, trailer-like vehicles that were used as classrooms in overcrowded schools. During an informal discussion about the inferior educational resources for Latino children, an Anglo teacher, a military veteran, rushed toward Yenelli in a threatening manner. She struck him. He rendered her unconscious for a few moments. They were subsequently both transferred.

49. Yenelli is referring to U.S. residency and the women's status as undocumented workers.

50. The Comité organized a labor solidarity committee in support of the mostly Mexicana/Chicana clothing workers on strike against the Texas-based Farah Company.

51. Gads Hill, a social settlement house in Pilsen, offers after-school programs and other activities for youth.

52. Saint Ignatius High School is a prestigious, private Catholic school in Chicago.

53. Latin Counts were one of the Pilsen-based gangs at the time.

54. Yenelli is using Chicano in this context to signify someone primarily socialized in the United States.

55. Pilsen Neighbors Community Council began in 1954 and initially served a primarily Eastern European community until the neighborhood became majority Mexican in the late 1960s. Pilsen Neighbors is now overwhelming Mexican.

56. Yenelli was fifty years old at the time of the interview in the late 1990s.

57. The August Twenty-Ninth Movement was an outgrowth of the Labor Committee of the Raza Unida Party in Los Angeles (Muñoz, 1989).

58. *Los de abajo* (the underdogs) is also the title of Mariano Azuela's popular novel of the Mexican Revolution.

Living the Life
I Was Meant to Lead

ISAURA GONZÁLEZ

On the Picket Line, 1972

Saturday is a busy day in Chicago's downtown shopping district.[1] Suburbanites come into the city in crowded buses and on trains. The more daring suffer through traffic jams in search of reasonably priced parking. On the streets, mothers push baby carriages and firmly grasp small, gloved hands that occasionally try to break free and run toward glittering holiday window displays. Mechanical toy figurines, gilded Ferris wheels, stuffed animals, and slender mannequins in evening apparel attract an endless queue of shoppers into the row of State Street stores. With every revolving-door rotation, small gusts of invisible perfume clouds escape from the fragrance counters where porcelain-faced women spray scents onto pearl-white sample cards that they wave gently in the air.

On the sidewalk, a group of protesters move in a circle. They lift placards and raise their voices in a collective chant. A woman whose raven hair falls down to her waist is on a bullhorn leading the crowd, "Boycott Farah pants! Justice for the Farah strikers!" A small squad of uniformed policemen stands vigil, watching the group of about forty, mostly young Mexicans. A few demonstrators step out of the line to hand flyers to those passing by. Two men unravel a banner at the curb that reads, "Boycott Farah pants!" The goateed man holding one end motions to the other with an army jacket and frameless, round specs to stretch the banner so that the organizational sponsor "Farah Strike Support Committee" can be read more easily. An elderly couple carries Chicago Jewish Labor Federation signs. Down the block at the street corner, a few White women sell their organizational newspaper. A tall brunette with her hair stuffed into a knit cap holds a stack of papers in one hand and lifts a copy high over the heads of the crowd, shouting, "Support the Farah strikers!"

Meanwhile, the long-haired woman with the bullhorn continues to lead the protesters in a chant. The marchers respond in a chorus, punctuating each word with gusto. Slogans are shouted in English and at other times in Spanish. The woman with the bullhorn steps in front of the picket line and begins to address those moving down the street angling toward the store entrance: "There are Mexicanas/Chicanas on strike in Texas that are demanding fair wages. They want their union recognized." A few shoppers stop to listen. Others take a flyer and smile sympathetically. A man in a long, tweed coat grabs a leaflet and crumples it before throwing it violently to the ground. After the first hour, the police begin to focus their attention elsewhere. They become involved in their own conversation and are lulled into numbness by the repetitive sounds of passing cars and the monotony of street activity.

A delegation of protesters demands to speak to the store's management. They wish to know why clothes made in sweatshops are being sold there. A dozen or so activists blend into the crowd and follow the shoppers into the store. It is only later that the police realize that there are smaller numbers on the picket line and begin to wonder if perhaps some have entered the building. They huddle and appear somewhat confused. Two uniformed men enter the store in search of those who may have entered.

Isaura stays on the line with one of the other members of the Comité. They walk behind the gray-haired couple bundled up in heavy coats and thick, fur-trimmed, Russian winter hats. The Comité members move around the circle holding signs and fall into a steady rhythm of conversation. A few more friends join them. Isaura suggests they meet at a nearby coffee shop afterward for a late lunch.

Inside, the young man in charge of the area watches a group of women move into his section. They cross over to the spinning carousel of pants hung on metal hangers. "Ladies, those are 20 percent off," the smartly dressed clerk informs them politely. They smile and continue to carefully examine the display of pants. Hands run over the cloth fibers, evaluating the weight of the fabric, assessing its thickness, wondering if the material is sturdy enough to withstand Chicago winters.

Women are such fussy shoppers, the clerk thinks to himself, but quickly returns to boxing items and ringing up purchases. More customers have joined the line at the register. A flurry of credit cards, shopping bags, and the continuous opening and closing of cash drawers occupies the attention of the three clerks behind the counter. Later, after the rush of sales has ebbed, the young supervisor scans the area for anyone who might need assistance. There is now only a white-haired woman at the sales section. "Those are 20 percent off," he says to the woman, but he is already looking at the man moving toward him, the holiday help and his relief. They nod at one another as the supervisor heads for the elevators to begin his break.

The elderly lady at the sales rack wonders whether she should notify someone. Almost every pair of pants in the Farah section has been damaged, sliced, it appears, by a razor. She thinks for another moment before deciding against it, moving away quickly. "They'll find out soon enough anyway," she says to herself as she walks down the aisle. Besides, there is just too much shopping to do before Christmas.

Outside on the thinning picket line, protestors continue to chant and pass leaflets. Isaura and her friends begin to shout loudly, trying to raise the level of enthusiasm of those still marching in the freezing cold. Soon they will be on their way. They want to make the last ten minutes on the picket line count. Victoria and Cristina wave good-bye as they leave the line for home.

From nowhere, a portly elderly couple breaks out of the crowd of shoppers and moves menacingly toward Isaura, shouting something barely intelligible, their cherry-red faces explode as they struggle in heavy Eastern European accents to convey a message that is reduced to one garbled word, "Go-backa-to-wherea-you-coma-from!" Before Isaura and the others can respond, the Jewish couple rushes forward. The small woman in the fur-lined hat releases a whipping verbal assault in her best native Chicago accent, "Get outta here ya DPs! Ya can't even speak English!"[2]

Home, Family, and School

FROM THE BORDER TO CHICAGO

I was born in 1944 in Blue Town in the valley near Brownsville, Texas, that I hear was under water at one point when the Rio Grande flooded. I think that was in the 1960s. We really didn't stay there long. My family lived in Weslaco, Texas, until I was four years old, at which point we came to Chicago. My uncle told my dad there were jobs here. My parents worked at the Morrison Hotel doing maintenance. My mother later prepared salads while my dad continued to do cleaning. We lived on Halsted Street at Madison Street, a little north of where the university stands today. There were all these little buildings. It was primarily a German neighborhood. In the late 1940s and 1950s, a lot of Mexicans started moving in. A little farther south was Saint Patrick's, where we attended school. Our backyard was where the expressway is today. Today, a bank stands where the Morrison Hotel once was.

My family moved to 18th Street in 1953. We were there for a couple of years until we moved again in 1955 to Milwaukee and Western Avenues. My parents had a hard time finding a place because they had six kids and they were Mexican. We went riding around and eventually found a large apartment. I don't know why my parents picked the Northwest Side.[3] They really had no plan in mind. They were not that organized.

When I was younger, I was in and out of the hospital. I had congenital heart disease. From sixth grade until I was eighteen, I went to a special school. By that time, I already had two heart operations. But I didn't see myself as handicapped. I saw myself as having a heart condition, but the kids I went to school with had more visible disabilities. They had polio and other illnesses and used crutches or wheelchairs. They had a difficult time getting around. A lot of these students died during their school years. So at an early age, I understood a lot about mortality.

I had regular visits at Cook County Fantus Clinic. After each checkup, the clerk would schedule another meeting a month later. One day, I had an early morning appointment, but they never called me. They called everybody else. It was one o'clock, and I was still there. Finally, I got up and left. I hated going there. After that day, I just said I'm not going back. I'll just lead my life. It was only after twenty years that I returned to that clinic for a checkup. I worried about it, but I was doing all right. I just said, "I'm tired of this, and I won't go back."

I have always liked the arts. I felt I was good at it because people praised me. After one of my surgeries, I was placed in a convalescent home that had after-school shop and arts programs. I was eight when I met a fifteen-year-old Latina who was volunteering. It was Christmas time, and she drew these little candles and hollies. I copied them and showed her my work. She said, "Oh, that's really nice." It made me feel good. Another time, we were doing portraits for our art teacher. She also complimented me. I thought, "Yeah, I can do this." It was easy. So I began to like art.

But when my family was around, I would put things away because they'd say, "What's that supposed to be?" My parents were very funny about art. Their general philosophy was also somewhat strange. They never tried to influence us. They never felt they should tell us what to do. Their perspective was that each person was going to do what they're going to do in life anyway.

They didn't even encourage us to do well in school. They thought things would just fall into place the way they were meant to. But outside our home, the assumptions were often more cynical. When I graduated from grammar school, I had the highest grade-point average in my class. A White girl I knew at my school had a mother who had a lot of hopes for her and wanted her to be successful. One day, my counselor, a very friendly lady, asked to speak with me. She said the student's mother had visited her. She wanted her

daughter to be valedictorian because she was going to go to college someday.
The counselor put her arm around me, smiled, and asked if that would be all
right with me. I didn't know what to say, so I said yes. Thinking back on that
incident, I think the counselor should have at least spoken to my mother.

My first job after high school was at the National Tailoring Company. The
company had a number of subsidiaries in the same building. There weren't
that many Latinos in the clothing company, maybe four or five out of fifty
or sixty people in the section where I worked. The men who did the selling
and the tailors were all White. Latinos basically had the lowest-paying jobs.
One Latina was an assistant to the accountant. I don't know how much they
paid her, but she was the only one that I felt had a better job. The other two
Mexican women were clerks. I stuffed envelopes. The management used to
say we were in advertising.

I was taking some classes at the Art Institute at the time and showed some
of my nude figure drawings to the ladies at the job. I should never have done
it because afterward they'd always ask, "Are you still drawing those dirty pictures?" I couldn't say anything there because people were too closed minded.
Then, there was Vietnam. Something was going on with the Vietnam situation
that involved Madame Nhu. I argued that the Vietnamese had rights, too, and
that the United States shouldn't be over there. Some people got angry at me.

One day, I had my hair pinned up. I look a little Asian anyway. When I
walked into work, one of the ladies said, "Oh, here comes Madame Nhu."
The woman didn't even know Madame Nhu was a member of the national
bourgeoisie who represented the interests of Catholics, not a member of the
armed resistance. I just thought to myself, "God, these people!" I didn't feel
I could discuss anything with them.

There were always things like that happening. I'm not a loud person. But
I say what I think. But closed-minded people like many of those I worked
with demand total conformity, and I am not going to pretend to go along
with something if I don't agree with it. All of the Mexican women supported
me on the issues. The White people in the office would say, "You guys . . .
you're always taking the other side. You're always against the United States."
A situation developed in Panama, and we said the United States shouldn't
be there. "There they go again," they exclaimed, throwing up their hands in
exasperation. But I always had certain ideas that placed me on the left.

MY POLITICS ARE JUST WHO I AM

I didn't think of myself as very political at that time, but I wanted to do something. When I returned from Mexico, where I had gone to take art classes,

I worked part-time at Carson Pirie Scott, a major downtown department store. Back then, I wanted to go to Washington, D.C., to march against the war, but I never followed through on it. I heard people talk about it, and I thought to myself, "I wouldn't mind going." But I didn't.

I also thought about joining the Peace Corps. I guess I wanted to make a contribution to humanity. I thought about going to South America. But somebody said to me, "Well, if you want to help people, why don't you help someone here?" I thought, "You know, they're right." There are plenty of people here that need help. It just seems more exotic to go somewhere else to volunteer. Later, I read something about another program called VISTA. It helped people in places like Appalachia, but I never joined. Instead, I got involved in radical politics, politics that attempt to get at root causes and ask fundamental questions.

Radical politics is who I am. I am more oriented in this direction. I don't think you move from nowhere to radical politics. At least this was true for me. I always leaned toward radical politics. I wanted to march. I wanted to do something. I wanted to join the Peace Corps, not the Young Republicans or the Young Democrats. Those weren't my inclinations. Radical politics was my natural progression because I placed a value on social justice, not conformity.

My family was still fighting the war with the United States. In the late 1950s, my older brother was in the Air Force. He was stationed in Fargo, North Dakota. He told my family about an experience he had there that made him quite angry. He and another soldier walked into a bar. They let my brother in, but they did not allow his Black friend to enter. My brother walked out of the place with his friend when that happened. He witnessed a lot of racism. He never hung around with anybody White. He was always with his Mexican friends. They would often ask each other what they would do if Mexico and the United States went to war. They agreed that they wouldn't fight for the United States. I think that was typical of a lot of Mexican people back then because of the racism they experienced.

I also had a brother who was in Vietnam around 1967. By the time I was in college, he was already out. My mother didn't want him to go. When he was drafted, my mother was very upset. She wanted him to go to Mexico. But my brother said, "Oh, I can't do that." So he went and did a thirteen-month tour. He's a mechanic by trade, and they had him working on helicopters. He never really talks about it. I tell people that those who know, who have been there, they really don't want to talk about it. My brother was in the infantry, but he was in a small place where they brought in helicopters to be repaired.

They got mortared a couple of times and had to carry their guns with them, but they weren't on the battlefield. When he returned, he didn't really feel pro-American or feel proud to have been there.

When people ask me what my parents thought about the war, I ask them, "What war?" My parents were still fighting the war between Mexico and the United States. They felt the United States was always taking advantage of everybody else. That was their position. Most people conveniently forget that one of the reasons for this country's land grab in the Southwest was about the expansion of slavery.

My dad never felt sympathetic to this country. He never really said much. I mean, I heard him talk about things on occasion, but I don't know where he got his opinions. He'd use the word *despot* a lot. He would say, "This all leads to despotism." I remember he said this with regard to [Juan Domingo] Perón and Evita [Perón] in Argentina. He asked, "Why do they want them?" My dad had it in his mind that he was going to go back to Mexico. He even bought a piece of land there. But my mother never talked about returning. Later, they realized they could not go back because of my dad's poor health.

It was common Mexican attitude to be critical about Vietnam from the beginning. Mexicans were more open minded, and they understood things because of the situation between Mexico and the United States. Mexicans saw the United States as always taking advantage of others and then rewriting history to make it look good. At least, I think the majority of Mexicans from Mexico thought that way at the time. Those that become Americanized, maybe the second generation, the ones born here, they may become more sympathetic toward the United States. They start feeling more like a part of it, like they have something to protect.[4] They begin to believe the lies, like that the United States government is fighting for freedom, *o quién sabe qué* (or who knows what).[5]

Getting Involved

BECOMING AN ACTIVIST

I began at Circle campus in 1971. I'd sometimes go to the university with my neighbor. I'd known her family for quite a while. She was the godparent of one of my nieces. She's my sister's *comadre* (co-mother or godmother). So we've known each other for a while. She had been involved with OLAS, but it wasn't so much through her that I became active. She dropped out after a year. It's just that she's one of the first people that I knew at the university. We used to go to the student union and sit at the tables where the Latinos congregated. There were so few of us at that time. People came and went, and I would spend a lot of time in the Pier Room drinking coffee.[6] I got to meet everybody. I enjoyed it. Then, I'd go to work after school, the whole day on Thursday, and on Saturday when the stores were open late.

A Puerto Rican activist named Rafael Pérez had a major influence on me. Everyone knew him. Different people would come up to the table in the cafeteria of the student union where Latinos would congregate, including many people who later become involved in the struggle to create the Latin American Recruitment Program.[7] I'd talk to Rafael a lot, and he'd invite me to an event or meeting. His group brought speakers to the university. I found their talks interesting. They were working around welfare rights, and they did concrete things. Twenty-five to a hundred of us would march into a welfare office and sit in to demand the welfare checks of mostly Black women who were getting the runaround from the system. We'd refuse to leave until they gave them the money for their families.

I thought I was hanging around with a Latino group because all the people around Rafael were Latino. He had Anglo friends, but most of the people around were Latino. I met Silvia Diaz, another PL person through him.[8] Rafael's group was pretty active, so I started gravitating to the events they sponsored.[9] I met one of the people that would later be active with the Comité at one meeting. That's when I learned that the group was part of SDS. I always heard the name of someone who later became aligned to Richard M. Daley, but I never saw him at a meeting. After I arrived at the university, I went to Washington to march against the war. In 1972, I attended the national convention of the Worker Student Alliance in Cambridge at Harvard. Then, I traveled to New York City to participate in a demonstration of tens of thousands of antiwar protestors. It was pretty exciting. I was involved in many different things.

When I started working at El Centro de la Causa, I crossed paths with the Cuadro people.[10] We had gone to the Sixteenth of September *grito* (cry) at the band shell.[11] My neighbor had been elected queen and was going to give a speech. We were still working with SDS, but we were involved with other groups on issues such as the 1968 killing of Mexican students and workers. A number of people at the grito had worked together in the past. Some had been active in OLAS and others in SDS. But it wasn't an SDS or OLAS demonstration. It was more like a spontaneous coalition. People went because it was about Mexico. Mexicans were interested in the issue. OLAS was a student organization at Loop College. But a lot of those people transferred over to Circle and started Cuadro.[12] Many were training to be in the classroom and joined a special federally funded program called the Teachers Corps. Some Latinos like Rudy Lozano were affiliated at that time with the Educational Assistance Program, a minority-recruitment program that focused primarily on Blacks. A few Latinos who were associated with EAP attended the Cuadro meetings as well.

I saw OLAS as a nationalist organization. It was not very interested in building alliances. Yet, when I moved into the community, I saw that there was a reason to be more nationalistic. At the university, I didn't see a reason, because we had so many international students around us. If you're working in a Mexican community, there is a reason to do more Latino organizing. It depends on your concrete situation.

People from Latino organizations never really talked to me or tried to get me involved in their groups. Cuadro had meetings, but the executive committee acted as if they were the leadership, and the rest of us were just an audience for them. Rafael's group would get people involved and make you feel like you were part of the planning. They'd ask your opinion. It was a different relationship. At Cuadro meetings, we sat down and listened, and that was it. There wasn't a lot of interaction. I didn't feel like I was part of the group. The same centralization of leadership happened when some of the members of Cuadro later founded the Mexican Teachers Organization.

I didn't feel like the Mexican groups at Circle really had many events, either. I felt like I stumbled onto those activities they did have. I was an education student, and once this classmate of mine, a Black woman, asked me to go to lunch. I told her I'd meet her after class. We heard from other students that there was some UFW program in the Illinois Room, and we walked over there.[13] It was a big event. I don't know if César Chávez or Dolores Huerta was going to speak there or what, but after the program started, a bunch of Latinos came into the room chanting.[14] They marched under a large banner. They were protesting because the university was serving scab lettuce in the cafeterias.

Here we were listening to UFW speakers, and the university was using lettuce that was not picked under a union contract. The group took advantage of the opportunity to expose the university for supporting agricultural interests over those of the workers who deserved decent wages and to work in safe working conditions. The protestors were mostly from Cuadro. The organizer was someone I recognized as one of its main leaders. But I didn't know in advance that the protest was going to happen.

After making a speech from the floor, the group left chanting. They formed a picket line in front of one of the cafeterias. I was sitting there with this other woman, and we joined the people going downstairs. We left with them. But

I wasn't made to feel part of that group. I later participated in some of their activities, but they just made decisions without involving people.

I moved closer to SDS people because I felt more included. They would sell literature at a booth. I would hang out with them. I got involved in a couple of events, concrete projects. They'd say, "We're going to have this march." Then it was, "We're having this big event." I suppose maybe some of the other groups did things, but at some point, they just weren't part of my circle.

I knew SDS was a radical group from the start. I enjoyed working with them. Rafael invited me to a dinner, and I began to meet more people in the organization. I agreed with what they were saying. They were against war and racism. They had a pamphlet that condemned the ideas of William Shockley, the academic racist.[15] Somebody at the dinner also spoke about Banfield's book *The Unheavenly City*.[16] It was really disgusting racist stuff that was being used in classes at the university.

Shockley was going to give an evening lecture at Wright Junior College. He was going to debate a geneticist from the University of Chicago. Everyone agreed that Shockley should not be allowed to speak without being challenged. But initially a few people thought we should be careful to respect his free speech. PL didn't think Shockley should even be allowed to speak. The group finally decided to shout him down because he had no right to promote his racist ideas as sound academic scholarship. It would be like granting legitimacy to someone who believed that Jews were racially inferior just because the person had academic credentials. Neither one was acceptable.

A few of us went to Wright during the day to leaflet. We were passing out flyers and met this one skinny White kid who was kind of nerdy looking. He was standing in the background looking interested. We gave him a leaflet. We said, "You know this man, Shockley? He's going to come here tonight to speak. He has this racist theory." But when we mentioned that Shockley was the co-inventor of the transistor and a professor at Stanford, the guy's attitude changed. He must have been impressed that Shockley was a renowned scientist. It didn't matter that he was speaking outside of his field. He casually said, "Well, he's probably right." Someone got mad and knocked the guy's books out of his hands. We intimidated the poor kid.

A few of us went to Northeastern Illinois University to pass out leaflets to students, informing them about the issues and the debate that night. There was a radio station that broadcasted out of the college. We met one of their reporters in the cafeteria, a hip-looking, long-haired, blond guy. He was excited about doing a radio interview with someone from SDS. "We need some controversy," he said rubbing his hands together, relishing the thought.

One of our members agreed to do it. "Yeah, I'll go on the air," he said. We began jotting down points in the cafeteria. But once we got to the radio station, the head guy wouldn't let an SDS spokesperson be interviewed. The student manager was pacing back and forth concerned. He had a petty dictator-like arrogance and was upset that one of his crew had invited SDS to speak. He finally said, "No, forget it!" As we were leaving, we shouted, "Up against the wall."[17] We thought, "So much for free speech."

MOVING OUT

I met Yenelli at Circle. A friend of mine said, "I know someone who's looking for people to work at a community center." I looked her up, and she hired me on the spot. I really didn't know her very well. I actually met her at a party that some other people had invited me to attend. The next time I saw her, I barely remembered her, but she hired a few activists from the university. I was just getting to know her when she mentioned that she was looking for a roommate.

I wanted to move close to work and school. Going home to the North Side every night was tiring. At that time, my family had lived in the house my parents bought when I was twenty. I felt it was too hectic to be traveling around, so I decided to move in with Yenelli. It was around New Year's when she and I went looking for a place. She found something by Centro de la Causa that was owned by the Podmajerskys, a Polish couple trying to gentrify the community by attracting artists. We moved to a second-floor apartment on Halsted and 19th Streets. Magda moved in a little later. I lived with Yenelli and Magda for about a year before moving north to Edgewater with some SDS friends and then later returned to Pilsen to live with several different roommates.

Some of us started working and organizing in the Pilsen community in the early 1970s. During this time, I was still an undergraduate. We did political work through Nuestro Continente bookstore near 18th Street and Blue Island and Centro de La Causa, which was located on 17th Street just east of Halsted Street and just south of UICC. We showed movies at the bookstore and had discussion groups. At Centro, I worked with the Right to Read program. It was a program to encourage youth literacy, but we also offered English classes and prepared people to take the General Educational Development examination, the high school–equivalency test. We started with young adults, mainly those not in high school, those who were out on the street. But it was very difficult to work with this population because we hadn't found a way to motivate them to participate. So we started doing more English preparation, teaching English to the Spanish-speaking.

It was around this time that Magda and Cristina invited me to go with them to La Raza Unida Party meetings. I didn't know the party existed until I went with them. We went to a meeting that was held on the second floor of a building on 26th Street. There were older people there. At least, at the time I felt they were much older. There was this guy there who was really thin and on the tall side who worked for the Board of Education. This was during the time that people began to get involved in the Angel Moreno campaign. The LRUP had its national convention in 1972. So I think it was around that time when Angel ran for office. I was already living on Halsted in Raza Towers. They were trying to get Angel elected to be a state representative. Ruth Mojica Hammer was also running for elected office. I think she had been a journalist and was the first Latina to run for a citywide position. An activist named Felipe Aguirre was there and played some role in Mojica-Hammer's campaign. Later, Felipe helped the LRUP in its campaign to elect Angel Moreno. Angel was running against Cardiss Collins, who was trying to regain her husband's state representative seat after he died. LRUP was going to propose someone else to oppose Vito Marzullo, the local city councilman. Collins and Marzullo were machine Democrats.

Magda took me around and introduced me to Angel Moreno. He was the last of the candidates to speak. Magda took the lead at some of these meetings. But I didn't feel real attracted to this group. Although I decided to go to some of the meetings, I didn't really feel part of it. I just felt like a supporter. But that's where I met Felipe. I'd seen him before, but I really remember him from working on those campaigns.

One of the Cuadro leaders didn't get involved in LRUP, maybe because it was not his idea. He was also very Mexican and very proud of that. The LRUP people were mainly Chicano. I don't think certain Mexican activists believed there was such a thing as a Chicano. Those from Texas like José Angel Gutiérrez and many of the others from Crystal City, which had seen big electoral victories, had been in the United States for most of their lives.[18]

At one time, activists were trying to convince everyone to mark *Chicano* on the census. They wanted people to write in *Chicano* because there was no box for it. They were getting everybody to say they were Chicano. Some Mexicans in OLAS were more open to thinking of themselves as Chicano, but others were not. The differences around identity might have played some small role in LRUP's short history in Chicago.

Some of the original members of the Mexican Teachers Organization had been in the Teacher Corps. The people I worked with did not want to be the leaders of the organization. But some of the others just wanted to control their own organization. I saw one of the leaders as an honest guy. I felt very comfortable with him and his group even though they were a little more Americanized, but they were not seeking power. They were more family oriented. They just wanted to have something for Mexican teachers. They wanted to contribute, but they didn't want power.

I was involved in some of those initial meetings when they were choosing the first president. That's when it almost broke apart because certain people were trying to assume leadership and there was a struggle. There were immediately two factions within the organization. People took one side or the other. The main group said they wanted to form an organization that would get people together and do something positive to move a Mexican agenda forward, although that's not what happened. The others wanted to have an organization that would have some pull with the big shots in the Chicago Board of Education. They wanted to position themselves as power brokers inside of the bureaucracy. I was doing my student teaching when I was approached to join.

"Would you be interested in having a teacher's group?" I said, "Yeah, I probably would." One of the guys that got involved was a person associated with Centro. He works at Pershing Road today.[19] I was left with a bad taste in my mouth because I felt many of those people were really just opportunists who were doing it for their own benefit. However, in the beginning, I never saw it like that. I naïvely assumed that people wanted to do good for the community.

Pablo Torres and María Torres were working at a factory in Cicero and organizing to start a union. They got together and founded an organization in the community to help Latino workers. So APO began around a real issue, something that was happening right there and then. They brought their concerns back to the community. They were close to the church and worked with a priest who was helping them.

Yenelli fought continuously with the priest. There were tensions between them. I think Yenelli always wanted to push the organization further left, and he was . . . well, a priest. He had a lot of influence over people, and the organization was based at the church. The priests didn't always show up at our meetings, but there were people who attended that were close to the pastor and met with him separately. We used to meet at the church. One of the most noted campaigns organized by APO was stopping the CTA buses in the community because the CTA rarely hired Latinos.

APO still exists today, but it's totally different. It's not the same. It really just serves as a building management board. It's run by one of the old guard in the community. APO was taken over. The person there has been in charge for the last ten years or so. People probably told them not to let the outside agitators come in.[20] Today, the APO building on 18th Street houses a community arts and cultural center.

I AM A MEXICANA

In the 1970s, I really didn't see myself as a Chicana.[21] I didn't define my activism in terms of a women's thing, either. I really didn't. I see it more like an us-against-them kind of thing, the them being the large corporations or big powers. We did struggle over what was called at that time the "woman question," and I went to an advance (retreat) for Latinas. The National Organization for Women was very strong in the city at the time. I thought it was good, but I never really felt I should be there with them.

Because we lived in Pilsen, the national question was a more sharply defined issue in terms of who one was, who one identified with, who one worked with. I saw myself as a Mexican. People like my roommate from one of the teatros at the time felt more like a Chicana.[22] In the beginning, I sort of rolled my eyes and asked myself, "Why do people call themselves that?" I asked a person who saw himself as a Chicano where Aztlán was. He said something like, "It's anywhere a Chicano is." For me, that was too abstract. It was too unreal. I couldn't identify with that. I would be negative about it. Also, I had a negative attitude about it because of how I saw some of those who called themselves Chicano. Some people had some good qualities, but sometimes they did not really have a job. I saw them as taking advantage of the women they were with, as if women should support them just because the men were activists or something.

I cultivated a friendship with someone who worked at a community clinic. I was looking for a place to live at that time and stayed with her for a month. Her boyfriend was staying with her. He and I traveled with a contingent of people from Chicago that went to New York for the Puerto Rican Socialist Party's bicentennial protest. He borrowed his girlfriend's car. I told him that I thought his girlfriend was nice to lend him the car to go all the way to New York. He just stared back at me as if that sort of thing was to be expected. He never acknowledged her generosity. I think he was more of a Chicano hippy. It left me with a bad taste in my mouth. We all have to work. When people like that told me about their beliefs, I really didn't put a lot of credence in them because I didn't trust their values. It was different with Chuy Negrete's sisters who were in Chispa, the singing group.[23] They considered themselves stone Chicanas, and I had a great deal of respect for them.[24]

THE COMITÉ

The group began the Farah committee around 1973.[25] We were located at the bookstore and had events there. These two Argentine guys initiated it and brought in other people. One of the Argentineans had an Eastern European name and was a medical student. They were members of the Sojourner Truth Organization. At that time, I was totally oblivious to where people were coming from. I would probably be more inquisitive today. The Revolutionary Union also had people that started coming around because they had a Farah strike support committee in California.[26] We didn't know that at the time. They were attracted to us because of the Farah committee connection.

The Comité wasn't always very organized. There were so many things happening. Yet, we had successes. I felt very much like we were together when we sponsored a big dance in support of the Farah strikers. We brought a Farah unionist to Pilsen. It was one of those things that make you feel good. Maybe people just came because it was a dance, but we felt good about it. We told the bands we hired about the strikers' situation. They were sympathetic and offered to play for less. We didn't have much money to organize, but there was a lot of sympathy. That entire evening was great. In between bands, someone did a presentation and spoke about the Farah struggle. Yenelli presented something that Cristina wrote. We'd sometimes ask Cristina to write something for someone else to say.

The Farah striker was from El Paso. There was a very nice turnout. It was overwhelming, really. Later in the evening at the Halsted apartment, I really felt fantastic. The striker told us some inspiring stories. She told us about how when they first got involved, some people had already walked out on strike. But not everybody had joined, and they needed more people to be part of the strike. There were a lot of people still working. The day came when another walkout was supposed to take place. There was talk about walking out, but the organizers were nervous. People were staring at each other, wondering if the other person was going to walk out. A lot of people were saying, "No, I can't walk out. You know, I need the job."

As the day progressed, the organizers got the feeling that very few people would actually leave work. The company piped in music through an intercom system. They had gotten wind of the plans for the walkout and were confident that most people wouldn't strike. But then the managers did a foolish thing. They began to play "Las Golondrinas" (the swallows), a Mexican farewell song that has a very special meaning. It's a sentimental tune sung when a loved one is going far away. For immigrant workers, this probably reminded them of the day they left their families and hometowns behind to come to the United States in search of work. The workers felt the managers were ridiculing them, making fun of their plight and their culture. The managers thought they were being clever piping in the music. But their joke backfired on them. The bosses ended up helping to convince people to join the strike. People became furious. Everybody walked out because they were so mad.

There were so many issues then. We began to ask ourselves why we didn't try to build a broader organization. People like the theater groups gravitated toward us, and when we had movies and other events, people came. At that time, we weren't really trying to recruit. We saw ourselves as primarily just educating people.

The group began to ask what we were going to work on after the Farah strike got resolved. We were leaning toward building a more politically focused organization that did work in a specific area. We held meetings to decide what we should be doing. Yenelli and I were among those who felt that we should work with the issue that was most pressing in the community, immigration. Maximo, Cristina's *compañero* (comrade), really didn't like that idea. He felt that meant joining CASA.[27] He was emphatic about not doing this. The other alternative was working with the farmworkers. We started a farmworkers support committee, which after much debate received the most votes from people.[28]

Farmworker support was what was happening. It attracted a broad spectrum of people. But although working-class people in the city empathized with the issue, it really wasn't their problem. It was something far away and didn't directly affect them. Yet, it was easier to do farmworker support work in Pilsen rather than other places because elsewhere people would snarl at you or in other ways show their opposition. In Pilsen you got sympathy. If you had anything to pass out, people took it. So you felt comfortable working there. That's how I felt anyway.

We used to picket the Del Farm grocery store. We picketed the Jewel on Cermak Road. We traveled all over the city, wherever the farmworker organizers would throw up a picket in front of a store. People from all over the city would come and join the protests that we held. But there was some opposition from the UFW organizers themselves.

Delegates from 1300 Wabash, the farmworker headquarters in Chicago, were not in agreement with us.[29] One of their representatives came over to a meeting of ours. He said, "No, you can't do this and you can't do that," and we said, "Well, it's our group." We weren't under their policy anyway. We realized if you work under their organization, you were expected to do what they told you. The issue was whether we should be encouraging people to boycott the items not under union contract or to urge people not to shop at the stores that purchased scab produce. We wanted to tell people not to shop at the store. We were more aggressive. The farmworkers at one time had called a primary boycott, but they might have been backing off under pressure.

End of a Collective Vision

SPINNING OUR WHEELS

I don't know if the Comité was fizzling out or something else was the problem. We organized the Community Safety Committee in honor of María Saucedo, who died in a fire.[30] The plan was to have a series of planning meetings, but things weren't getting done. It was very aggravating. We'd get together, and there would occasionally be an event, but the group was just not doing too much. There were just these long meetings. I could see that some people were more interested in theater, which they should have pursued. I mean that's all right. But I think the Comité . . . the political, theoretical arm of the collective wasn't doing anything. We lost direction. I became very aggravated with the long meetings. I felt we were getting nowhere.

One of our last collective projects was to pressure the city to provide adequate fire equipment for the community. But after that, I don't know if we had any really outstanding events. There was some investigating, and we discovered some valuable information, but we couldn't get ourselves together. The group was unraveling. I know Cristina felt aggravated. I felt the same way.

There were a series of long meetings to decide what to do next. It was finally decided to form a study group. However, some of us would be arriving to the meeting, and the couple's whose house it was would be going out the front door. They'd say, "We have something to do. We forgot about the meeting."

The positive thing was that there was initially an enthusiasm to jump in and get involved. When the group organized, it produced results. I just don't think we had a good sense of direction. The tendency was to react to crises and not give leadership to an issue and take it to a higher level. We sometimes spun around in circles and didn't have a handle on things. So, that was the beginning of the end.

REFLECTIONS

I have gotten great satisfaction from being a teacher. It wasn't initially on my mind to work in a school, that was not my mindset when I started out. However, when you work with the kids, you do feel you are contributing.

You feel very much a part of the community. Through the years, I came to feel like I was in a war, and as a teacher, I was in the trenches. Teachers are right there with kids and parents and where everything is happening, right in the middle of the community. That is satisfying.

I also felt good working in Chispa, the singing group. I thought it was a good way to educate and communicate with people, because they enjoy listening to music. The arts were an easier and more enjoyable way to communicate and educate. I was only with the group for a few events. It was difficult to adjust to the demands of a semiprofessional schedule. I sometimes asked myself why I was doing this. I couldn't really sing. But I think I helped keep the group on track, reminding them of the reasons why we were doing what we were doing.

When I came to Pilsen, I saw myself as politically open. I had the time, and I didn't feel I had anything more pressing to do. I might have been politically conscious because of the atmosphere of the day. But people around the arts are usually pretty radical, philosophically anyway. Then again, if you're too involved, you can't do other things. I wasted a lot of time. At times, I was more involved in running around and socializing in the student union, talking with people, especially in the Pier Room. I wasn't focused on my studies. I wasn't ready to do that until much later. I resigned from the Chicago Public Schools in the mid-1980s and around that time began to take photography classes at Columbia College, where I earned a second bachelor's degree. In 1989, I returned to the public schools when an art position became available at Kanoon Magnet, a grammar school in the Little Village Mexican community, just west of Pilsen.[31]

But I wasn't involved in other things as much as when I was an activist. I liked events and people. I liked going to different programs and listening to discussions. I enjoyed my role with the singing group. I didn't always think through what I was doing or at least I wasn't thinking about the long-term consequences of my commitments, and I'm not sure I was always doing it for the purest of reasons either. There was a time when it was exciting to be in the Movement. I met interesting people who were socially committed. It became an important part of my life. I enjoyed observing everything that was going on around me. I wasn't part of the Brown Berets, but I enjoyed interacting with them. I'd say to myself, "Wow, look at them," and be fascinated with what they said and who they were. I learned to appreciate their point of view. Many people become who they are because they feel the full weight of oppression. I never felt so directly oppressed. I mean I never felt singled out. No one ever shouted, "Hey, you, spic!" to me. I didn't feel personally affronted.

I did feel sympathetic. I don't know if this was because I am Mexican. I think it's because I was religious when I was younger. I think that has had a lot to do with it. I didn't see the Catholic Church and priests as always being retrograde like some other activists did. I saw many of them trying to help people. They were trying to do the right thing to educate and to help the needy and sick. I saw them as basically good. I didn't see them doing it just to convert people. I saw them doing it because they wanted to help the poor. One of my nuns when I was a kid actually tried to warn us Latinos about the injustice we would encounter in our lives. At least, I think in her own way, that's what she was trying to communicate to us.

When I was young, I saw myself going to the Art Institute and being an artist. But looking back, I didn't take it as seriously as I should have. I was too laid back. I wasn't painting all the time. It was more an idea. I really wasn't practicing my art like I should have been. I did take art classes in Mexico in Ciudad Victoria from 1968 to the summer of 1970 before I enrolled full-time in college. If I could do it over again, I would be more active in the arts and blend this passion with my political work in a better, more productive way. I'd definitely spend more time doing art. If you want to be good at something, you really have to devote the time. People who are good at sports devote many hours a day to it. It's really the same thing with anything else. In any case, I don't see how my life overall would be different. I may not be as much of a fatalist as my parents, but I think it was my fate to be active and to respond to this calling. I don't see it as any more complicated than that.

Notes

1. This introductory vignette was developed in collaboration with Isaura González. The substance of this chapter is derived from several interviews that occurred mainly in 1998 but that continued through 2008.

2. DPs, displaced persons, is a term used to refer to those forced to leave their country such as those who came to the United States during both world wars.

3. María's family moved to a low-income, working-class community on the Northwest Side of Chicago.

4. For a conservative assimilationist perspective, see L. Chavez (1991).

5. The phrase *o quién sabe qué* is often used as a dismissive phrase, similar to the common English expression "whatever." Interestingly, Isaura sees first-generation Mexican attitudes as more ideologically resistant to incorporation while others like Moraga (1993) associate radicalism with those who, regardless of immigrant generation, undergo the transformation from a Mexicano to a Chicano identity or from an immigrant consciousness to one that stakes a claim on this country. Ogbu (1974,

1991) sees the immigrant generation as typically more optimistic and less prone to an oppositional consciousness with respect to education.

6. The Pier Room is a cafeteria located in the UIC student union.

7. Latino students, community, and sympathetic faculty conducted a long-term and often combative campaign to establish an independent Latino student-support program. The program was initially founded under the name of the Latin American Recruitment Program (LARP) but was renamed in the mid-seventies the Latin American Recruitment and Educational Services program (LARES).

8. PL had roots in the American Communist Party and provided leadership to the Worker Student Alliance faction of SDS.

9. By 1972, Latinos represented a good percentage of the UICC SDS chapter. This was largely because of the organization's decision to recruit Third World students and the dedicated work of the two Latino PL members mentioned by Isaura.

10. Those who founded El Cuardo Latinoamericano (the Latin American Group or Cadre) included students transferring from Loop Junior College that had been members of the Organization of Latin American Students (OLAS).

11. Mexican Independence Day celebrates the proclamation, call, or "cry" for independence from Spanish rule.

12. Prior to the consolidation of the Chicago campuses of the University of Illinois, UICC was known as Chicago Circle or Circle campus.

13. The Illinois Room is a large conference and special-events space at the UICC student union.

14. César Chávez and Dolores Huerta founded the UFW agricultural union and became icons of the Chicano Movement. While acknowledging the contributions of Chávez to the Movement, Muñoz (1989) argues that Chávez never saw himself as a member of the Chicano Movement.

15. William Shockley, known for his work in the development of semiconductors, advanced the notion of dysgenics. He was accused by the left of promoting racist and sexist social polices, such as the sterilization of women with IQ scores below one hundred.

16. Edward G. Banfield's controversial book (1970) blamed the problems of cities on urban pathology stemming from the dysfunctional cultural values of poor people.

17. "Up against the wall" is a phrase used by the poet Amiri Baraka. It was adopted by a 1960s New York City anarchist group Up Against the Wall Motherfuckers. For more about this group, see Neumann (2008).

18. Crystal City is a town in Texas where LRUP won its greatest victories, gaining the majority of the city council at one point.

19. Pershing Road at the time was the location for the central office of the Chicago Public Schools.

20. One of the criticisms used by the opponents of the Comité was that its members were actually not from "the community," even when the majority lived in Pilsen. It often took the form of red-baiting that was similar to the "outside agitator" label used

by conservative politicians to isolate individuals and groups. However, the criticism was also used by sectors of the left. Being called an "outsider" sometimes referred to perceptions of individuals as coming from a more privileged social strata and, therefore, divorced from community realities, as well as someone new to the *barrio*.

21. There are many theories as to the derivation of the term *Chicano*. However, it has a long been considered a derisive term but was appropriated as a positive one by the Movement in the 1960s. Chicanos located their cultural and racial identity in hybridity—*mestizaje,* a mixture of the Indian and European and culturally between the United States and Mexican experiences. Chicanismo was associated with the development of a critical political consciousness. Chicano activists often portrayed themselves as the spiritual children of indigenous tribes that eventually settled in Mexico. Indigenous groups such as the Aztecs claimed to have come from a homeland in the north, which Chicanos argued was the U.S. Southwest. Martha Menchaca (2001) gives some historical credence to this perspective.

22. The reference is to Chispa (spark), a group of women that previously had been affiliated with a street-theater troupe but spun off and formed a Latina singing group. The core of this ensemble was the three Negrete sisters. For a brief time, Isaura sang with the group. Several people in this cultural-political ensemble were associated with the Comité.

23. Jesus "Chuy" Negrete remains a Chicago Chicano cultural icon. He was the Chicano Movement's troubadour who often performed with a guitar in tow for the UFW and other Movement groups. He was active in OLAS's theater company, Teatro de la Raza, and afterward became the director of the South Chicago–based Teatro de los Barrios.

24. A stone Chicana is sixties urban slang for an uber Chicana, so to speak. A stone anything was comparable to today's extreme anything.

25. Two 1970s pamphlets on the Farah strike were produced by San Francisco Bay Area Strike Support Committee (1974) and Coyle, Hershatter, and Honig (1979). Mata's (2004) dissertation focuses on the legacy of Chicana working-class resistance. Honig (1996) examines the long-term impact of the Farah strike on the lives of Chicana union activists.

26. The Revolutionary Union, today the Revolutionary Communist Party, led by Bob Avakian, was associated with the Revolutionary Youth Movement II faction of SDS. For more on the RCP, see Avakian (2005).

27. Centro de Acción Social Autónoma (CASA) was initially headed by longtime community activist and labor organizer Bert Corona, who resigned from the organization, which was subsequently led by a new generation of activists that provided services and advocacy to immigrant workers but also saw itself as a political organization. The politics of CASA wavered over the years and at times shifted from a blend of radical nationalism, "Tricontinentalist" socialism, and traditional Communist Party politics. After the organization dissolved, a few of these Chicago activists eventually adopted electoral strategies and became involved in local politics as independent

Democrats. Rudy Lozano, an ally of the late Chicago Mayor Harold Washington, is probably the most well-known CASA member to enter electoral politics. Many believe Lozano's killing in 1983 was an assassination.

28. The more commonly known of the various farmworker organizations is the UFW, but the Comité also worked with the Texas Farm Workers Union (TFWU) and the Farm Labor Organizing Committee (FLOC).

29. The office of the Catholic Archdiocese of Chicago was located at 1300 West Wabash Street. The UFW and other organizations had offices in the building.

30. María Saucedo was a very active Comité member. At one time, the CSC was also referred to as the María Saucedo Community Safety Committee. A local school was later renamed the María Saucedo Scholastic Academy in honor of her educational contributions.

31. The full name of the school is Gerald Delgado Kanoon Magnet School.

Una Chicana en la lucha

MARÍA GAMBOA

The Froebel Uprising, 1973

Warmer weather brings everyone in Pilsen out of their homes. College students join other young people who congregate in community centers, church basements, and parks.[1] For some time, there has been talk of a new high school. However, the Chicago Board of Education and Pilsen Neighbors seem to be embroiled in a frustrating cycle of fruitless meetings. Many suspect that the board is using bureaucratic tactics to delay, discourage, and derail the creation of a new community school.[2]

In a small room at Casa Aztlán, two veteran leaders sit around a table talking with young activists. The two older organizers know that others would not like that they are meeting with these young people. But they fear that without some action, a new school will never be built, at least not in time to rescue generations of young people from overcrowded classrooms, rat-infested buildings, and inferior education. Among those gathered that day, there is a general belief that the educational needs of Mexicano/Chicano youth are a low priority for the CPS politically connected bureaucrats and board members whose own children attend privileged learning centers in the city or well-equipped schools in tree-lined suburban enclaves. This secret meeting is known only to a few. It ends with heads nodding in agreement and hearty affirmations. "Let's do it," someone says as the group rises in unison determined to move the agenda forward at any cost.

The mood in the community had already begun to shift a few years earlier at Harrison High School. Some community leaders felt that a new, impatient generation of students was pushing things too fast and sometimes too hard, going against authority and often demanding rather than attempting to engage officials in productive discussion. This new attitude was apparent at the high school's Pan-American Festival. A theater troupe of young activists from OLAS was at the center of a comical tug-of-war. The issue was whether the actors would be allowed to present their play at the main assembly.

The day of the scheduled event, the curtain rose, then fell, and rose again only to fall and rise several more times on the Teatro de la Raza (people's theater). The company was eager to perform the controversial play *The American Dream*, which questions the relevance and meaning of this theme for Chicanos. On one side pulling the curtain ropes open was the bilingual-education teacher, and on the other pulling them closed was the faculty sponsor of the Spanish Club, a supporter of General Franco, Spain's dictator. In order to escape further embarrassment, school authorities finally allowed the play to be performed.

The year after *The American Dream* incident, staff members of the *People of the Sun* student newsletter along with others at Harrison High School led a series of walkouts. Protestors demanded that a new community school be built immediately. Community residents, including parents, students, teachers, and counselors from the local alternative school, as well as employees from social-service agencies, joined in marches that on several occasions culminated in downtown rallies.

These events led to the Aztlán meeting where activists decided to take action. On an early weekday morning without drawing attention from authorities, a handful of young organizers and students entered Froebel, the freshman and sophomore branch of Harrison High School. Once inside, organizers moved from classroom to classroom shouting, "This is a takeover. Everybody leave." Students rushed out of their rooms, some to seize control of the school while others formed a picket line in front of the building. A group of young people inside the building climbed the stairs to the top floor, the school gymnasium, where they shoved chairs and equipment in front of doors, barricading themselves.

The Chicago Police arrived quickly and moved to regain control of the school. A row of riot police formed a power wedge and broke through the crowd demonstrating in front of the building. In the ensuing scuffle, a brick was thrown. A police officer's nose was broken. He was brought inside where several student negotiators urged those in charge to rush him to the hospital. But the commander seemed less interested in getting the officer cared for than making sure he remained soaked in his own blood until the photographers arrived. The policeman was whisked away only after a picture was finally snapped for the morning edition.

The situation was tense and getting worse. Desks and heavy equipment were launched from the school roof. Several police cars were smashed below. The faces of police hardened behind their plastic shields. The young negotiators miraculously convinced the principal to let those who had taken over the top floor to leave the building without being arrested. Students spilled out of the gymnasium and rushed down the stairs, chanting loudly as they exited out onto the streets. Groups of students dispersed into side streets. The cops followed close behind, waiting anxiously for the right moment to strike.

A neighborhood *señora* signaled to a large group of youths.[3] She invited them to come into her yard to keep them safe. The police sent word to the woman that the large numbers of students congregating on her property constituted a fire hazard. The cops surrounded the students; riot squads formed outside the front of the home and located themselves strategically on the other side to block the exit from the alley. The moment seemed near. The leaders knew they must get the students off the side streets where they were the most vulnerable. Surprisingly, the negotiators were once again able to convince the school principal to intervene and grant safe passage to the protestors. They were able to gather the various contingents of students and guided them to 18th Street, the major avenue of the community. Once on the main thoroughfare, the organizers breathed a sight of relief. They knew that the police were less likely to attack with so many witnesses present and people that could provide support to the protestors. The march ended with a rally at Casa Aztlán and speakers demanding a new school for the community.

Pilsen Neighbors not wanting to be associated with the day's violence denounced what young people on the streets were already calling the Froebel Uprising. The administration closed the school for the rest of the week. However, each day students marched in front of the building to continue their protests. Shortly thereafter, the Board of Education announced plans to build a new high school in Pilsen. Pilsen Neighbors resumed its role as the negotiator for the community. The students and leaders of the Froebel Uprising felt that they accomplished what they set out to do. The community was going to get a new school, although they understood that they must remain vigilant and the struggle would continue.

Home, Family, and School

THE FATHER, THE SON, THE HOLY GHOST, AND RACISM

Before we moved to Pilsen, we lived farther north. I attended Catholic school in that mostly White neighborhood. You could feel the racism there. The majority of kids were Polish, although there were a few other Latino kids in the school. The nuns still used corporal punishment even after I think it became illegal. They used belts and even broomsticks on the same old kids. I know those kids had problems, but all they needed was to be sat down and talked to, and an understanding needed to be developed with them. But the nuns would beat them. Back then, parents would put a fear in kids. They would say, "Listen to the teacher. They do no wrong." I couldn't even say to a teacher, "I didn't do that." So I would get punished for things I didn't do.

The little White kids, the Polish kids, they were always put first. They always got the credit. They were always being praised by the nuns. They got everything first. I don't remember any Latino kid being singled out or brought in front of the class and told how well he or she did. Of course, Chicano culture was never mentioned in school. That never came up even though they didn't see us as White. They had to see us as people of color. But they didn't even acknowledge that we were different. So we were never taught to be proud of who we were.

I really wanted to do well in school, and I was doing well. As a matter of fact, the nuns used to pull me out of reading class. They put me outside in the stairwell to work with the kids who had problems reading. But I was the one who lost out. It wasn't a good experience. That's why I'm not a practicing Catholic to this day.

My cousin and his wife lived in Pilsen. That's how I got introduced to the community. I didn't move to Pilsen until I entered eighth grade. It was a big change for me. Pilsen was a Mexicano community. The kids at Cooper Upper Grade Center were Mexicanos with only a few Whites enrolled there. We lived on 23rd Street and then 21st Place and Damen. My father finally bought a house on 21st and Damen, near Froebel High School. I lived there until my husband and I bought our first home in Little Village.[4]

Initially, Pilsen was a brighter spot. I felt the release, the freedom coming into a Mexicano community. Seeing that the people there were like me, I didn't feel isolated like I did when I was on the North Side. But academically, well, I felt it was just another public school, and the education wasn't good. I thought all public schools were alike. There were some good teachers. But most of the teachers were there to babysit you. They just read the newspaper. When I entered Froebel High School, it was the same. In one of my history classes, we had different teachers every month. We never had one teacher. But what I really loved was socializing. There were dances in the school gym. That's how I got to meet the kids from the neighborhood. The kids really got together there.

I was supposed to graduate from Harrison High School in 1972, but I graduated in 1973. I loved cutting school. The education I was receiving wasn't very good. We had very few teachers at the high school that really cared. There was no interest there from them, and so there was no interest there from me. I had a lot of friends and a lot of bad influences. At Harrison, one of the biggest problems was the gangs. The fights and shootings happened inside and outside of the school. The Latin Kings would stand right across the street harassing the other kids.[5] You'd put yourself in danger just going to school. That's one of the reasons why I really clung to the Chicano Movement.

Harrison didn't prepare you for college. It was a factory. Either you got ahead on your own, or you didn't. At that time, the opportunities were there for kids to go straight from high school to jobs, even if it was factory work. Most kids weren't really thinking about college. It was about making money. At that time, there weren't a lot of programs or centers to encourage high school students to continue their education.

It was OLAS, a student organization that began at Loop Junior College, that worked with high school students. They did not wait until students got to college. It was about encouraging and supporting them before they got there. One of their best projects was to motivate high school students to study and get more of them accepted into college: "This is what you can do. This is what it means to be an educated Mexicano and to share your knowledge with other people." They would encourage young people. That really made a big difference. I don't see that happening anymore.

In high school, there were the gangbangers and the Mexicano clique, the newly arrived immigrants we used to call the brazers.[6] It was not cool to hang around with brazers. But there were other groups. There were the more-mellow kids that just got educated and went their own way. They didn't get involved. It was the hippie era, so there was that, too, a lot of pot smoking, antiwar activity, long hair, and the music. Then there were the Chicano militants who pushed culture, the unity between the Mexicano and the second and third generations. That's the lasting impact of the Chicano Movement. That's really what it did. The only reason I didn't drop out of school was because that's when the Chicano Movement began. It was the most powerful influence on me in the 1970s.

Getting Involved

DANCING WITH CHE

Even though I lived in Pilsen and got to know my neighbors and all that, I wasn't very active in anything in the community. It wasn't until high school that I was introduced to the OLAS people. I went to visit them on 17th Street where they had an office. I liked what they had to say. OLAS was the start of teatro. Chuy Negrete got us interested. He started Teatro del los Barrios. I hate to say it, but he didn't really have a need for women. The guys got most of the roles. They mostly did Teatro Campesino plays so again there really wasn't really anything about women.[7] But it was fun.

Some of us women started voicing the notion that Chicanas were a valuable part of the Movement. I started asking why just Chicanos? Why not Chicanas? It wasn't just based on fighting politically for the rights of Chicanas/os. It was also just about socializing. A friend and I began questioning those things, and then we got an idea. We got together and decided to organize a dance. We sponsored one of the first OLAS dances in the community. OLAS had a Pilsen branch that had space at Saint Joseph's Church.[8]

There was an old bowling alley on the first floor. It was real messy, and nobody was using it. We went to the OLAS leadership and asked to use the hall to throw the dance. We wanted to do a fund-raiser. It wasn't for OLAS. It was for our benefit. They thought it was a good idea and told us to clean it up because it was really messy so we did. It took all day, but we cleaned it out. We swept it. We mopped it. We moved junk. We also got three bands. We brought in a group called Che. They were very good. We wanted to introduce them to the community. We hired two other music groups that charged us $25 each. One of my girlfriends was married to one of the leaders of Che so they didn't charge us anything. We used our own money to do the posters and flyers and pay for the printing of tickets. We did the publicity, decorated the hall, and even managed to get a strobe light.

We called the dance "Chicanas Can, Too," because it was organized by us. It promoted who we were as women. We made about a $250 profit, which was a lot for that time. It was very successful. People from OLAS did come to it, but only one of the OLAS guys volunteered to help. Sure enough, at the end of the dance, the OLAS guys said they wanted a percentage. I said, "Well, where were you guys when we needed help?" But they still wanted a cut.

It was about that time when I began to link up with María Saucedo again. I had known her since we were in grammar school, when we lived on the Near North Side. Her parents and my parents were friends. She moved away so I kind of lost track of her the last year I was in Catholic school. But we got back in touch when I moved into Pilsen because her family had moved there, too. María lived on 17th Street. She was going to a Catholic high school, but we still got to see each other again.

We linked up at a really good time. She was very active in the farmworkers' struggle. You know, she had something to share in terms of the Movement. I had something to share through my work with teatro. I introduced her to my friends from school and to people from OLAS. María's mother thought I was a bad influence. At that time, she didn't like me hanging around too much. But I think María and I were good for each other. She was looking for something more than the Catholic schools could offer. We really developed strong bonds because of the Movement. We had the same interests, and we got to know each other as friends.

María had a big influence on me, politically, in terms of the woman question. That's not to say that I wasn't very conscious about being a woman or the issues that faced us as Chicanas. As long as I can remember, I always questioned why there were double standards for men and women. Why was it that men could hit their wives or girlfriends or abuse them verbally? Why was it that every time you watched a TV program the woman was always the victim? Why was the woman always getting attacked, and why did she just stand there and scream? I recall challenging those things. Personally, I said to myself, "This is not who I want to be." I made up my mind years ago that I was never going to allow any man to tell me how to run my life or tell me what to do or what to wear or how to talk. I was never going to allow anybody to tell me to do anything I didn't want. I challenged my own father. I certainly wasn't going to allow any man to control me again. María and I shared these ideas.

María's mom was a very powerful woman. She was really the one that carried the family. That's where María got her strength. Politically, and in terms of education, María had a lot more to offer. She already had a lot of leadership experience because of her work with the UFW. She was a leader in high school. She already had developed those abilities much more so than I at that time. Those are things that she offered me.

Before we got into teatro, we started doing skits on the radio. We got involved with a radio station, WCYC, the Boys Club station on Ridgeway in Little Village.[9] That's where we met this guy who introduced us to the station. We went to a workshop there to become junior radio announcers and took some classes. We started our own little program called "Mi Chicano, WCYC" (My Chicano, with Chicanos you can). I think it was once a week for an hour. We DJed our own music and did skits on the air. From there we started our own teatro group.

THE IMPORTANCE OF CULTURE

My parents were raised in Mexico. We did *posadas* every year at our house.[10] It was on one of those occasions that I realized how important culture was. I invited some of my friends to our Christmas party. Since it was my family's house, I had to follow their rules. My friends had to come upstairs and join in the posada. I felt so humiliated. I said to myself, "Oh no." Each person had to hold the little baby Jesus and put Him to sleep and all that. I had all my friends there. Some were gangbangers or were from OLAS, and some were just kids I was trying to get to know, boyfriends and the like. I felt so embarrassed.

There was a guy there, though, who made me feel differently. He was a gangbanger that I invited. When we were alone, he started crying. He told me how much he wished his family was like mine and how important it was to keep our culture. So that really had an impact on me. But the Chicano Movement was starting to become more and more visible.

I met my husband, Héctor, about 1968 in my freshman year of high school. We started going out in senior year. I sometimes went to events that OLAS sponsored. At that time, I wasn't that involved with teatro, maybe I went to one or two performances, but eventually some of us became interested in being in a skit. Chuy was doing performances at Harrison High School. At a Pan-American Festival, he performed *The American Dream*.[11] That must have been 1971 or 1972. By then, he was working closely with my husband. Héctor had decided to go to the University of Iowa, where he resumed his involvement in theater. I stayed in Chicago and continued working with some of my classmates and María in teatro. In 1972 or 1973, María and a number of people, including two humorous guys from my high school, started developing the theater group we called Trucha. We added more people later. Trucha started when we were in senior year, but we really got going after high school. María was already at NEIU at the time. She had been double promoted in high school.

COMPAÑIA TRUCHA

Trucha is Chicano slang for "Watch it!" or "Watch out!" or "Beware!"[12] I think Trucha lasted a good five years, on and off again. Many of us were students. It was really a wonderful experience, but my family and Héctor's did not like that we were involved in theater. We heard it from both sides of the family, my husband's and mine. "Why are you guys wasting your time? Why are you in the circus?" I mean our families really didn't understand what we were doing or what we were trying to accomplish. We didn't get very much support from them. My father objected to many of my ideas.

There was one incident in particular that I remember. I brought home *Salt of the Earth* for the family to watch.[13] At that time, it was in large, bulky, 35 mm reels. We borrowed a movie projector, and I showed it to my family at home. My father was furious, especially because my ma saw it. He told me never to bring any kind of crap like that home again. We could never agree. We could never talk politics, my dad and I. We didn't see eye-to-eye on anything.

I got married after a teatro conference in Mexico City. When my first daughter was born, we were still very much involved in teatro. This was my main political work, to write plays and struggle politically about what we were going to convey. There was always a lot of discussion among the members of Trucha. One of the main issues within the Chicano Movement was the disagreement between women and men. Men could not see women fitting into the roles of leaders. We had those same struggles in our group. I wanted to make sure that our own plays reflected the full spectrum of women's roles. A lot of my politics and my beliefs came out in these plays, and many focused on women as leaders.

Other teatro groups we came across had women playing the same old types of characters. Either the woman was the victim or a grandmother. She either accepted a traditional role or the woman wanted to be married to an Anglo who had money or she was *La Virgencita,* or the bad woman.[14] We began to challenge that. We didn't want to promote those kinds of stereotypes. So we started writing our own plays. But it was a struggle. It was a struggle not only in teatro but also between my husband and I and how we saw each other's roles. It wasn't easy when we first got married. I mean we loved each other, but it was a struggle. It's still a struggle. It's not negative to struggle. It's good to struggle. That's why I feel we're kind of united now.

Compañia Trucha performed across the Midwest and even the Southwest. We performed throughout Indiana, Missouri, Michigan, and Wisconsin. People heard about us because there were good opportunities to network with other teatro groups across the country. We were lucky enough to establish linkages all the way to Mexico. There was a big teatro conference in Mexico that many of the groups attended.

At that time, Héctor and I had a storefront and lived in the back in a little apartment. It was on the corner of Throop and 18th Streets. I was married and had Tonantzin. The Mascarones spent a couple of days with us when she was a baby.[15] They did workshops with us and performed at Casa Aztlán and other places. We even had a Midwest network of teatros. It developed into a kind of a coalition; Teatro del Barrio, Chuy's group from South Chicago, and Bread and Roses, a progressive White group, and a group from Indiana. We hosted a Midwest conference. We invited teatros from the Southwest to come to Casa Aztlán. So we became well known. Even when we went out to the Southwest or when we traveled to the teatro conference in Mexico City, people had heard about us.

Compañia Trucha was very educational. A lot of the teatros were connected with universities. The ones we met outside of Chicago were mostly connected to colleges. Teatro de la Gente, a group from Indiana, and Teatro del Barrio were different. But our teatro was very working class. We were nationalists. Left groups would appeal to us depending on their line on the

Chicano question. We felt closer to groups that dealt with the national question.[16] We later started aligning ourselves with groups like Bread and Roses who were Anglo but were very much a working-class theater group. We did see it as our responsibility to educate people on the national question. But even then it wasn't just about being Chicanos.

THE MOVEMENT BROUGHT GOOD THINGS

The Chicano Movement here in Chicago opened people's eyes. It said okay for those born here—second or third generation—we're all Mexicanos even though this guy just came from Mexico. Your parents came from there. You respond to your family's culture, so you know you love that part of your family. However, I didn't feel very Mexicana because I really didn't know anything about Mexico, the language, and customs other than what my family exposed me to. I started thinking, "Why am I against this guy who just came from Mexico? Why am I against this brazer?" Addressing these questions is what really built the strength in Pilsen. The division between Mexicanos and the second and third generations—in addition to the gangs—was the biggest issue in Pilsen at the time.

There was also the problem of the poor education young people received. The vast majority of teachers were White. There were a few Blacks and only a handful of Mexicano or Chicano teachers in the schools. I didn't start seeing Mexicano teachers, I think, until I went to Harrison High School. There was someone who was the head of the Bilingual Center, but she wasn't a mainstream teacher, if I could use that word. She was more of a resource person with an assistant. The school put a Spaniard in charge of the Spanish Club. But she was reactionary. Before they even put in a Mexican administrator, they brought in an Asian principal. We finally got a Mexicano vice principal in the 1970s.

There were plenty of good things about Pilsen. There was the Chicano Movement, and with it came the mural movement with artists like Ray Patlan and Marcos Raya. They had a major impact on that community. There was a philosophy advanced by Mexicano/Chicano students at the university, mainly the OLAS people. It was a philosophy that emphasized the need to reclaim our culture. The artists were putting that philosophy into practice out there for the community. The ideas about brotherhood and how we're all connected and that we're all part of the same *raiz* (root) was becoming more visible. It was helping to motivate young people. The music also came along, teatro started growing. This all helped bring identity to young people, and that's what one started to see. You didn't have that fear and embarrassment about listening to the old Mexicano songs anymore. I could appreciate my father's music and the new artists as well.[17]

CASA AZTLÁN

After we began our involvement in OLAS, we started meeting friends at Casa Aztlán. It was when I had started hanging around with María again, and we began to get a sense of what Casa Aztlán was about. When Héctor came back from the Denver Chicano Conference in 1969, I remember him talking about it. I didn't have permission to go. However, the conference really gave us a sense of direction. It was not just Pilsen now. This meant people from all over the United States were deciding to be a part of this Movement. That's when I first started recognizing that it was a Movement. It wasn't just a Pilsen thing.

After that, you started seeing the development of Mujeres Latinas en Acción, APO, Latino Youth, Centro de la Causa, and Librería Nuestro Continente.[18] All that started developing, but especially Casa Aztlán. I learned a lot there. If you were any type of Chicano in Pilsen, you had to tap into Casa Aztlán. To me, it was the center. It was really the Mecca of the Chicano Movement in Chicago. It showed in its art, the community meetings, and the issues it dealt with, like the fight for immigrant rights, César Chávez, and the unionization of *campesinos* (agricultural workers). All that started at Casa Aztlán. The Brown Berets started to get organized then, too. A lot of the people connected to Casa Aztlán also went to the Denver conference. Casa Aztlán was trying to live that philosophy of self-determination, the whole concept of the Chicano nation. The Chicano nation was right here in Chicago, too. The flag hung there at Aztlán, the three faces of our identity. That was very symbolic, the Indian, the Spaniard, and the *mestizo* (mixed blood).[19]

NO LONGER ASHAMED

For me, all that I was starting to learn meant that I didn't have to be ashamed anymore. I didn't have to be ashamed because of my connection to Mexico. Even if you might never have stepped foot in that country, those were your roots. I could recognize and appreciate that I had something to offer. Knowing who you are and where you came from gives you a sense of where you're going. To me, that is what that flag represented.[20] Now we are here, and there are a lot of issues to fight for here in Chicago and in the United States. We were not just doing it for ourselves, but we were doing it for the recently arrived Mexicano and for those that had been here for many years. Harrison High School didn't offer very much. What it did offer was very limited. The Spanish Club and the Bilingual Center were mainly for monolingual kids.

But we Chicanos were starting to see it as okay. Now, we had something to connect us with those kids. We could connect with what they knew. We could go there and find out what Mexico was about.

The Chicano flag was also an alternative to the corrupt Mexican government. A lot of Mexicans put aside their history because all they saw was corruption. There was the contradiction that poor people were being oppressed and killed there. In other words, they saw the Mexican Revolution not really as a liberation but just an excuse to kill more people, more Indians, more poor people. They didn't even want to exalt the Mexican image too much because of this. So Chicanismo was something new, an opportunity, something pure. Something that wasn't corrupt. It was something true.

I didn't fit in any of the different cliques of kids at school. The hippie thing gave you music and opened a lot of doors, but I didn't feel like I was about that.[21] Even though I had to repeat a whole year because I was having too much fun, I knew education was important. I knew I had to stick it out and try to learn as much as I could. I didn't see myself as a genius or even as a bright kid. I just felt that there's got to be a place where I could finally feel comfortable and fight for the other generations of kids that would come after I left. That's why I was part of the fight for the new high school.

OPPRESSION AND INJUSTICE GOT ME INVOLVED

The fight for Benito Juárez presented an opportunity for Chicanos. Toward senior year, a few other kids and I got together with the same idea. There weren't very many of us. It was not even half of the Latino/Chicano kids at school who were very active. It was only a few. But those few were very good leaders. The leadership started surfacing at Harrison High School. A lot of good leadership came from there. Even though some of them later became corrupt, many others from that generation became professionals and made an impact. They went through the same bad education without a lot of support. Yet, they were able to get a college degree. They understood that they needed to get as much education as they could, and they needed to find the support necessary to help them do it.[22] Groups like OLAS offered that support. Iowa offered it at that time through the Chicano House for my husband. Later, even UICC started becoming a little more open. Students were not encouraged at Harrison to go to college. If it weren't for OLAS students coming and saying, "You can do this," some would not have been inspired to go on. I think that's what made a difference.

A lot of things that were happening to us were unfair. I didn't fit into any of those groups until the Chicano Movement came along, and I wanted more. I wanted support. I felt that support coming from those young people from OLAS. They offered that opportunity. Education was important to my father and my mother, but they didn't know how to support us in that. The expectations were there. My father saw me going to college. He wanted me to go to college, but my parents didn't know how to make that happen. You got your support through organizations like OLAS. I only attended UICC for a year or less because I wasn't prepared, and the support wasn't there at that time to really make it. But Latino students later started demanding more from UICC.[23]

My family motivated me to get involved in the Movement. My family was very traditional. My mother stayed home and raised a family. My father went to work. He was a very good breadwinner. He really saw to it that all our needs were met. I mean we never went hungry, never, even if it was just tortillas and *sal* (salt) and beans. We never went hungry. Even when he got drunk, he went to work. He never wanted to miss work. However, in that man-of-the-house tradition, there are problems. A lot of men feel isolated and demoralized at work. My father drank. He had a drinking problem. Those who have a problem with drinking sometimes lack control. He was abusive to my mom at times. That had a big impact on me.

The media was always portraying women as victims. I thought, why are these women so stupid? Why don't they just run or pick up a bat and hit the guy over the head or whatever? Then to see it in your own family . . . I asked myself, "Why isn't my mom strong enough to fend against my father? Why is she allowing this to happen?" So, even when I was growing up, I said to myself, "I will never ever allow any man to make me a victim." This was back when I was ten or twelve years old. When I started high school, I was very clear. I thought, "I deserve more." I would never allow a man to dictate to me. I would never allow anyone to do that. That was something missing from the Chicano Movement. I think that's why I started bringing up the idea that "Chicanas Can, Too."

OLAS didn't offer very much for young women. I don't remember any women taking us aside and saying to us, "Hey, girls, this is what we got to do." The only feminists that I looked up to were María and her mom. I thought there has to be more out there than what's being offered to us. I saw older men hitting on high schoolers. I didn't want that. That was bullshit. I think that also made a big difference for me. I wanted more as a woman.

I decided to try college for a year after graduation though I didn't have the discipline that it took to be a college student. My political life was more important because it fulfilled something inside of me that I didn't have at home at that time. There were too many issues going on with my family. That was a time when you challenged your parents in their thinking and everything else. The most progressive and positive way of doing this was doing the kind of political work that we were doing in teatro.

BECOMING LEADERS

We got to meet members of a California-based political group, the August Twenty-Ninth Movement.[24] We linked up with some of these members through people we worked with. Basically, the organization was about giving leadership, giving support to some of the issues that were going on in Pilsen, because as a teatro group, we got involved in community issues as well. Compañia Trucha had to take a position. There were a lot of issues out there that needed our support and that needed connection and leadership from us. So, besides being a teatro, besides doing an analysis of the issues and educating through theater, we took positions like on the Rush Presbyterian Saint Luke's Hospital struggle.

I think I was pregnant with my second child at that time. We were connected to Casa Aztlán. That's where we used to practice, and that's where we discussed a lot of political issues with some of the more active people in Pilsen. Magdalena's firing for being an advocate for Latinos and other injustices at Saint Luke's were brought up in a meeting. The speaker said, "Look, these are her issues." So we developed a play and performed in the community to gain support for her.

People eventually called for a sit-in at Saint Luke's because we weren't going anywhere. The organization was part of those activities. We were networked, and others got involved like the people from South Chicago. We were going to support it. We were going to be part of the sit-in. Some of our people in Compañia Trucha were also influential within the leadership of ATM. After the action and the arrests, we had to take it to the next phase, which was defending those who got arrested. ATM got together with Compañia Trucha and people from South Chicago to strategize. We met with people from Casa Aztlán to determine how we were going to defend ourselves. Casa Aztlán brought people to court. We continued as Compañia Trucha but were taking leadership within ATM. We even met late at night at our Compañia Trucha Center to strategize and identify resources. We were the leadership that took this issue to the next level, and we were able with the help of Casa Aztlán to carry out the campaign to get the hospital to offer better quality care to Latinos and not mistreat them. We operated behind the scenes developing strategies.

Even though I was pregnant, we met at our center, and it was not as difficult as it might have been for me. You can say we met in my living room. We discussed the role of women and took the position that we needed to support all the women in their work, and if that meant providing childcare for them, that's what we had to do. So this allowed me to do what I had to do. I think this helped my family life. It was not like anyone said, "María, we need your husband in the struggle, so you know you got to excuse him for not being around." No, it was like, "Okay, we'll take turns watching the baby." It made my husband conscious that he had a responsibility to the Movimiento—to whatever work we were doing—but also to his child.

MOVING FROM MIDDLE GROUND

When I started high school, I found myself on middle ground. I grew up with a lot of misconceptions about Mexicanos. In school, a Mexicano was a brazer. You know, if you were not a brazer, you were a gangster, or you were just in the middle, neutral. You didn't really identify yourself by any name. As I built a consciousness through the Chicano Movement, I saw it more as a unifying effort, a uniting force so we could stop the kind of backwardness that saw people born in Mexico as very separate, very different. You were here with your Mexican parents speaking *pocho,* eating tacos but always being forced to be somebody else.[25] You know, you were caught in the middle. Not until the word *Chicano* appeared and truly knowing what Aztlán was about did we begin to understand that it was not our fault that there was so much ignorance and misunderstanding among second- and third-generation Mexicanos. It was out of ignorance that we were dividing ourselves.

I consider myself Chicana. When people ask me, though, people I don't really want to spend a long time dealing with, I will say my parents were raised in Mexico, and I was born here. I'm Mexicana. Back then I would use Chicana because *Chicano* and *Chicana* had a meaning. It had a very powerful meaning but not anymore, not for people my age who are not very political. To some of the youth, it still has a good meaning, especially for the kids who are in college and are starting to build their consciousness and getting to know their history. For them, Chicano/Chicana still is a powerful name and identity. Calling myself Chicana really gave me an identity. My father was born in Mexico, and my mother was raised inside of Mexico. I am second generation, and I had no real linkages to Mexico other than through my parents, other than being in Mexico one time, when I was very young and my father took us to San Luis Potosi to visit his homeland. I couldn't identify with Mexico.[26] I didn't know the history. People didn't accept me as being Mexicana because of the way I spoke.

But the term *Chicano* brought us together. Chicano meant unity. It made us see each other as one. We were all Mexicanos, that's our nationality, but you just happen to be born on one side, and your history of struggle is one, and the history and struggle of people born across the border is another. The struggles on both sides of the border are still not over. So that's what *Chicano* meant to me. It's a history of struggle. Just because the United States took over Mexico's land didn't mean it was going to wipe out everything. The word *Chicano* represents struggle. It represents a political position. Groups like CASA were totally denying that struggle and the people on this side of the border.[27] The struggle in the United States is very different from the struggle in Mexico in many ways. If you really want to support the struggle in Mexico, if you're always talking about building the revolution in Mexico, fighting imperialism, then your struggle belongs in Mexico. You belong in Mexico. You need to go there and struggle. To me, it was a big contradiction that people ignore what people have accomplished and what people have worked for here on this side, in the United States.

I don't agree when people say we're all Mexicans just transplanted here. No! We're not Mexicanos all transplanted. I've never lived in Mexico! I've never struggled in Mexico! I've never felt the oppression that people in Mexico have. I support Mexico. I support the people of Mexico in their struggle. I will do that with money, through sending whatever help I can, but my struggle is here. That's where I'll always put my efforts in the struggles here . . . being part of the ongoing struggle of immigrants, doing farmworker support and participating in the labor movement here in Chicago. There is too much to do here for me to want to go and struggle there. Reality is what you make it. You struggle where you are. Of course, you support everyone's struggle. You do it in many different ways. It's that I chose to struggle here in my home. The oppression continues, the ignorance continues, and the development of young minds and consciousness continues. That's where I want to put my efforts. That's where I'm going to put my energy in helping new leadership develop through the work that I do with high school students and the work that I do with my daughter through her school. Wherever one can do it, I'm going to do it.

End of a Collective Vision

We're going through another phase. What we have is the growth of people coming to the United States. They bring along their ideals and also a lot of their ignorance.[28] That's why the term *Chicano* right now doesn't have the same meaning with people my age. Today, people struggle with me about why I call myself Chicana. They say I'm a Mexicana. It's an ongoing struggle about terms. They think I am just trying to separate myself. But it's a word to unite. It was a word that began to unite all of us. The Mexicanos, the ones that are coming in, have gained from the struggles we took up years ago. It doesn't mean that there is not going to be another struggle tomorrow, such as for bilingual education, bilingual interpreters in hospitals, and jobs, or like the campaigns to get Mexicanos and other Latinos employed with the CTA and with the post office. Those are all things we struggled for during our time. And we made some gains. People now are benefiting from our struggles. The Mexicanos coming in are benefiting, and so are their children. But the struggle is not over, because what we gained sooner or later, they will try to take away. We see them doing it. We see the attacks against immigrants. We need to struggle again, but how do we unite Mexicanos and Nuevo Mexicanos to fight the enemy?[29]

There is a popular adage that warns that "one is doomed to repeat history if one does not learn from its lessons." There is some truth to that quote if we look at what is going on currently in this country. The struggles of the 1960s and 1970s seem to be repeating themselves today. As Mexicanos/Chicanos, we struggled to stop attacks and deportations on undocumented immigrants.[30] We are once again facing attacks on undocumented workers, even more severe and with increasing aggression. Families are put in detention centers or in some cases in county prisons. Detainees unfamiliar with immigration laws are being unjustly charged with felonies.

Then we protested against an unjust war in Vietnam. Fast forward and there is an unjust war in Iraq that has gone on for years and is costing us $170 million a day. In spite of the massive demonstrations against the war at home and abroad, both the Bush and the Obama administrations have proven effective at sidestepping the will of the people of the United States and the world.

Back in the day, some of us searched for a national identity that reclaimed our history, culture, language, and political position in the world. Today young Mexicanos, unaware or not interested in history, are facing a dilemma. The same dilemma we faced . . . who are we . . . Hispanics, Latinos, Mexicans, or Chicanos, and what is our social responsibility to our *gente* (people). . . to our community? I am sometimes disheartened by the message of division or lack of unity around identity. Mexicanos are the largest minority population in the United States, and our economic power has grown exponentially. However, we are still lacking in educational and political representation that impacts our economic independence and social development as a constituency in this nation. The path to liberation is a protracted struggle, and becoming a better-educated populace is crucial. Having political representation that can present and push through a progressive agenda does not hurt the cause as long as the electoral process is seen only as a tactic and not the main or only strategy.

As women, we declared our independence and demonstrated our leadership ability within the movement. However, we have come across *hermanas* (sisters) who are still struggling today with issues of sexism. I recently encountered some women developing their own art and cultural center because their male counterparts refused to take them seriously. These women on their own opened the Centro de La Cultura (the Cultural Center) in the Pilsen community. Again we find ourselves divided by issues of identity and gender.

We as a people need to learn from history and find the strength to challenge the status quo. Just like during the Chicano Movement when we unapologetically dared to disrupt cultural norms. We must again disrupt the existing cultural, political, and gender relationships with unity and purpose. We must not give in to labels that divide us but find the unity in our political positions that can help us to secure justice for our gente. What made us unite and struggle as sisters is still the case . . . discrimination, attacks on immigrants, political and social inequality, and war.

My main focus in the 1970s and what I tried to focus on in teatro was the working class and recognizing women's leadership because women were a big part of leadership in many movements including the labor movement. But it was not recognized, and it was always a struggle for women to put it forward. During the Reagan era, people were not really about getting an education and coming back to the community to teach or to have an impact. It was not about the need for more Mexicano teachers or engineers. It was about one's own career and how much money one could earn. How you can make it individually. How you can buy into the American Dream. This was the 1980s Reagan generation.

I started seeing a little different trend in the nineties. I raised two girls and put them through college and looked for support to help them. I mean I think that's what helped my daughter stick it out. It wasn't because of the college itself. For the four years that Tina attended Knox College, a private upper-middle-class school outside of Chicago, I had to be on that phone almost every week, listening to her cry, "Ma, I can't take it anymore." It wasn't so much the academic part of school. It was the social part of school, feeling isolated away from her community. My goodness, four years of having to support her, to say, "Stick it out. What you're going to get out of there is much more, and after that, you can socialize. You can do whatever you want to do. You can organize."[31] Even though she was involved a little bit, she had a very difficult time because Knox College really looked toward those kids who could afford to pay, the upper-middle-class kids. That's who was in leadership there. It's a different type of leadership when you have upper-middle-class students than it is if you have working-class kids or kids with good community politics and a sense of their culture.

When my other daughter went to college, they offered more. She started at Madison but transferred to UIC.[32] There was the MeSA group at UIC.[33] But again that group was not reaching out to kids. She had to reach out to the groups. That's the difference. You have to have a friend to be a part of the clique. That's how you get involved. They are not aggressively recruiting students, trying to really win them over and getting them involved. It is more of a social circle. That's what's going on now.

When I was in alternative education, I would make the effort to take our students to MeSA's events and try to make a connection. The MeSA students didn't even follow up with them and say, "You guys come back, and we can do this or that. You know college is important." It doesn't happen like that. I think right now there is a leadership vacuum. Kids do want leadership. They do want guidance. I see that. They just don't know how to become leaders. They're too busy trying to stay in school.

At some point in the 1970s, money was thrown around to keep the lid on the kettle. You had resources. You had the funding to do many things. We don't have that luxury anymore. Let's say if a college thought it was so important to have a cultural center to really support Mexicanos and keep them there, why wouldn't they provide the necessary resources? Why not offer a class for credit if a student wants to get into organizing and go out there and recruit kids? That's not going on. Universities don't feel it's important. We have to push for those resources.

Society has deteriorated so much. We're not really critically thinking of kids' needs. There are so many problems with gangs and drugs. The drugs have grown tremendously. People have no jobs, and all of this plays into kids' motivation, what they see themselves doing with their lives. We still have that pull-yourself-up-by-your-bootstraps mentality from the Reagan era that says, "If I can do it, you can, too." We know it doesn't happen. There are so many variables. We're not all the same. The best opportunities are still for upper-class people, and most of those are Anglos. But for Latinos, well, it's not fair. It's not going to change unless we make that a part of our agenda and struggle to get back what we have already lost. Latinos generally don't get the quality of education that many Anglos and upper-class people get.

Look what UIC is doing. It's changing its entrance requirements and changing who gets into the university.

Chicago is a working-class town. Unlike Teatro Campesino that concen-
trated mainly on the *campesino* struggle, we saw our people being cheated
and kicked out of the companies where they worked for organizing. I began to
see beyond just Chicanos to think more broadly about issues of class. Sometimes you get class consciousness through your education in college, even
though I didn't really go. I depended on my role models who were learning
about the workers' movement—those like María, my husband, and others
who attended college. That's when I started learning about working-class
politics. Through teatro, we also had an opportunity to meet other groups
from around the country and Mexico and South America. Their issues were
focused on working people, the class issue. That's when we started learning
more as a teatro. We started developing our own skits rather than just doing
what Teatro Campesino had been doing.[34] Women's issues were also a very
important part of our struggles. It wasn't just about Chicanos. It was about
the working class and women, equality for women as well as equality for
workers and Latinos.

When I think back on all of this, I realize we accomplished a lot. I think
through the teatro, I as a woman was able to start raising women's issues.
That's something that we did not find among other teatros. That was a criticism we made.[35] They were doing the same old traditional *la mama* (the
mother) and the whore kind of stuff. We were out there saying women have
to be seen as the leaders because we are the leaders. Some male activists
used to argue that only until after Chicanos have equality can women in the
Chicano Movement get their equality. That's bullshit. I think that was one of
the things that was important for me because this is what helped me raise my
daughters to be strong Chicanas, strong leadership, and I saw it when they
were in college. You see it now in their work in their struggles. For me, that
was the main thing I was able to offer them.

There still needs to be education about those times. It really upsets me
when I hear some people speak about the word *Chicano*. How people see
it as a divisive term, not just divisive but a put-down. That's how some students describe it, like it somehow means you're second class, like this is a
dirty word. For us, it was ultimately the way we were able to unite Mexicanos
with the other generations because of the working-class issue. We were able
to raise our consciousness. That's why we have conferences like the NACCS
(National Association of Chicano and Chicana Studies) Conference, and we
have so many more writers and academics.

My work with Compañia Trucha is what I had to offer my community. That's something that was missing. That's what we were recognized for in the community, for raising issues, because teatro was not just about entertaining. It was about educating. It was at least providing a way of saying to people, "Okay, these are opportunities; these are issues that you need to get involved in." Maybe we were not involved in all the issues, politically, I mean, but we were involved in many, not just as the teatro but also in terms of other forms of organizing. Maybe today I'm not the director of a center, but what we were able to do, what I was able to do at least was keep my principles and my practice. I think I've been able to influence people and the projects that I've developed for students. I was able to integrate my beliefs into the philosophy of the school and how we treat our high school students.[36]

My involvement in the Chicano Movement gave me the opportunity to meet other women leaders. We were able to connect as women. Now we have respect for each other because of our involvement. A lot of my friends helped me raise my daughters. Because of who they are, the kind of role models that they are, they had a great influence on my kids.

María was fighting on the *campesino* front. Then there was the teatro and dealing with the cultural part of the Movement. There were people working at UICC and that front trying to change things going on at the college level. Then you had working-class women fighting in the community and on other fronts. We struggled and made inroads, and we got some of what we fought for, but it's not that simple. Whatever we won we know we're going to eventually lose again. We're going to have to fight for it again. Even though we made gains like with bilingual education in schools. They're being threatened. They're being taken away. Opportunities for Latinos through affirmative action . . . we're losing them. We've lost it in some universities already. So that's another struggle that needs to happen over again and again. Our kids are not being given a fair opportunity. To me, leadership has to come from the students at the university. They have to start making those things happen. I know there are a lot of conscious kids in those colleges. It's just that they need leadership. They need the support. How we get there I don't know yet. But we have to try.

SOME REGRETS AND HOPE

Sometimes when we move to the left, we forget how to remain human. There were definitely a lot of mistakes made. Some of our comrades were very honest. But then we didn't find out until much later that some people we trusted didn't live up to our expectations. This helped to divide the teatro. We never really sat down to analyze how we could avoid making that mistake again. Sometimes, we got so involved that we didn't take care of ourselves. I didn't finish college. I was too busy with the Movimiento. Héctor wasn't able to finish college because he was too busy. So he doesn't make the salary that he could have made.

Still, there was so much that was gained. The Movement brought unity between young and old, working-class mothers, parents, and the undocumented. We worked together hand in hand to make changes. It brought us together for the same cause. You know we learned from each other. We had *compañeros* (comrades) who came from Mexico and struggled in Mexico who brought us lessons from their fights that we were able to use here. They brought a lot of motivation, not just to Chicago but nationally. We still have those contacts, that closeness.

The Chicano Movement created passion, a passion for philosophy and principles, like self-determination, and a respect for other cultures, starting with respecting ourselves, our own culture, so that we could respect everybody else's. The Chicano Movement generated so much passion on so many different levels: a passion to stand up for bilingual education, a passion to stand up for Mexican history, a passion to stand up for the undocumented, a passion to organize. I have kept my cultural philosophy through all of my life. Even in the face of misunderstandings from today's generation that say that *Chicano* is a bad word. They don't understand. But to us, it gave us a passion to speak up and to speak openly. Through the contacts we made with the people in Mexico who had more of a class perspective, we learned to develop better strategies. That passion is still useful. All the raw materials are still there. We can still reach back into that freezer and take out some of what we had in the past and mold it into different things. I think Chicago is tremendous. A lot of things have happened here, and I think a lot of things can still happen here.

Notes

1. The chapter's title translates as "A Chicana in the struggle." This introductory vignette was developed in collaboration with María Gamboa. The substance of this chapter comes from several interviews that occurred mainly in 1998 but continued through 2008.

2. Pilsen Neighbors Community Council was founded in 1954. It remains one of the major civic organizations in the community (Pilsen Neighbors Community Council, n.d).

3. A *señora*, a title of respect, is a married woman or older lady.

4. South Lawndale, or Little Village, lies directly west of Pilsen.

5. The Latin Kings is a major street gang that exists in many areas of the country.

6. *Brazer* is a disparaging term to refer to an immigrant who clings to his or her Mexican culture that is often perceived as "rural" by young urban Chicanos. The term is derived from the Bracero Program, a guest-laborer program that brought Mexicans into the United States. In the 1970s, one of the local Pilsen gangs called itself the Brazers and recruited primarily among Mexican immigrant youth.

7. Luis Valdez founded El Teatro Campesino, the most successful Latino street-theater troupe. For more on El Teatro Campesino, see Broyles-González (1994). While appreciating their contributions to the UFW, their plays were criticized by some Chicana feminists for their male-centered material and the stereotyping of women. For a critique of Teatro Campesino leadership, see Treviño (2001). The Valdez brothers, Luis and Daniel, were active with the California farmworkers and eventually went on to have major careers in music and film.

8. St. Joseph's name was changed in the 1970s to El Centro de la Causa (Center for the Cause), a social-service agency that housed youth and educational programs and offered services to the Pilsen community.

9. WCYC was a small, twenty-watt radio station at the time. It later became Radio Arte (Art Radio), which today is associated with the National Museum of Mexican Art, previously Mexican Fine Arts. It is based in Chicago's Pilsen community.

10. *Posadas* is a nine-day Latin American Catholic Christmas celebration that uses small figurines to reenact Mary and Joseph's search for shelter.

11. These political skits sometimes offended conservative school personnel. Over time, it became more difficult for OLAS and other Chicano activists to enter the schools. Jesus "Chuy" Negrete was a major figure in Chicago street theater and Chicano culture and was for a time employed by the Latin American Recruitment Program at UICC.

12. The common Chicano expression was *ponte trucha,* meaning "get wise" or "get with it."

13. *Salt of the Earth* is a film that focuses on the tensions between a Mexican couple during a mining strike. When the men cannot walk the picket line, the women get involved. The husbands eventually learn to accept the role of women as partners in the struggle. Some of the actors and those affiliated with the production of the film were blacklisted during the McCarthy era.

14. *La Virgencita* is a diminutive of the Virgin Mary.

15. The Mascarones (masked ones) is a well-known and innovative Marxist-oriented theatrical troupe based in Mexico City. The Mascarones act and incorporate music and choral poetry into their performances. For more on the Mascarones and Don Mariano Leyva Dominquez, see Dominquez (2004, November 16).

16. The Chicano national-question debate related to the nature of the oppression suffered by Chicanos as a consequence of the U.S. appropriation of the Southwest and the various solutions advanced to address the conditions of Chicanos.

17. The paradox of Chicano cultural identity was in the manner in which for some it served to create a "new" not-so-Mexican identity—initially, a distancing mechanism—that eventually blended the culture and history of two countries, an idealized or hyperbolized Mexico with *barrio* Chicano realities across the border. Therefore, it provided a special lens for the generation and a half and those born in the States to view, appreciate, and perhaps ultimately even return to a "Mexican" cultural identity, albeit as viewed from a unique and hybridized perspective. Mestizo (the mixture of races) identity lauded by Chicanos in the 1960s gave birth to indigenous perspectives advocated by subsequent generations.

18. Mujeres Latinas en Acción (Latina Women in Action) began as a consciousness-raising group and shortly thereafter transitioned to become an advocacy and community-service center for women and young girls.

19. Mestizo encompasses the Mexican and Chicano identity, the product of the blending of cultures.

20. The Chicano flag comprises three faces, the indigenous, the Spaniard (European) facing east and west, and at the center facing forward the mestizo.

21. María's issue with the alternative youth culture was related to some of its more cynical adherents who minimized the possibilities of achieving fundamental change and its tendency to emphasize personal liberation over collective action and social change.

22. Ovando (1977) documents a case of a Midwestern high school where contact with highly politicized college-student activists may have increased the college aspirations of a sector of poor, Latino secondary-school youth despite what academic research might have predicted.

23. María is referring to the successive struggles in the 1970s at UICC for outreach and academic-support programs, Latino studies, and other mechanisms of student support, including a Latino cultural center.

24. ATM was a socialist group named in commemoration of the 1970 Chicano Moratorium, an antiwar demonstration attended by approximately thirty thousand people that ended in the deaths of three, including journalist Rubén Salazar. Many in the Movimiento believed he was intentionally singled out for assassination.

25. *Pocho* is "Spanglish," commonly seen by Mexicans as a vulgarized form of the language.

26. María is using the term *second generation* to mean the first generation born in the United States of first-generation immigrant parents.

27. Centro de Acción Social Autonoma (CASA, Autonomous Center for Social Action) is an immigrant service center and labor-organizing and community-activist group initially associated with Bert Corona. CASA was based in Los Angeles but soon had various affiliates across the country. The *Sin fronteras* (without borders) slogan was also the name of CASA's newspaper and is suggestive of the unity of the struggles of Mexican workers, no matter on which side of the border they reside. María's criticism of this political perspective is that it seemed to imply that the Chicano struggle

should be subsumed or appended to the political strategy of the Mexican left. Her belief is that an understanding of Mexicano/Chicano life in the United States should be the basis of an effective politics of social change.

28. Moraga (1993) provides a message of hope: "A new generation of future Chicanos arrives every day with every Mexican immigrant. Some may find their American dream and forget their origins, but the majority of Mexico's descendents soon comprehend the political meaning of the disparity between their lives and those of the gringo" (155).

29. The phrase *Mexicanos and Nuevo (New) Mexicanos* alludes to the inclusion of Mexicans from both sides of the border.

30. For essays related to anti-immigrant and racist events in the 1990s, see Martinez (1998).

31. María is contrasting "socializing" or collective action and community progress with the individualized manner that students are generally moved through at all levels of the educational system. This is often felt by Latinos to be an intensely isolating and psychologically painful process that separates one from community and social-support networks.

32. *Madison* is short for University of Wisconsin–Madison.

33. MeSA (Mexican Students of Aztlán) is a local, university-based student group with similarities to MeCHA (Movimiento Estudiantil Chicano de Aztlán, Chicano Student Movement of Aztlán) groups still found in the Southwest and historically linked to the Chicano Movement.

34. Local theater groups often produced versions of plays or skits developed by nationally known companies such as Teatro Campesino.

35. For an overview of some of the criticisms raised by Chicana feminists, see Garcia and Garcia (1997).

36. María is referring to an alternative educational project with which she was involved at the time of the interview.

Figure 1. Jane Addams Hull-House Museum, May 2009. (Photo by Claudio Gaete-Tapia.)

Figure 2. Centro Social Mexicano, 2431 West Roosevelt Road, full-length view (prior to removal of back portion of building), 2006. (Photo courtesy of HHZ.)

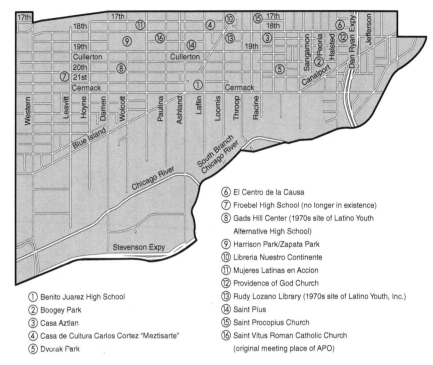

⑥ El Centro de la Causa
⑦ Froebel High School (no longer in existence)
⑧ Gads Hill Center (1970s site of Latino Youth Alternative High School)
⑨ Harrison Park/Zapata Park
⑩ Libreria Nuestro Continente
⑪ Mujeres Latinas en Accion
⑫ Providence of God Church
⑬ Rudy Lozano Library (1970s site of Latino Youth, Inc.)
⑭ Saint Pius
⑮ Saint Procopius Church
⑯ Saint Vitus Roman Catholic Church (original meeting place of APO)

① Benito Juarez High School
② Boogey Park
③ Casa Aztlan
④ Casa de Cultura Carlos Cortez "Meztisarte"
⑤ Dvorak Park

Figure 3. Pilsen Community.

Figure 4. OLAS community event flyer. (Courtesy of Magda Ramírez-Castañeda.)

Figure 5. Centro de la Causa (formerly Saint Joseph), 731 West 17th Street, community site for OLAS, June 2009. (Photo by Claudio Gaete-Tapia.)

Figure 6. Original site of APO (former site of Saint Vitus Church), May 2009. (Photo by Claudio Gaete-Tapia.)

Figure 7. Current site of
APO, Casa de la Cultura
Carlos Cortez and Mestizarte
arts organization, May 2009.
(Photo by Claudio Gaete-Tapia.)

Figure 8. National Youth Liberation Conference pamphlet.
(Courtesy of Magda Ramírez-Castañeda.)

Figure 9. Casa Aztlán facade, May 2009. (Photo by Claudio Gaete-Tapia.)

Figure 10. Teatro de la Raza flyer, ca. 1970. Courtesy of Magda Ramírez-Castañeda.)

Figure 11. Flor y Canto (flower and song) singing group, Rosa Negrete and Jesus "Chuy" Negrete, ca. 1975. (Photo by Rico Garibay, courtesy of Juanita Negrete.)

Figure 12. Isaura González, right, at UFW march, ca. 1973. (Photo courtesy of Isaura González.)

Figure 13. Community protest against Chicago Transit Authority, corner of 18th Street and Ashland Avenue, July 1972. (Photo courtesy of Magda Ramírez-Castañeda.)

Figure 14. Providence of God Church, May 2009, where during the 1970s, Father John Harrington was pastor, and many Movement activities took place. (Photo by Claudio Gaete-Tapia.)

Figure 15. Facade, Librería Nuestro Continente, 1642 South Blue Island Avenue, ca. 1973. (Photo from Chicago Department of Development and Planning.)

Figure 16. Flyer, Latino Women's Education Awareness Conference, June 9, 1973, cosponsored by El Centro de la Causa and the National Education Task Force de La Raza. (Courtesy of Magda Ramírez-Castañeda.)

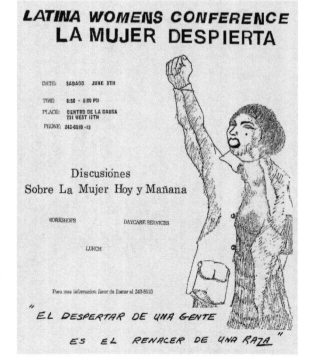

Figure 17. Compañia Trucha, ca. 1975. *Front row:* Filiberto Ramírez, María Aguilar, Héctor Gamboa; *back row:* Joe Murillo, Antonio Zavala, Jose Gaspar. (Photo courtesy of María Gamboa.)

People's theatre

COMPANIA TRUCHA

Compañia Trucha was formed in March of 1974, as a means to communicate to the people the struggles and problems that face the majority of people of the world. We believe that theatre is a very important part of expressing the feelings, problems and successes of the people in fighting to get what is justly theirs.

Peoples' Theatre is a theatre that is born and grows from the roots of the multi-national working class. Trucha means to be aware, to open your eyes, to wake up. It dedicates itself to present an analysis of the lives of people by means of plays, songs and poetry, and also as a means to communicate to people possible solutions to our problems.

To us there is no reality to the statement of "Art for art's sake", all art-theatre, poetry, music, movies, etc..... is a reflection of culture and makes a political statement--the question of who's culture and who's politics enters here.

We draw our plays from our experiences at work, in the neighborhoods, from the schools, from our friends and families. The members of Trucha are active in many ways trying to learn from the people, and to do what we can in the working-class and national liberation movements.

We appreciate any criticisms of our work and if you would like to join us in doing peoples' theatre or would like more information on theatre and/or performances--come talk to us or call us. We'll be glad to answer any questions.

COMPANIA TRUCHA
C/o Casa Aztlan
1831 S. Racine
Chgo, ILL 60608
666-5508

Figure 18. Compañia Trucha flyer, ca. 1975. (Courtesy of María Gamboa.)

BOLETIN DEL PUEBLO

NO. 1

LA SALUD ES UN DERECHO

NO UN PREVILEGIO

Figure 19. Bulletin, Coalition of Latino Organizations, on health care and firing of Magdalena Garcia and Victoria Pérez, 1976. (Courtesy of Magda Ramírez-Castañeda.)

CORRIDO DE SAN LUCAS

Llegamos hasta san lucas peliando por la justicia,
luchando por los derechos de un pueblo discriminado,
toda la gente gritaba, bast ya ya no aguantamos.

No fue hasta el 12 de Agosto cuando la accion fue tomada
gritaban por entrevista sin que resultara nada,
y el hospital respondia, no cumpliremos ocn sus demandas

Cuando llegaron al punto, la gente no se detuvo, (Coro)
tomaron las oficinas y el derecho se obtuvo,
aunque se llevo algun tiempo, al hospital le dieron duro

Entraron 20 policias con los garotes en la mano
se acercaron a la gente, pensaban encarcelarnos,
en poco tiempo saldria, no era tan facil como creian.

La lucha les cuento senores, no es solo contra el hospital,
pero contra un sistema que roba nuestra igualdad,
y mandan la policia, que solo sirve la burguesia

Cuando llegaron al punto, la gente no se detuvo,
tomaron las oficinas y el derecho se obtuvo,
aunque se llevo algun tiempo, al hospital le dieron duro.

Eran obreros y obreras, estudiantes y madres de ninos,
unidos en una lucha que realmente era justa,
y una cosa todos vimos, un pueblo unido nunca es vencido.

Este corrido fue escrito por Teatro del Barrio en apoyo
de la luch contra el hospital San lucas. Las pasadas de
la guitarra son A-E-D.

This corrido was written by Teatro del Barrio in support
of the struggle against St. Luke's hospital. The guitar
chords are A-E-D.

Figure 20. Ballad written by members of Teatro del Barrio to protest Presbyterian Saint Luke's Hospital and published in *Boletin del Pueblo*, 1976. (Courtesy of Magda Ramírez-Castañeda.)

Figure 21. Magda
Ramírez-Castañeda
at downtown Chicago
demonstration against
the Shah of Iran,
ca. 1979. (Courtesy
of Magda Ramírez-
Castañeda.)

Figure 22. Compañia Trucha performance in downtown Chicago in support
of the Puerto Rican community and against police brutality, ca. 1977.
(Photo courtesy of María Gamboa.)

Figure 23. Chispa performance at Daley Plaza for women's event, March 16, 1978. *Left to right* Santa Negrete, Juanita Negrete, Isaura González, and Rosa Negrete. (Photo courtesy of Isaura González.)

Figure 24. María Saucedo and Filiberto Ramírez at their wedding reception, June, 1977. (Photo courtesy of Victoria Pérez.)

Figure 25. Marcos Raya mural, main floor, Casa Aztlán, ca 1975. *Middle group,
left to right:* María Saucedo, Jose Valdivia, and Marcos Raya (with glasses),
painted from photographs taken during interviews for principal of Benito Juárez
High School. (Photo courtesy of Victoria Pérez.)

Figure 26. Benito Juárez High School, May 2009. (Photo by Claudio Gaete-Tapia.)

Figure 27. Casa Aztlán, gathering point for María Saucedo commemorative march, 1981. (Photo courtesy of María Gamboa.)

Figure 28. March down 18th Street in honor of María Saucedo, 1981. María Gamboa (*holding right side of banner*), girl in front of banner is student of Saucedo. Banner reads: "teacher, mother, revolutionary, friend." (Photo courtesy of María Gamboa.)

Figure 29. *Pots of Promise* book reception, April 2004. Left to right: Cheryl Ganz (author), person unknown, Margaret Strobel (author), person unknown, Isaura González, Victoria Pérez, Cristina Vital, and Magda Ramírez-Castañeda. (Photo courtesy of Victoria Pérez.)

Figure 30. *Tributo a nuestra compañera* (tribute to our comrade), Saint Pius Church, Sunday, March 7, 2010. *Left to right:* María Gamboa, Cristina Vital, image of Isaura González, Victoria Pérez, and Magda Castañeda. (Photo by Thomas Elizalde.)

Figure 31. Homage to María Saucedo by Marcos Raya. (Courtesy of the artist.)

A Woman of My Time

CRISTINA VITAL

Living the Movement, 1973

It is almost eight A.M. on a Friday morning, and the meeting space at the back of the bookstore is a mess.[1] The blackboard, metal folding chairs, and tables from the night before are scattered in an inexplicably, haphazard way as if children had upended things in the course of their play. The vestiges of last night's class, a language workbook, candy wrappers, scraps of paper, and other debris, remain on tables and littered across the floor. As usual, the twenty or so men and women who had arrived last night tired and droopy-eyed strained to remain focused on English lessons after a long day's work at nearby factories and restaurants.

Yet after the class begins, the energy begins to return. Even under such trying conditions, it is pleasant to have an opportunity to socialize with others. Students linger after class inside the bookstore and in front of the building, holding onto the last vestiges of the evening until they must accept the fact that it is time to return to families and prepare for work the next day. After all the students have finally left, Maximo pulls down the blinds and checks every lock. He examines the mess but decides to leave it for the next morning.

In the morning there is just enough time to put a pot of coffee on the stove and straighten things up before the day begins. Cristina strikes a wooden match and lights a burner before she surveys the situation in the bookstore up front. Against one of the walls are racks of organizational newspapers, bulletins, and journals that must be put in some order before the store opens. Maximo will have to take care of storing the tables in the basement. The chairs must be rearranged for the movie tonight. The Comité expects a full house to see the documentary film *Mexico, the Frozen Revolution*. Tonight's special guest is a veteran of the 1968 Mexican student movement now living in exile in France. Yenelli and María are in charge of refreshments, but Cristina remembers that she also promised to help Yenelli pick up food donations from local grocery stores.

Maximo enters the bookstore meeting space from the apartment in the rear and hands Cristina a cup of coffee. She asks him to take the folding tables to the basement so she can continue cleaning. He shakes his head and informs her that the Comité will have a brief meeting before the program. The tables cannot be taken down until later. It is just before nine o'clock, the opening hour for the store, but someone is already pounding on the glass door up front. Héctor is dropping off the movie reels and projector for this evening's event. Cristina is still not sure why the tables must be left standing.

"The guys can help take the tables down and set up the chairs for the program. Just leave them," Maximo insists.

An extrawide bookcase separates the front of the store from the multipurpose space at the back. It is one of three library-sized wooden bookcases that hold the entire store's stock. One can walk around either side of the central wooden case and enter the meeting room, where shelves of newspapers and other periodicals can be found against a wall. There is another knock at the door. It is time to begin the day. Cristina does not recognize the voices of the people speaking to Maximo. He brings them to the back where she has started drafting a paper on the role of women in the Movimiento. Three men from a Minnesota collective are passing through on their way to a conference in Ohio. They have heard about the Librería and decide to stop in on their way. Maximo leaves them talking with Cristina.

He retreats to the small neat kitchen to fill mugs. The small apartment contrasts sharply with the disheveled room up front. The blue-and-white–tiled counter and the yellow molding bordering the ceiling evoke a traditional Mexican home. An earthen-colored *sarape* covers a daybed.[2] Framed wall posters of Che, the Mexican Revolution, and works of the great Mexican muralists are sealed behind glass and add more color to the room. Maximo empties a bag of *pan dulce* (sweet bread) onto a platter and places it on a tray with a milk container and sugar bowl.

The phone rings. Someone is inquiring about tonight's program. "Yes, it begins at seven. . . . Yes, childcare will be provided," Cristina reassures the person on the other end. Throughout the course of the day, she will receive a dozen or so calls like this. Maximo and Cristina are talking to the *compañeros* (comrades) from Minnesota when she hears the chimes above the store door. Cristina makes herself available to the two customers who walk in and browse the shelves and the table of books on sale. They leave after purchasing a volume on Bolivian miners and another on the Uruguayan Tupamaros.[3]

Cristina smiles at María and Cookie waving on the other side of the store window. After exchanging greetings and embraces, she offers them coffee, but they both have had two cups already this morning. They are doing work with a group of Mexicanos organizing at a local factory. A decision to strike has already been taken, and María will ask the Comité to help support the workers. Sticking out of the front panel pocket of her painter's pants is an assortment of colored markers. Several political buttons are pinned across the front bib of her overalls. A red bandana covers most of her head. It is part of her regular *campesina* (agricultural worker) look that she projects. Cristina asks about the markers. She had almost forgotten. María wants to know if she and Cookie can make posters and a banner for the strikers there at the store. They have the paint in the car out back, and signs need to be delivered to the workers before this afternoon's union meeting.

"Sure." Cristina agrees readily. Cookie leaves to get the paint and materials. Yenelli appears out of nowhere. There are more hugs and greetings. She wants to know when Cristina will be able to walk the neighborhood with her soliciting food donations. "I'd love some coffee," Yenelli responds readily to Cristina's offer. On her way to the kitchen, Cristina realizes that she will probably not be able to make it to class today. The summer term has just begun so there is still time for her to catch up. When she returns, she finds Yenelli, María, and Cookie at the back of the store talking with Maximo and the friends from Minnesota. Maximo turns to Cristina with a large smile and informs her that the *compañeros* will be staying for the program tonight.

María hands out markers and poster board to everyone, including the men from Minnesota. Cookie is unfolding material across the floor, pushing chairs and tables to the side, preparing to make the banner. On her way to the kitchen, Yenelli shouts to Cristina, "I hope you don't have anything planned for tomorrow. There's an emergency meeting at APO. We need you to be there."

Home, Family, and School

I am a third-generation Chicana.[4] My parents were born in the United States. My mother's parents were *betabeleros* (beet farmworkers). Like so many other Mexicans at that time, farm contractors lured them to the United States to harvest sugar beets in the Midwest. My mother was born on one such farm in Iowa. One fall in the early 1920s after the harvest, they migrated to Chicago, where my grandfather's brother was living and working. The family settled on the north side of the city in the area today known as Lincoln Park. My mother stayed in that neighborhood for almost seventy years. It was a working-class, European-immigrant community when my grandparents first arrived there. My mother started public school knowing little English.

Like other immigrant schoolchildren, the school system traumatized her, and she quickly learned English as part of her Americanization. Although the family was Catholic, a parochial-school education for my mother and my aunts and uncles was out of the financial reach of my grandfather's salary as a restaurant kitchen worker. Yet they all managed to do well and graduate from high school. My two uncles went on to college after the war with help from the GI Bill. They were probably some of the first Mexican Americans in Chicago to earn advanced degrees. My mother even went to college for a while. However, she only lasted a semester at Wright Junior College because she claimed college was too stressful. She found work as an office clerk.

I think those were some of her happiest times. She was earning her own money, going to dances and movies with my aunts and friends. She married at twenty-three at a time when eighteen or younger was the norm. She always cautioned my sisters and me not to marry too young, to enjoy ourselves. After my mother married, she quickly had children and never worked outside the home again.

My father was born in Colorado. His father was working in the coal mines there. My grandfather was a labor organizer, helping the miners to unionize. After a cross was burned at his front door one night, my grandfather and his family escaped to the coal mines of Pennsylvania. I only recently learned about my grandfather's labor activism. I thought the only one in my family with a meaningful past was my uncle, my mother's older brother. A budding artist in high school, he attended Saturday art classes at the School of the Art Institute through a program run in partnership with the Chicago Public Schools. Art teachers affiliated with Hull-House were in this program. These teachers had a lasting influence on my uncle, and he spent much of his early youth at Hull-House.

This was in the late 1930s and early 1940s when Hull-House was the center of a great deal of social and political activity in Chicago. My uncle's activism was mainly confined to painting, which led him to create the first Mexican mural in Chicago, painted on the inside wall of a Hull-House building. Unfortunately, gentrification destroyed the mural when Hull-House was torn down to make way for the Chicago branch of the University of Illinois. There is a photo of the mural in a recent publication on Hull-House.[5] It looks Diego Rivera inspired. My uncle went on to earn an architectural degree, and many years later his firm designed Benito Juárez High School in Pilsen. He also was the architect for the National Museum of Mexican Art and El Hogar del Niño in Pilsen and South Chicago.[6] He died in 2004.

EDUCATION WAS ALWAYS IMPORTANT TO MY FATHER

Although my father was born in the United States, he was raised in Mexico. Shortly after my father's family relocated from Colorado to Pennsylvania, my grandfather took the family back to Mexico to claim an inheritance. My father was just a young boy then. The inheritance my grandfather had returned to claim failed to materialize, and the family fell on hard times. My father did not have the opportunity to receive much of a formal education in Mexico. Drafted into the army during World War II, he returned to the United States to work and eventually married my mother. But he has spent his lifetime self-educating himself. He would often read until he fell asleep with one of our schoolbooks or with a volume of the encyclopedia set he bought my older sister when she was only a year old. Like most parents, he wanted his children to have what he could not.

Because my parents believed in the value of a Catholic school education, one they were deprived of, my father often worked two jobs to pay for this privilege for us. When my parents first married, he worked as a furniture patcher. Later, he was able to get better paying jobs by claiming he had earned a university education in Mexico. Still, it seemed it was always a struggle to scrape up enough money for school, clothing, and food for the eight of us. When each of us turned sixteen, we were expected to find jobs to help pay for our educational and personal expenses.

LOSING MY LANGUAGE

My mother's family never had thoughts of returning to live in Mexico. They embraced life in the United States. Though proudly Mexican, my mother had grown up entrenched in American culture, and she was very assimilated by the time she had met my father. That my mother married someone like my father always puzzled my sisters and me. It was a clash of two cultures. My Mexican father ruled a house full of women, six daughters, with a bewildered detachment but a firm hand. My Americanized mother was always at odds with him. However, they both believed in the American Dream for their children. It was easier to achieve this, they believed, if they thought and acted "American," not Mexican.

My mother helped my father relearn English before they were married, and as good Americans, they raised their children as monolingual English speakers. My mother did not want us to suffer the same humiliation of not knowing English as she did when she entered school. My parents still spoke Spanish to each other and to my grandparents who lived downstairs from us. One event particularly early in their married lives convinced them of the importance of the English language. One day, my mother took my older sister, then just a toddler, to the doctor and spoke to her in Spanish. "Do you want her to grow up stupid?!" the doctor said, reprimanding my mother. After that, there was never any question about Americanizing their children and the language they would use to speak to them.

There weren't any Mexicans in the neighborhood I grew up in when I was young. My family was still living in the Lincoln Park area. The immediate vicinity where we lived was still primarily White. Naturally, my friends were White. In the *Leave It to Beaver* era of the 1950s, White was the only color to be.[7] I thought I was White, too, although maybe a darker shade. Some of the kids on the block, however, would remind my sister and me of our "place." Whites did not invite us to birthday parties because Mexicans were not allowed in White homes. I remember us kids being caught in a storm on the way home from school one day. The White kids were brought in from the rain into a neighbor's house, but my sister and I were excluded. My mother hired an older White girl to take me to school, but the girl made me walk behind her and her friends because she didn't want to be seen with me.

The first wave of Puerto Ricans began to settle in the area in the early 1960s when White families moved away because they believed the neighborhood was in decline. Gangs of White boys formed, and so, too, did rival Puerto Rican clubs. *West Side Story* played itself out on the streets of my neighborhood.[8] These were rough times. To White people, all "Spanish" people were the same, so I had to prove to my White friends that I was not like the Sharks, not a spic.[9] I tried to dilute the Mexican in me and began to tell people I was part Native American. This to me somehow seemed more American and acceptable. The gang wars soon petered out when urban renewal rolled in with a vengeance, destroying much of the neighborhood. Whole city blocks were torn down, mostly where Puerto Ricans lived, and these families were forced to relocate to other parts of the city. My grandparents' two-flat, which they bought after the war and where I grew up, survived the wrecking ball, and I survived the gang wars.

Growing up thinking White, I thought I should marry a White guy, too.[10] I could see the conflicts between my United States–raised mother and my Mexican father, and I didn't want to go through that. Until I entered high school, I figured I would take the path my mother took, work a while, then marry. My mother always prided herself on the fact that she didn't marry right out of high school. She had her independent life for a few years before she had all those babies. Because she found college so stressful, she didn't think we should go unless we wanted. There was never a college fund set aside for us. My parents were barely able to afford our grammar and high school tuitions. If we were to go to college, it would be on scholarships and income earned from part-time jobs. This is how my older sister did it. I didn't consider attending college when I started high school. I was content to enroll in secretarial classes and search for a White guy to marry. Midway through high school, my outlook on things changed dramatically.

THERE HAS GOT TO BE SOMETHING MORE

My high school was unique. A single building, it was divided down the middle to form two separate schools and maybe even two separate worlds. There was the boy's school on one end and the girl's school on the other. Each had its own faculty and administration. Walls and classrooms intentionally segregated us. We even had different starting and closing times so that we wouldn't mingle. The boys' side of the school offered college-prep courses while the girls' side had typing and shorthand classes. A few girls who knew they were going on to college, like my sister, were able to take some advanced math and science classes with the boys on their side of the school, but the majority of the girls remained behind the designated barrier. While other schools had college-admission recruiters on their campuses, Saint Michael's School for Girls invited human-resource staff from Loop offices to tell us how to dress for a job interview. As Saint Michael's parish began to lose families due to urban blight and flight, its economic base shrunk, too. After I graduated, the Chicago Archdiocese was forced to combine the two high schools. By the time my youngest sister was in high school, enrollment had fallen considerably, and the school finally closed. It remained vacant for many years and was finally sold and turned into condominiums when the neighborhood turned trendy.

When I was in high school in the late 1960s, the world was undergoing profound changes. Perhaps, it was inevitable that they'd affect me. I found new friends that didn't think like the kids I had grown up with. A few progressive teachers who made their students think about what was happening in the world around them influenced me. My childhood neighborhood was changing, too. Hippies were moving in and bringing with them a psychedelic counterculture too cool for me to resist. Wells Street with its head shops and coffeehouses was right around the corner.[11] The civil rights movement, drugs, antiwar protests, all of it was in the news and on the streets of my neighborhood.

In late August of 1968 at the start of my senior year, the Yippies were camped out just blocks away in Lincoln Park.[12] The Democratic Convention was in town, and the "whole world was watching" while I was sitting in religion class.[13] I felt so alienated. I wanted to be out in the streets, too, but I felt trapped by the secretarial career path I had somehow chosen for myself. I was fed up with my schooling and the hypocrisy that passed for education. I had to find anther way out.

In high school I made new friends. They were waiting to hear from college-admission offices while my old friends were planning their weddings. I decided to take the ACT examination.[14] Not surprising, I did poorly. I had not taken any college-preparatory courses, and I was ill prepared for the mathematics and science sections of the test. I applied to UICC anyway. Denied admission because of my low ACT scores, I enrolled in the less academically discriminating Wright Junior College.[15] Like my mother, I lasted there only one semester but for entirely different reasons. I thought college life would be like all those news stories. I expected hip professors, campus protests, and student movements. Instead, this school was stuck in a time warp. The students were passive, and the instructors not very dynamic. I transferred to Loop College the next semester, and though it would never make a glossy news spread of *Radical Student Life,* it did introduce me to a diverse student body.[16] By this time, the Chicago City College system had instituted open admissions. Anyone with a high school diploma or an equivalency examination could go there, regardless of one's ACT score. Tuition was free, too. I think because of Loop Junior College's downtown location, it attracted people from all over the city. There were students right out of high school, older students taking classes after work, as well as Black students, White students, foreign students, and Latinos.

Getting Involved

ORGANIZATION OF LATIN AMERICAN STUDENTS

Around this time, with the Black Power movement in full force, women and other minorities had started to organize themselves, too. Magda was one of my few Mexican friends from high school. She had gone to the Denver Chicano Youth Liberation Conference. It wasn't until we had already graduated that I found out about this conference and began to learn what all this Chicano stuff was about. It sounded good to me. I wanted to be a Chicana, too. Magda was going to UICC but knew some of the Latinos at Loop College. Some of them had attended the Denver conference and had formed OLAS on campus. OLAS was not only organizing at Loop but in the *barrio* as well.

Magda took me to a meeting in Pilsen and introduced me to the OLAS people. I was terrified. Everyone was speaking Spanish. I felt like an outsider. The meetings were male dominated with one particular macho in command. I wanted to be part of the movement, but the task for women seemed to consist of taco making along with other "womanly responsibilities." Magda wanted to do more than make tacos. She criticized OLAS's decision-making structure and frequently got into arguments with male members.

OLAS had narrow ideas about some things, but it was a viable organization and did a lot of good as far as promoting Mexican culture and getting the students and community involved in issues affecting Mexicans and Chicanos. OLAS members also tutored students at Harrison High School and encouraged them to go to college. I joined the Loop OLAS chapter, where it was the strongest. OLAS put on cultural programs and sponsored guest speakers on campus. It was also instrumental in initiating Latino studies. Colleges funded student activities more generously in those days, and OLAS members were able to attend many out-of-town Chicano conferences. I was able to participate in the first National Chicana Conference in Houston while an OLAS Loop student.

WORKING CLASS BUT NORTH SIDE

With the arrival of Chicanismo, I thought, "Well, I am Mexican so maybe I should start acting like one. I should start learning about who I am." That was the whole purpose in the early years of the Chicano Movement, cultural awareness and deflating the arrogance of White superiority in the United States. However, for some people, this whole Chicanismo thing turned into a way of proving how Mexican one was. There's an *acto* (act or skit) where Juan Raza ("John man of the people") claims to be so Chicano that he wears *huaraches* (sandals) even in the winter.[17] Theater groups meant it to be funny, but some people actually took it seriously and lived it. I didn't feel too Chicano around the OLAS people. Even though I was spending more time with them at school, I still felt like an outsider in front of them.

OLAS was a very nationalist student group. Many of its members were born and raised in Mexico. I had grown up differently from them. I don't think OLAS people were that comfortable around me either because I wasn't living in the barrio and couldn't speak Spanish. I was shamelessly living on my own then, not under my parents' roof. It was hard for them to relate to me. Magda persuaded me once to host an OLAS party at my apartment, and these cultural differences were brutally evident. That night I dressed up for the party in denim bell-bottoms. The stereo was loaded with 1960s rock albums. The OLAS people came to the apartment, decked out in their idea of party wear, the guys in slacks, no jeans, and the girls in dresses and heels. When they found out there wasn't any polka or ranchera music to dance to, they began to leave very early.[18]

I don't think OLAS accepted me until Maximo and I got together. Maximo's acceptance of me made it easier for them to overlook my shortcomings. Maximo wasn't a student. He had recently arrived from Texas but was more Mexican than Chicano in many ways. He wasn't like the other OLAS Mexicans, but he earned their trust through his maturity and intellect. He was drawn to OLAS by the work they were doing in Pilsen, where he lived. As part of OLAS's cultural-awareness campaign, they had produced a play about the Mexican Revolution and were performing it in *barrio teatros* (community movie theaters) throughout Chicago. Maximo had a leading role in that play, the one that another major OLAS leader wanted. It fed the growing rivalry between the two that eventually led them to part ways. Magda, the drama queen, was, of course, in this theater production, also. She introduced me to Maximo. Magda and I were roommates at the time, and she had invited Maximo to the apartment for a small gathering. Maximo and I found we had similar perspectives. We hit it off that night and ended up together for the next twenty years.

I liked the fact that Maximo wasn't like the other OLAS guys. He didn't have to prove his *Mexicanidad* (Mexicaness) and was aware and interested in things outside the realm of Chicanismo. Our common aspirations clouded our underlying differences. He was attracted to the active, independent Chicana image he projected onto me and made me feel like a slacker. He was always pushing me to read more, study harder, and have a stronger will. He didn't drink or smoke and discouraged my participation in such "backward" behavior.[19] It was hard to argue the merits of getting wasted (getting intoxicated on alcohol or other drugs) when there was serious work to be done for el Movimiento. So I figured, well ok, it's time to grow up. My pseudo-hippy days were over. The movement began to take a front seat to everything else in my life.

I became a Chicana after I started getting involved in OLAS with Magda and even more so after I met Maximo. It was easy to identify myself as Chicana because I was not from Mexico. I wasn't Mexican. I wasn't American. I was Chicana, someone born in the United States of Mexican ancestry. It was also a political statement to call oneself Chicano instead of Mexican-American. Only the backward, unenlightened sellouts were hyphenated.[20]

Moving to Pilsen was a life-changing experience. A true North Sider, I hadn't ventured farther south of downtown before I took the bus with Magda to OLAS meetings on South Halsted Street. The first time I went on my own to Maximo's apartment, I took the elevated train. Stepping off the Hoyne Street Station, I was shocked and terrified. The disappearing sunlight couldn't mask the decrepit apartment buildings that sagged in front of crumbling or vaulted sidewalks. I had never seen sidewalks that stood higher than the entrance of houses. You had to maneuver your way carefully around the gaping holes in the sidewalks or you might end up below street level. A pair of local *cholos* in black leather jackets followed me from the El stop.[21] I made it OK to Maximo's that night, but this first impression of the barrio stayed with me a long time. I always thought the neighborhood of my childhood was rundown, but Pilsen was so much worse. The community was crowded, deteriorated, and dirty. There was no greenery. Two small patches of grass that passed for city parks were hardly an oasis to escape the grittiness of the neighborhood. Every city service was inadequate. At that time, Pilsen was divided into two city wards run by White Democratic machine bosses who were uninterested in their Mexican constituency. This barrio living was a big cultural shock for me, but it was all the more reason to get down to business.

OLAS wasn't the only organization in Pilsen working to change things. There were other segments of the community that were beginning to organize around social issues like housing, education, and jobs. The success of the La Raza Unida Party (LRUP) in Texas, which had scored some electoral victories in that state, appealed to many Chicanos fed up with the indifference of the two major political parties. In 1972, an LRUP convention in El Paso, Texas, called for Chicanos to organize nationally. I was a Chicago delegate along with Maximo, Magda, and a few others involved in community organizing. The convention drew Latinos, mostly Chicanos, from nearly all fifty states. Delegates drafted national agendas without too much debate as a common bond to change the existing White status quo seemed all that was required to unite us. We were to go back to our home states and barrios and form LRUP chapters with our candidates on the ballots.

In Chicago, we slated a fellow conference delegate, Angel Moreno, to run as representative of the Illinois Congressional district that included Pilsen. He lost the election, of course, but those of us involved in his campaign got a good introduction to electoral politics. The differing ideologies of LRUP's members also surfaced during the campaign. The Chicano power slogans that had united us in El Paso couldn't sustain us after the election, and we drifted off in different political directions.

Around the same time of the campaign, Maximo got laid off from his job and had time to spare. An avid reader, he could never find anything to his liking in the barrio. His dream was to open a bookstore in Pilsen that stocked serious literature, not the *fotonovelas* (comic book–like magazines often with a romantic theme) and *discos* (records) that were the common staples of the *tiendas* (shops) that passed as bookstores. I thought it was a good idea, too. We found a storefront on Blue Island Avenue that had some living space for us in the back rooms. With money borrowed from family, the dream became a reality. We opened Librería Nuestro Continente (Our Continent Bookstore) in 1972, specializing in Chicano/Latin American literature. The books were in Spanish and English. The bookstore was not only unique in Pilsen and in Chicago but for much of the United States at that time. Customers would come from outside the Pilsen area and other parts of the Midwest because they understood the importance of the store. Sadly, over thirty-five years later, there still isn't a comparable bookstore in Chicago.

The store also had room to hold events and meetings, something we specifically had wanted when we were looking at storefronts. We showed political films and encouraged discussion afterward. We also offered free English classes there, too. The support committee for the striking Farah workers was based there. The bookstore became something of a community center. The Comité operated out of the Librería. Later, when ideologies and dogmas began to divide the community, the bookstore was still able to attract different strata from the neighborhood. By the time political lines of demarcation were seriously drawn, we had closed shop.

UNITED FOR CHANGES

A core of us were becoming less Chicano focused and broadening our points of view. What initially brought us to develop a common ideology was our involvement in the Farah strike. Almost unheard of outside Texas and New Mexico, where the Farah pants plants were located, our committee brought the issue of this mainly Chicana workers' movement to Pilsen and Chicago. We organized fundraisers for the strikers and led picket lines on downtown streets in front of the stores that sold Farah pants. Most of all, we tried to make broader connections to the international movement of workers' and women's rights.

Although the Farah Strike Support Committee was our common activity, we were involved in other projects. By this time, I was at Circle Campus. Isaura was also a student there. We were active in various student groups that were mobilizing. The Latino students' presence on campus was finally making an impact, and we played a part in forming a progressive Latino student union that was involved in various actions that sought greater Latino representation on campus. We also initiated an accredited class on women that associated the origins of patriarchy to economic structures along the lines of Friedrich Engels's analysis.

In the community, Isaura and I became founding members of Mujeres Latinas en Acción (Latina Women in Action), a focus group that had grown out of a women's conference we had earlier helped to organize.[22] We were both also working at the time at El Centro de la Causa, where other Mujeres members worked. We participated in many of the first organizational meetings of Mujeres that were held at the bookstore. There was a decent-size *Mujeres Latinas* (Latina women) contingent at the first International Women's Day Demonstration in Chicago around 1974. Eventually, our commitments to the Farah strike and school activities overshadowed our involvement in Mujeres, and Isaura and I left the women's group.

There was a flurry of activity in Pilsen in the early 1970s. We seemed to be at the center of it as a bookstore collective, as a community of activists, and as neighbors. I was finally feeling comfortable living in the neighborhood because I knew the people around me. Though I still felt like a displaced North Sider at times, I was mostly feeling like a member of a community. It was a good feeling. Before the activists divided along political party lines and became suspicious of each other, there was a shared community spirit among us. Everyone seemed to have the same goal, to organize for change.

End of a Collective Vision

CLOSING THE DOORS

The bookstore was only open a few years. It seemed a lot longer considering all the work we put into it and the many activities that were held there. The store itself was never profitable. We knew going into the business that we wouldn't be making any money. Maximo was called back to work at about the same time his unemployment-compensation checks were depleted. These checks had been our major source of income. I was still in school and working part-time. We couldn't keep the bookstore open by ourselves, and although there was discussion of a collective effort to keep it open, for all practical purposes, we knew it wouldn't work.

I was secretly relieved to have the bookstore close. I was beginning to resent my lack of privacy and looked forward to living in a normal environment, some place where I could lock the front door whenever I wanted. Many good things came out of the bookstore's short existence. I'm proud to have been a part of it. However, the twenty-four-hour commitment was too much. After we closed, Maximo and I were still involved in things but at different levels and in different projects. After he returned to work, he became more active in his union and labor-related issues and less so in neighborhood ones. I was trying to concentrate on finishing my undergraduate degree. Our core group was fragmenting, but we made attempts to unify around the then-developing crisis in Central America. We participated in mass demonstrations against United States' involvement there and tried to organize a Pilsen-based solidarity organization. It was becoming increasingly difficult to work with other community-based groups who were now under the influence of national organizations and their stiffening political perspectives. Where there was once a strong community spirit with people working toward a common goal, there was now a growing mistrust of everyone. Real or imaginary, the infiltrators' trashing (bad-mouthing, criticizing, and rumormongering) campaign nearly led us to lose sight of the real enemy. I became pregnant around this time, and it was a good excuse to distance myself in a quiet way from it all.

Maximo always felt that I didn't take a strong enough leadership role in the Movement. In our relationship, he was clearly the dominant figure, and it was hard to win any argument against his determined point of view. He always made my counterarguments seem petty. The ultimate attack in those days was to call someone petite bourgeois, and in his eyes, I was. To him, if you were not committed twenty-four/seven, you weren't a real revolutionary. I used to feel like I let him down because I was not playing Tania to his Che.[23] He prided himself in understanding the basis of women's oppression, but he didn't really get it. He didn't understand me. I was tired of trying to have to prove anything to Maximo. He eventually pushed me out of the relationship. Did I finally get the upper hand in leaving him as some of my *compañeras* suggest? I don't know. But when we finally split up after twenty years, I felt a lot freer. The woman question affects everything. Until sexism is eradicated, women will always feel like they have to work harder to prove their worth.

TODAY'S DISCONNECTED YOUTH

The many early battles fought in Pilsen for community control are largely unknown to today's young people. This unrecorded history has left them disconnected to their past. I've tried to relay this period of the Movement to my own children, to give them a perspective on current events and what they can learn from the past. I'm a little disappointed, though, in their lack of intensity to any kind of real commitment to a cause. I hope my own burnout didn't affect them negatively. I think it's just the times. The fervor of those early civil rights and revolutionary movements is missing today, especially among the youth, although the same issues that ignited the movement still exist.

Working in the movement was a good experience. I don't regret anything I did. This was probably the most constructive period in my life. Many good things came out of the work we all did. I matured growing up living through those experiences. It laid a foundation for how I see the world today. I'm sorry to say I'm not active in anything right now. It's not that I'm complacent, just lacking the drive. It's hard when you get older. You come home from work and don't have the energy to do anything. This shouldn't be an excuse, I know. I admire and have respect for the older people in the movement we worked with who were saddled with full-time jobs and children and still found time to become actively involved in things. I especially salute the women and mothers of Pilsen who trumped the passive-Latina stereotype and played strong leadership roles.

I no longer live in Pilsen, but I had a job there until 2004. I hope my many years at that job in the community made a difference. My job was a daily struggle, trying to provide quality library services amid shrinking book budgets and the administration's self-interests. One of my job duties included giving library orientations and tours to ESL (English as a Second Language) classes and school groups. I always tried to incorporate the history of Pilsen and its many struggles in my talks. I would tell them that the shiny new building they were touring was a result of years of struggle with the city, as was the high school down the street. It seems the Pilsen community has always been involved in one struggle or another, even from its earliest times as an immigrant Bohemian neighborhood. Historic labor battles such as the McCormick Reaper strike in the 1860s were staged in Pilsen.

Pilsen has physically changed for the better since I took my first elevated ride to the neighborhood. However, the underlying problems are still there. There's a new library but old books, a world-class museum eats up precious public park space, new schools but a staggering dropout rate. Pilsen is currently facing a paradoxical development, the betterment of the community in some ways but along with that comes the threat of gentrification and the displacement of Mexicano/Chicano residents. The city's land grab in conjunction with UIC is creeping farther and farther south. It's already destroyed much of the Black community that separated Pilsen from UIC. Developers, working hand in hand with the city, have been busy renovating abandoned warehouses into trendy condominiums and tearing down Maxwell Street and transforming it into a university village that its former residents can only dream of inhabiting. Pilsen stands on the brink of losing its former identity. As the Mexican population explodes throughout the Chicago area and the suburbs, Pilsen is no longer the main port of entry for immigrants. Newcomers are now more likely to first settle in Arlington Heights or Cicero than on 18th Street. Current Pilsen residents are moving out as higher rents and property taxes make living there unaffordable. It's important to document Pilsen's history and its legacy before the new neighbors gentrify and bury it.

Notes

1. This introductory vignette was developed in collaboration with Cristina Vital. The substance of this chapter comes from several interviews that occurred mainly in 1998 but continued through 2008.

2. A *sarape* is a rectangular textile product from Mexico or Central America often used as a covering or as a blanket.

3. The Uruguayan Tupamaros were a urban guerilla group that obtained widespread support in Uruguay as well as from social justice advocates from across the continent, especially youth. The Indian rebel Tupac Amaru led an uprising against the Spanish in the eighteenth century and became a symbol of Peruvian resistance and independence.

4. As used here, the first generation is the immigrant generation. The one and a half generation then signifies those of the immigrant generation who crossed the border early in their lives and whose socialization has mainly been in the United States.

5. The first Chicago mural painted in the Mexican tradition was done by Adrian Lozano and located in the Benito Juárez Club Room on the second floor of the Boys Club building. Only a part of this mural was captured in the background of a photo displayed at the "Pots of Promise" exhibit and published in Ganz and Strobel (2004).

6. El Hogar del Nino (the child's house) childcare center is located in Pilsen.

7. *Leave It to Beaver* was a popular TV sitcom that was one among many of that era to project an idealized vision of White middle-class normalcy and a monolithic prosperous "America."

8. *West Side Story* was a popular Broadway play that was later adapted into a film in 1961. It utilized a Romeo and Juliet plot structure to highlight racial tensions between Whites and Puerto Ricans in New York City.

9. In *West Side Story,* the Puerto Rican Sharks were the rival of the Jets, the White gang.

10. For an investigation of an urban legend that focuses on the attraction-revulsion of Mexicano/Chicanos to Anglo culture, see Limon (1994).

11. Wells Street is the main avenue of the Old Town district, the center of the Chicago hippie phenomenon in the 1960s. A head shop is a store that typically sold drug and other counterculture paraphernalia. Head shops were popular among youth as well as tourists of all ages.

12. The Yippies were members of the Youth International Party, led by Abbie Hoffman and Jerry Rubin. The Yippies were a countercultural political group known for

their use of street or "guerilla" theater and dramatic carnivalesque or outlandish public acts of defiance. Yippies distinguished themselves from hippies by not dropping out but by dropping in and by their involvement in political theater and their active campaign to lampoon the political establishment and erode its legitimacy as a step toward creating social change.

13. Antiwar demonstrators at the 1968 Chicago Democratic Convention repeatedly chanted, "The whole world is watching!" as police charged the crowds and beat journalists and protesters indiscriminately.

14. The ACT is a test of the American College Testing program, one of two major college-entrance examinations used in the United States.

15. Cristina eventually transferred and graduated from UICC and later completed a master's degree at the University of Michigan, Ann Arbor.

16. Cristina is alluding to a general disappointment she felt at the relative lack of student activism at community colleges when she attended. Of course, there was no such glossy magazine that focused on student activism, but many publications at that time featured stories on student protests and movement activities on college campuses.

17. *Huaraches* are sandals originally crafted and used by the indigenous poor in Mexico.

18. Traditional *Ranchera music* originates from the state of Jalisco.

19. Among some militants at that time, *backward* was a critical term used to refer to those not politically serious or those given to indulging "weaknesses," such as smoking, drugs, or alcohol.

20. To be Mexican-American or hyphenated at that time was considered a mark of colonial, obsequious, or "backward" thinking.

21. *Cholo* originally meant a mix breed of dog. The Spaniards later used it to describe racially mixed people. It is often used derogatorily. In Mexico and the United States, the term has also been used to depict someone from the lower classes or someone with an unsavory character. However, Chicanos sometimes used the term more neutrally, or at times humorously, or even more positively to depict community streetwise youth who although marginalized were generally insightful about life.

22. Mujeres Latinas en Acción eventually went on to establish various community services including a shelter for battered women.

23. Tania, or Haydée Tamara Bunke Bider, is the Argentine-born communist of German parents. She became a guerilla fighter with Che Guevara in Bolivia.

Defending My People and My Culture

VICTORIA PÉREZ

We Got to Change Things, 1976

I learned about Magdalena's case on an ice-cold Saturday afternoon.[1] Forty people were walking a picket line in front of the Daley Center. One sign read, "Magdalena, fired after seventeen years of service." I had heard something about this in the community. However, meeting Magdalena face-to-face that day was how I really learned about her story. Magdalena and I walked the line together while she told me about how she had been helping Latinos at Rush Presbyterian Saint Luke's Hospital, talking to them about medical issues, giving them information. I knew what kinds of things went on at the hospital because I worked at Rush Presbyterian Saint Luke's satellite office in Oak Brook, Illinois.

Magdalena was a lab technician, and like other Latinos, she was constantly pulled away from her job to translate. That's how she began to see patient abuses. Many people didn't know what was being done to them. They were just expected to sign the consent forms. The hospital administrators began to suspect that Magdalena was advising patients about their rights and didn't like it. She was eventually fired because the hospital believed she could no longer be trusted.

Months passed, and the hospital still refused to cooperate with the committee that had been organized to defend Magdalena. The hospital's community representative kept refusing to meet with the committee. The hospital was invited to send representatives to community meetings, but it refused. Hospital administrators only wanted to meet with one community person. The hospital disliked the idea that a group of Mexicano/Chicanos was questioning their policies and taking action. The hospital wouldn't budge. Something else needed to be done. Members of the Comité, Casa Aztlán, and APO decided to confront the hospital administration if they continued to ignore the issues.

On the day of yet another protest, I came out of Saint Luke's employment office and saw a rally taking place in front of the Professional Building. I had taken the day off. I had just finished requesting a transfer to a different job so I could work closer to home. I took my son's hand and crossed the street. I told him that I was going to join the picket line. At first, he stood on the side but later walked the circle with the others and me. He was only nine years old, but he was familiar with picket lines. He had joined his aunts and me on many picket lines in support of the United Farm Workers. I explained that Magdalena had been fired for helping her people.

When it was clear no one was going to come downstairs and speak to the demonstrators, a contingent of protesters decided to go upstairs. I thought about it for a while and felt compelled to go. I joined the group. I left my son downstairs with a person I knew from the community who said, "Don't worry. I'll take good care of him. I'll look after him. He'll be here with us." I trusted that and trusted my friends, the people I knew in the group. So I went upstairs with the others. Perhaps thirty people entered the building that day, including someone I knew from South Chicago and my good friend María Saucedo.

It was August 1976 when the sit-in took place. For almost six months, the teatro had been practicing a skit about the racism and injustices at Saint Luke. We performed it that day in the lobby of the hospital on the administrative floor for all who passed by to see. It helped to keep our spirits high. Some had been at the demonstration since the early morning. We were told that if we did not leave by five o'clock, we would be arrested. Shortly thereafter, the Chicago Police Department came and began making arrests. We resisted. That day, twenty-three people were taken away, nineteen men and four women. Two people from the picket line had the misfortune of being arrested by accident. They were not even upstairs. The police just took them because they were in their path. One was a young teenager.

As we were put in the paddy wagon, I saw my son standing on the sidewalk with my friend. I felt very strange, not like I imagined I would at all. I was surprised at what I was feeling. As I watched my son's face, I couldn't help but think that my arrest would mean something to him one day, that it would be important to him in the future. They transported us to Monroe and Racine. They kept the four of us women apart from the men.

We were handcuffed, María, the other two women, and myself. We were later transferred downtown to be processed. María was strip-searched, but they didn't do that to the rest of the women. They took photographs and fingerprinted all of us. Then they put us in separate cells. We couldn't see each other. However, we were on the same floor. We actually had bread and water for our first meal, just like in the movies. The men got out quickly, as expected. But we women stayed in jail until midnight. We were taken to a downtown lockup on 11th and State because there was only a men's lockup on Racine and Monroe.

People later said we had fun when we were in jail. Well, we had to keep everybody's spirits up so we started singing songs, protest songs. We were sensitive to the young girl's situation. She had not been with us upstairs in the administrative offices. She was caught completely unaware. She was picketing and supporting the issue just like the rest of the community people out there. However, it turned out she was not only young but wise. She said, "No, it's OK. You were doing the right thing. This is not fair." We gave her the whole history and background about Magdalena. She was very supportive. She felt bad that she had to be arrested, but it wasn't devastating for her. It didn't freak her out.

All the other women were all very socially conscious. We all knew what we were doing. As time went on, regular women prisoners were brought into the lockup. I think they were mostly prostitutes. They heard us singing in Spanish. They started saying, "Right on, sisters." They were supportive. They heard us and said, "Oh wow, that's a good song. What is that about?" or "That sounds good." So we told them that we were singing songs of protest and songs from the struggles of our lives and about people getting together, believing in a cause, and believing in helping their fellow man and woman and about the need to change things, to change society so it would be better for all people. "OK, right on, right on!" and they asked us to "sing that song again," and shouted, "Oh, I like that one!" María and a woman from South Chicago and I were into street theater, and we knew a lot of songs in Spanish.

When we got out, the women we left behind said, "Good luck and right on, keep on."

I said, "You, too. Keep up the struggle. We got to change things."

"Yeah, you're right. We got to change things."

And that kept up our spirits. Well, actually singing kept up our spirits and talking to the young woman that was arrested with us, telling her the history and explaining why what we were doing wasn't frivolous, that it wasn't for naught. A friend said he saw me on the news that night. Presbyterian Saint Luke's Hospital fired me.

Home, Family, and School

LOOKING FOR A HOME

I was named Victoria after my mother. I was born in 1939 in Chicago and am the fourth of seven children, the fourth girl. There were six women and one man. I grew up on Seminary Street, between Lill and Wrightwood Streets. That's where I spent the first twenty-five years of my life. I attended

Agaziz Grade School until I was ten when we were evicted. We moved just two blocks away.

One day, we put on our Sunday best, and my father told us we were going to court. My father was given time to find another place. I heard from family members that the judge gave my father the maximum amount of time to relocate because our landlady was pushing us out of the building. There were seven children living in a one-bedroom basement apartment. She said that she wanted it for her son and daughter-in-law, who had no children. That's what I heard growing up.

I thought it was fun because I got to sleep at a friend's house. That was probably the most exciting thing about the eviction for me. I didn't understand the hardship. All of our furniture was put out in front of the house. My father put ads in the paper, and finally he came home one day and told my mother he had found a place for us. It was a house. It had formally been a warehouse for Weiler's Soup Factory. He walked into the company one day and talked to Mr. Weiler directly. He said, "Well, Mr. Pérez, as far as I'm concerned, we're renting the building for a warehouse, but you talk to the realtor who is handling it for the owner, and we'll clear out and replace the two windows that were broken and fix the sidewalk, and it's yours." Within two weeks, we moved into this house, a single-family home.

There were these huge glass jars that were left behind. My mother used them for flowers and condiments. When we went into the dining room, we could see outside because there was a separation in the wall between the floor and the foundation of the house. But it was great. When we moved in, my sisters were fourteen and fifteen, and I was ten. They had to do all the work. They helped my father paint, clean, scrape, whatever had to be done. They painted the whole house, six rooms, and there was a shanty attached to it and a garage in the back. It was our home for the next fifteen years.

The new neighborhood was a complete change for me. Living in the new neighborhood was traumatic. I learned later that it comprised blue-collar workers like people who worked for the gas company. I'd meet them on the El on their way to work. They'd have their work clothes on and wore heavy shoes, and they carried their black lunch buckets with them. Many of my neighbors were Irish. There were a few German families, but the area was predominantly Irish and Italian. I was ten and in the fourth grade. I went to Knickerbocker Grade School, which was located at Clifton and Belden, which is now where DePaul University is located.

I graduated grade school three years later in 1952. I wanted to graduate in summer so I went to summer school. I was thirteen and a half when I entered

Waller High School on Orchard and Armitage. There it was a potpourri of nationalities and races. There were Asians, Blacks, and a wide variety of ethnic groups. It reminded me in many ways of my first-grade school, where there was also quite a broad representation. I liked it very much. Upon my father's urging, I joined the band and orchestra and played the clarinet. I participated in parades and had to wear funky army uniforms from the Second World War that were made of itchy wool and that were terribly out of shape, especially for larger women. I did that for the next four years and graduated in June of 1956. I had ambitions of going to college. So I worked part-time and attended Crane Junior College, which was on Jackson Boulevard. Crane was a high school, but there was a section of it that was being used as a junior college.

I thought I wanted to be a schoolteacher. That's what I was pursuing. I was only in school for a year. I wasn't a good student. It was difficult. I didn't have my mind only set on college. I was interested in doing a lot of other things. I belonged to a dance group at the time. I enjoyed being a member of the Fiesta Guild. I was thirteen when my father encouraged me to join the guild, and I stayed until I was about twenty-one.

LOVING MEXICAN CULTURE

José and Angelina Rico started the Chicago Fiesta Guild. They were devoted. It was a family-run organization. Their kids learned the dances. Ellen Rico, the only girl, had three sons and a daughter. She went to Mexico to study so that she could learn the dance steps and become familiar with the costumes. The Rico kids would make them. My mother made some costumes. It was like an extended family. It was a wonderful experience. We'd meet weekly to practice.

I can remember as early as the 1940s dancing at the Museum of Science and Industry. There was an annual fiesta at the science-and-industry museum, depicting how Christmas was celebrated in Mexico, its music, dance, musicians, singers, and decorations, especially the *piñatas*. The father, Mr. Jose Rico, would make the piñatas. They were just elaborate. They were just beautiful, just wonderful.

I was also vice president of the citywide Spanish Club of Chicago while I was in high school, and that took me out of my neighborhood, so to speak. In many ways, I was already going out of my neighborhood, going to the Fiesta Guild at the age of thirteen, prior to that going with my parents to the Centro Social Mexicano, which was located on Roosevelt Road and Western in Chicago. It was formally a Turner Center owned and operated by Germans in that community and later sold.

The Lincoln Turner Centers originally were where activities of the German Association of Soccer Teams took place. They had a gym that was very elaborate. They had ringers. They had ladders. It was on Roosevelt, just west of Western. It is still standing, and for a while, it was a Black-owned church. But back then, it was elaborate in the sense that the building was extensive. They had different levels, and it provided many meeting rooms. They had a bar and a dancing room in the basement. Then on the first floor, you had this huge auditorium with seating for maybe three to five hundred, perhaps more. There was a stage that was set up for production. It was created for the complete participation from that particular community. I'm not clear as to whether the Mexican community owned it or leased it. There is some dispute. I discussed this with some family members, and they weren't certain if it was purchased by Mexicans or if it was just rented. As a child I remember going there and meeting these girls. They belonged to a dance group that was directed by Diego de la Rosa. I'm not sure if he was Mexican or Spanish, but he taught Spanish dancing. I got to know that group of girls. That's where Diego had his group practice so we met each other there.

We went to Centro Social on Friday nights in the early 1950s. I was a bug-eyed kid, thirteen years old. The Ziggy González band was very popular at that time. He, of course, was playing for the young crowd, maybe sixteen to late teens, early twenties. We'd sneak around by the stairway to see who was going up the stairs. I recognized some of the people, but they were a little older than me—maybe by two or three years—so they could go upstairs. I wasn't allowed, but we'd sometimes sneak all the way up to the top of the stairway and peak in and listen. We'd see the couples dancing. Tables were set up around the dance floor, and they had candles or little lights on each table. It was a dimly lit room, and the music played was mambo and cha-cha.

THE REVOLUTION BROUGHT US HERE

My father would tell me things as a young girl. I was still in grade school, and he'd say, "You know sometimes you'll meet people, and they'll say they're Spanish, but they're Mexican, but they feel it's better for them to say Spanish." He came to Chicago after he was married around 1929 or 1930. His sister was here. According to my father, there were more job opportunities in Chicago than back in Cleveland, Ohio.

My father was one of five children. He came from Mexico with his family, his mother and five children. It was during the time of the Revolution, around 1917. His mother had a dream that she wanted her children to be educated in the United States; then she wanted to return to Mexico. She came with her five children when my father was about sixteen years old. She brought a couple of dear, close family friends. I don't know if they were cousins or what but two or three other young people. The story was that my paternal grandfather's brother helped her monetarily to support her dream.

They ended up in Texas. Several of the children, my father included, attended Holding Institute, which happened to be a Methodist Episcopal–run residential school.[2] It was in Laredo, Texas. Several of them attended there. The story went that they had first gone to San Antonio, where the Catholic school refused the admittance of my grandmother's children. These are stories I've heard secondhand from an aunt. Anyway, they ended up in Laredo, Texas, and spent several years there.

Then, my father and his brother, Ricardo, went to Kansas, and they worked for meat-packing companies. My father joked how my uncle worked in the area where they chopped up everything, the bones, muscles, ligaments, whatever. He smelled worse than my father. Nobody wanted to sit near my uncle on the bus. Meanwhile, my Aunt Beatrice and Aunt Lupita went to Cleveland, Ohio, to explore job opportunities. They were social workers of some kind. I don't know about the schooling they had. There was a missionary school in Cleveland, Ohio, that my Aunt Beatrice had learned about. They were going to explore that and work. My grandmother joined my aunts in Cleveland. My father, his uncle, and my father's younger sisters eventually arrived in Cleveland as well. That was to be their next place of residence. They resided on the east side of Cleveland, the poorer section.

A MARRIAGE ACROSS THE LINE

My parents met in 1922. My mother was eighteen, and my father was twenty-two. My mother was born and raised in Cleveland of Italian parentage. She had three older brothers. She was the first girl to get married. She had gone to a coworker's wedding. It was a "Spanish wedding." My father and uncle happened to be there at this Spanish wedding, and my mother danced with my uncle first. My uncle and my father ended up driving my mother home. My father proceeded to court her, and they got married four years later.

I asked my mother what her family thought. I never got my parents' full version of the story, but at some point, the issue arose that my grandmother, my maternal grandmother, did not attend my mother's wedding. I think I was a teenager when I learned of that. "Why didn't your mother attend the wedding?" I asked. "Well," she said, "because I was the first girl to get married." My father once told me somewhat humorously that my mother's brother Dominic said, "Who's that Jap you're going out with?" My Aunt Lupita also had an Asian look about her. I suppose not being knowledgeable about Mexicans, he might have seen my father as Japanese.

MY FATHER WAS INVOLVED

My father was socially active. My mother was a housewife and supported him but not vocally nor publicly. She supported his involvement in the radio. She supported our going to the Fiesta Guild. She would make our *trenzas* (hair braids). She would get the ribbons. She made the costumes. She ironed the slips and starched them. If it weren't for her, we wouldn't have gone. She didn't have any family here. She left them in Cleveland. She was the only child to leave her home. My mother, father, and uncle stayed in Cleveland for a year or so, then came to Chicago.

I came across my mother's papers when she passed. My father had been involved with a Bishop Sheil in Chicago, a Catholic priest.[3] Sheil was a pastor at Saint Andrew's on Addison. I don't know where he was located when my father worked with him; it was post–World War II. Mexicans were coming home, and Bishop Sheil wrote a paper and was a radio guest, addressing the issue of Mexicans having the largest ethnic representation in the Second World War but not being treated well in the United States.

When I was about five or six, I remember going to this huge car dealership. I later learned it was Emil Denemark on Ogden Avenue. I used to ride a tricycle around there. In the early to mid-1940s, my father was a Spanish radio announcer. My mother was a housewife. She took care of the home and the children.

My father would record and announce out of the radio station. He invited Bishop Sheil to address the issue of the returning Mexican boys who were coming home and had no jobs. They were being discriminated against. They weren't being given opportunities. They weren't being accepted into the mainstream. Yet, they fought and died for their country. My father also asked a rabbi to talk about the same issue. Yet I don't recall if the rabbi actually guested on his show. We have a record where my father talks about *El Día de la Revolución* (the day of the revolution) in November.[4] He made announcements about that. He appeared to be very proud. I don't know how long my father worked there.

When I was a child, my father would tell us stories about Mexico. I loved them. Every Sunday morning, I would jump on their bed and shout, "Tell me more! Tell me more! What was it like growing up in Mexico? What did you do? Where did you go? Who were you with?" He actually was a great storyteller. My mother was more reserved about that. But ultimately, she began recalling things about her childhood. It was natural for my father. He told me he was called *un mosco en leche* (a fly in milk) because as a little boy they'd get dressed up on Sunday and wear white suits. Because he was dark, they would refer to him as un mosco en leche. He was very tickled about it. He appreciated it and enjoyed the memory.

His father died when he was about nine years old, and, I believe, he was the third child of six children. He had an older brother and sister. Francisco died in 1916 before my father and my grandmother came to the United States. There are a couple of competing stories as to whether or not he died in the Revolution. You know, one aunt tells it this way, the other one tells it another. My father used to say that my grandmother didn't want to lose any more boys in the Revolution, and that's why she was driven to come to the United States during this period, so she could educate her children and then return to Mexico. That's where she wanted to live her life out.

The oldest sister, Beatriz, died after Paco. After Paco died, she was the eldest and always took charge. These are stories I've heard from my aunts or my father. My father was very devoted to Beatriz. He looked up to her a great deal. He respected her. She returned to Mexico at some point during the time everyone else was in Cleveland. So we're talking the early twenties. She left to get things organized, get a house, and set it all up for their return. She died in childbirth. My grandmother was always very intuitive. One day she asked my father, "¿Ay, Rafa, que pasó con Beatriz? ¿Por qué no llamaste? ¿Por qué no escribiste? ¿Hay, Rafa, por qué? ¿Por qué?" (Oh, Rafa, what could have happened to Beatriz? Why haven't you called her? Why haven't you written her? Oh, Rafa, why? Why?) It seemed very close to the time that she had these premonitions that they got a letter. Of course, it was in black. That's how death notes are sent from Mexico. Death announcements come in black envelopes with a white face. So, well, her worst fears were realized about her daughter. Beatriz died in 1921 or 1922. From that point onward, the tide changed. My father suffered a great deal from the loss of his sister, possibly from a loss of direction. Beatriz had always been the strong woman, the one to take charge. My grandmother had always looked to Beatriz as the force in the family, and now my father was the oldest.

My father attended some university in Cleveland. It may have been affiliated with Case Western Reserve. I have the papers at home. But I did get his papers from Western Reserve. They had the records. He knew Yenelli's father, who also attended college. I think at one point, he was at Navy Pier, but I don't know for sure or where he went subsequent to that. I have no idea if he went down to UIUC. I know they became friends. His name was listed on papers I found. My father became a director of the West Side Mexican Civic Committee. It was located on Blue Island and Polk in Chicago. This was in the forties. I remember going to the office. They provided English classes for incoming Mexicans, the ones new to the community. They offered sewing classes for the women and art and cultural classes for the children. They had a dance group. They celebrated the Mexican fiestas, the *fiestas patrias* (patriotic holidays). Again, the family, the community was involved. I went to the place when I was young. I think I was nine or ten years old. I always remember seeing a lot of people, a lot of families, always children, that was at the West Side Mexican Civic Committee. My father left school and worked as an auto mechanic for a period of time. I don't know for how long, perhaps when he was first married. My parents married in 1927 in Cleveland, Ohio.

Getting Involved

A CONCERNED FAMILY

My father had a great passion for issues. I can recall as a child the way he would talk about his experiences growing up in Mexico. His family was very important to him, his siblings. My Aunt Lupita was very active. She was repatriated in the 1950s during the McCarthy era. She died in 1984. As a youngster, she came to the United States and made it very clear that she did not want to be in the States forever. She wanted to return to Mexico. "No, I don't want to be here. . . . This is not my home. This is a place where I am for a time, but I want to be in Mexico." The earliest recollection I have of her was that she worked for Sears Roebuck. She worked closely with General Wood.[5] This is probably in the 1930s or 1940s.

Beatrice and Lupita attended Holding Institute in Laredo, Texas. It had a high school and maybe lower grades as well but definitely a high school. I visited there myself when I took a trip to Mexico. It still exists. Beatriz and Lupita were close. They became social workers or semi-professional social workers. While she was at the Holding Institute, Beatriz, the oldest, wanted to celebrate the fiestas patrias. She started forming a group. There weren't many Mexicans, a handful. However, this was an important celebration in Mexico, in her culture. The school told her no, she couldn't do it. But she had already gotten plans underway for a program. Well, she did it underground. She proceeded to do it, anyway. They didn't expel her, but they let her know that it was not acceptable. She was very determined, very stalwart. She said, "This is my culture, and I think it's important that I celebrate it and that everyone else celebrates it."

That was one of the earlier experiences I learned about Beatriz, and, of course, her sister Lupita, was involved with her. I don't know about her actual participation in the program, but I know they were in school together at the same time. They went to Cleveland to work at a missionary school in Ohio. Beatriz was in her late teens then. My Aunt Lupita had a child when she was sixteen. She wasn't married. This was extremely traumatic for my father. It was a Mexican boy. I am not clear as to where the boy was from or whether this happened in Texas or Ohio, but my grandmother embraced the child and brought him home. He was raised as a family member. My aunt married a Brazilian Jew in Cleveland. He brought her to Chicago and bought her a home in Villa Park, which in the 1920s must have been country out there. He was a lithographer. He had an accent. I remember him saying, "Que-di-ash? Que-di-ash?"[6] They had two boys together. Well, for whatever reasons, they separated. She never talked about it with me. I met Uncle Joe only a few times.

After her marriage to her first husband ended, she became involved with a man named Teofilo. They married and had two children, a boy and a girl. Teofilo was Mexican and was writing for a paper called *Información* (information). It was just a local community newspaper, two to six pages long. We used to sell it at Centro Social Mexicano for twenty-five cents a copy. That's where I remember seeing my Aunt Lupita. I was a teenager, in my early teens. She was active in committees and groups, including the mother's club. We had programs for the children and for adults. They had a parents' club as well.

Eventually, she became involved at Jane Addams's Hull-House. She knew Ellen Gates Starr. On the day of the Republic Steel strike, Ms. Starr was the one that suggested Lupita go and check out the strike. My aunt's husband was involved in it in some way, although I don't believe my uncle worked at Hull-House. But his picture was in the paper. He was hit on the head with a billy club. That's what she told me. A film was taken of it. I saw the film as an adult when I was in my fifties. There's my aunt climbing over bodies at the 1937 Republic Steel strike, at the Memorial Day Massacre, as it later came to be known. I didn't know of it as a child. I learned about it later, maybe as late as my teens or early twenties.[7]

My father and his younger sister had a strong devotion to each other. My family had frequent family gatherings. My father's two sisters and the rest of us always got together at holidays. I grew up with my aunts and uncles around me. I knew my cousins very well. It always seemed that each holiday there would be a dinner-table discussion. It always included something about labor issues. My Aunt Lupita was prolabor, prounions. My uncle, my Aunt Carmela's husband, was German born. He was a tradesman, and he was against unions. He was a tool-and-die maker. He used to say to my aunt, "Are these all your sisters and brothers? You're all so different." My father told me as a teenager that he loved his sister very much. I don't know what specifically had transpired. But I understood why he was saying this. She was accused of being a card-carrying communist during a very intolerant period of history. My father use to say he was in alignment with her ideas with regard to those issues related to the plight of Mexican people.

My father made a decision after being a car mechanic that he would work with his mind, not his hands. He eventually became a social worker. When John F. Kennedy assigned resettlement monies to the Cubans, my father became a social worker. He was working at Cook County Hospital doing casework. There was an ad for Spanish-speaking caseworkers. He applied and got the job. That's what he did for the last three or four years of his life.

As a teenager, when these dinner-table discussions were happening, they became heated. I never participated, of course. It was only the adults who after dinner was finished and the table was cleared took part in them. Some food would be left on the table for people to munch on, and they would have their beers and coffee and whatnot. I overheard discussions about labor and unions.

"Well, look at the issues . . . look at the workers. What are the workers getting?" These are words and phrases that I recall my Aunt Lupita saying, holding firm in her stand. Carmela pitched in, but, again, her husband was a craftsman, a tool-and-die maker, and not pro-labor. I don't know where my father stood on unions, but he was concerned about the plight of Mexicans. He certainly felt they needed to pursue higher education. That was a must. He saw that for many people, this wasn't possible. They weren't given the opportunity to get an education. He would say, "Look what's happening in Texas." Of course, he was a young man when he lived in Texas. But he remembered going to a dance where there was a sign that read, "No dogs, Mexicans, or sailors allowed." He remembered the separate bathrooms and drinking fountains for Mexicans there.

I ingested all of this. But I didn't know how to handle this table communication. It would get so heated. I saw it as conflict. Yet, they all embraced each other at the end of the night, and we saw each other again and again. My mother was not involved in the discussion. She just sat there and listened. I don't remember my mother participating. She may have. But she was very quiet and passive.

I found papers where my father was promoting El Día de la Revolución in Mexico. He would also talk about *El Cinco de Mayo* (the fifth of May) to us.[8]

He explained to us about that conflict with the French. In his words, "How the Mexicans beat them up and sent them home." The ones that stayed loved Mexico, and they embraced Mexican culture. I think he was nationalistic in that respect. He didn't become a citizen until 1945 when he had been in the country already more than twenty years. I understand that when the Second World War came, he applied. He was told that since he was a social worker, he was already doing a good job at home, and he didn't have to go. There was some talk that he was handing out rations during the war.

PILSEN

I knew of Pilsen because my father would sometimes take my younger brother, sister, and me on Saturdays to a Mexican Restaurant, La Veracruzana, that was nearby.[9] It was on Roosevelt and Halsted. I also went to Roosevelt Road because my Aunt Lupita lived on that street. We used to go shopping on Halsted and 13th or what was called Maxwell Street. There was also a 12th Street Department Store. I recall going down there as a kid before I was in my teens.

My mother would go shopping in the area because at that time the grocery stores on Taylor and Halsted Streets were primarily Mexican and Italian. My mother would go in one store and speak Italian and enter another and speak Spanish. I just loved going in those places because they smelled so good. It was wonderful. We'd always get samples of whatever was offered. When Milagros Restaurant came about in the early 1950s, the owner opened his first shop on Halsted and 13th Street.[10] He would come around with a huge industrial tray filled with *taquitos* (miniature tacos). He passed them around, and we were in there packed like sardines. That was my introduction to Milagros tortillas. I also went to Roosevelt Road because my Aunt Lupita lived on that street.

There was a gentleman who had a realty business on 18th Street who was active in Mexican community civic affairs. The group my father belonged to, the West Side Mexican Civic Committee, had dissension over this man's politics. I think they worked together earlier, like in the 1930s and 1940s. But later there were problems. Maybe that's why I heard of him.

To me, Pilsen was little Mexico. My connection started with my learning about the plight of the farmworker and the UFW. We're talking early 1970s. I went to Centro de la Causa in the 1970s. It was on 17th Street. I don't know if César Chávez visited Centro during this time, but farmworker rallies and benefits were held there. My sister was very involved with these farmworker projects. She'd ask her family to come, and most of us did. We would go and help prepare food. There would be a program with speakers and usually a dance at the end of the night. That's how I learned more about the farmworker issue. I wasn't involved at that time. I was divorced and raising two children. My sister became involved with the UFW, and I went to a few of the programs. I guess it lit a candle. It lit my candle of interest. Maybe it was latent, but I certainly saw myself as being Mexican. I'd always say Mexican Italian. People would just recognize the Mexican, maybe because of the name, maybe because of the way I look. I was just beginning to begin my involvement in the Movement, which would later evolve.

TEATRO

I saw teatro for the very first time and liked it. I thought it was an excellent way of delivering a message to people. It was amusing, and yet it was meaningful. It could address issues theatrically, dramatically, and humorously. I thought it would hit home. I began to get involved in about 1975. There were teatros from out of town that would often come around. I saw Teatro Campesino. I saw Teatro Esperanza (hope theater) and Teatro del Barrio from South Chicago. Then I saw Compañia Trucha. I heard they were housed on 18th Street. They were often at the farmworker benefits. I saw myself aligning with them. The way they performed appealed to me. It was maybe 1975 when I decided to move to 18th Street and get involved with Compañia Trucha.

Earlier that year, I had learned of Magdalena García's issue with regard to being fired after seventeen years at Rush Presbyterian Saint Luke's Hospital. I was working at Rush at the time in their satellite office in Oak Brook. I was a paraprofessional, health counselor. It was a federally funded research study on heart disease. The campaign to defend Magdalena was organized by APO and Casa Aztlán. I started attending meetings and felt that the issues of employment and education were important.

At the time, my children were roughly nine and eleven. My daughter was beginning to express some preadolescent energy. I thought she was going to be influenced by the kids around her, and I didn't want her to mimic middle-class kids, to have the kind of values that prioritize money and status over people. I asked myself, "What's her culture going to be?" I understand I am mixed, and my daughter is mixed even more than I am. So what culture would I like her to embrace? What culture would I like her to know about? I thought I can't eradicate the fact the she is of many cultures or many nationalities, but I introduced her to my Mexican and Italian cultures more than anything that came from her father's side. He claimed to be "American" or, as he puts it, an American of Irish and German descent.

It just seemed natural to leave the North Side of Chicago and move my children to 18th Street. That's what I did and got involved with teatro. My children both attended Komensky Grammar School. My daughter was finishing sixth grade. Well anyway, she was moving on to Little Cooper from there. My son was finishing fourth grade and in September went to Jirka Elementary School.

If I told my family there was a march, they pretty much all supported me. My sisters supported the farmworker benefits. We all did. She took the lead because she was working closely with them on the support committee. We always knew when there was going to be an event. Now, I was becoming involved myself, not in the farmworker committee, but I was getting involved. I was involved with Compañia Trucha. However, I don't recall my family ever seeing anything put on by the teatro.

They were puzzled when I moved to Pilsen, like, "Well, why are you doing that? That's quite a change. You don't have to live in Pilsen to be Mexican."

I said, "No, but I just feel like it's closer. I won't have to travel." Being a divorced mom with two kids, I thought I can't be leaving them with babysitters. I can't afford babysitters. I want that we all be together. I told my children, "It's important that we're all together, and this is where we're going to be all together." So that's what I did.

End of a Collective Vision

WOMEN IN THE MOVEMENT

Women in their individual lives are often held back, maybe their ambitions, their dreams, and their goals demeaned. I saw that some women who wanted to get an education were held back. I thought maybe it was not the right thing to do because of their husbands. He won't be able to watch the children, or the husband wouldn't pitch in. Some women didn't think that they could really put that upon him "because he works all day and for him to come home while I go to school, well maybe I'll wait until the kids are older."

I saw it in the Movement. I saw it in Compañia Trucha, where we were trying to deal with the woman question. People in relationships or those who were married seemed to be more sensitive to these issues. I didn't initially see it so much. I guess my eyes gradually became open to it. I would hear people say, "What's the problem? Why aren't you letting me speak? Why can't I bring out an idea?" I don't mean me personally. I saw young people—younger than myself, maybe by a good ten years—whom I admired addressing the issue of women's participation. I thought, "Maybe women should participate more. Maybe she should be upfront as opposed to sitting in the back while the men get up and talk."

Personally, I didn't see it as a political problem. I thought, "Well, this is the way things are. You just go ahead and do what you want to do and don't deal with it as a women's issue." Like if a woman wants to pursue education and advance herself or do what is not considered appropriate for a woman, you just go ahead and do it. I guess in some ways it was rebellious on my part because I didn't want to work it out. I didn't want to struggle. I said, "There's no struggle. If a woman wants to do what she's qualified to do, then she should just do it."

As time went on, I heard these conversations and thought maybe there is a reason why this issue has to be addressed. But then I thought, "Why are we even talking about why women shouldn't be in the forefront? Why women aren't educated? Why women are considered the sole caretakers of children?" I began to undergo a self-searching process about these questions and was introduced to political analysis from some of my friends and associates who were reading Marx and Lenin. They looked at it from a Marxist perspective. I started hearing language that I had not heard before. I asked myself if I was too old for this, whether I should take this on. I felt somewhat overwhelmed. I thought, "I don't know if I can study, raise my children, attend meetings, and go to functions." I think I made a decision, but I didn't discuss it with anyone.

I just decided that it was important to support and advance the issue of education for people that don't have opportunities, to support the issue of medical care for people who don't have choices. I saw these as citywide issues, not just 18th Street or community concerns. If you have an insurance card and you go in with it, you get treatment, and if you don't have an insurance card, you don't get treatment. You have to fill out many forms, and you have to show evidence of being able to pay, and if you can't, then you have to go on welfare. From that perspective, I saw it was important to represent and support these issues. What that meant for me was being active, continuing my work with teatro, participating in whatever way I could, and otherwise showing my support.

When it came to political analysis, I saw myself as someone in the audience. I didn't see myself as a Marxist expert. I couldn't get into the polemics. I would be lost. I saw myself as one of the masses. As part of the masses, was it correct to advance the idea of having proper education? Access to education? Access to medical care? Access to a job, regardless of the color of your skin? Yes. Absolutely. So it was on the foundation of that premise, on the force of that premise that my efforts were based.

I did begin to analyze my own experiences as a woman growing up as a child, as a sister, as a girlfriend, as a wife, as a mother, as a worker. I said,

"Well, have I experienced being considered not equipped to do a job because I was a woman? How did I feel about it myself? How do I perceive myself as a woman? Did I perceive myself as having the right to voice an opinion? How did I see the issue of child care?" In some ways, I was considered politically backwards because I saw it as my job, as my responsibility, to raise my children, not to put it off on my husband or their father. I would never consider giving them to their father. When I heard the "woman question" being discussed, I thought there were issues that I didn't agree politically with. I thought in the real world, this is the way it is. But if we lived under socialism, the little I understood about socialism, I thought, "That would be . . . wow! That's unbelievable . . . that would be wonderful, beautiful! Men and women working side by side and raising their families together. . . . If it's the husband's turn to stay at home with the children, okay, and if it's the woman's turn to go out to work, we'd work in a community, maybe a commune." Now I was really fantasizing!

There was a contradiction between the reality of raising two kids alone in Pilsen and what people were reading. I often went to meetings, and I didn't have child care. So the woman question wasn't really being addressed. I would leave my children home alone. Even though my daughter was twelve and my son was ten. I didn't like it, but I didn't think it appropriate to bring them to all the meetings either. To some I did. But, at some point, I said I can't bring them to everything, so that's the way it's going to have to be. I saw that question falling short. I mean the struggle. I would bring it up, but I didn't expect to get it resolved by the group because we weren't organized yet. The movement was not organized enough to take care of children. Sometimes, there would be a man and woman team put in charge of little ones, young children under five. But I didn't like the idea. I don't know why. I didn't trust it.

I did get involved with a group of women during the late 1960s. They were in the feminist movement. I didn't understand that term *feminist* then. Anyway, they were women on the North Side where I lived around Belmont near Broadway. They started providing child care. They were not just giving lip service to it. They were actually doing it. It was very organized, and they even held classes. Maybe you'd go to a session, maybe two or three times. They were reading books women had written, and you'd discuss the book. I probably went about a total of ten times over a period of two years. They would have day care. I felt comfortable with that. I don't know why. Maybe, looking back, I thought they were organized. I think it was also because they were women. I didn't know the women that came to do the child care personally, but whenever we met in groups, one of them would come to my house and take care of my kids. There was no cost. It was a grassroots movement, although some of the people in Pilsen would have described them as "those middle-class White women." They were all Anglo, but it was very comforting. I felt secure. The people in teatro were younger than I. They had babies. But mine were ten and twelve. I stayed in Pilsen for four years until I married for the second time.

LOOKING BACK

I saw my life moving forward at that time. In retrospect, my son didn't do too well in school. He had learning problems before we moved, so for him, it wasn't as successful as I would have liked. My daughter was better able to grasp the change. Both of my children had encounters with gangs. They managed to keep it from me. So that was not productive. I was disappointed to learn that they were doing things that I didn't know about and that were detrimental to them. Later, my daughter told me, "You know, mother, we moved into a community that was totally alien to us. We knew of it because you used to take us there, and we'd go shopping or go to a restaurant. But those kids were mean." My children were called names, especially my daughter. She was called a Nazi. I don't think my son ever joined a gang when we were on 18th Street, but there was something possibly appealing to him about that culture.

I suppose between my idealism and the reality that my children experienced a better scenario might have been commuting from the North Side. As the adult, you go into things with no idea what children age nine and eleven experience coming into a brand-new community. Then it dawned on me. I was ten when we moved two blocks away from our old house, and it was completely different. I went from a middle-class to a blue-collar, working-class environment. I don't ever remember being called names in the first school I went to. Then when I moved, I was called names, set aside, so to speak . . . referred to as a lesser being, having to hear derogatory comments like, "Hey, Blacky! Hey, Nigger! Smile so we can see you."

As for myself, I saw what power can be obtained with a group of people with an ideology and with a purpose that benefits the people. I didn't always see it as being embraced by the masses. I thought we have so much to overcome. We don't have the media. We don't have newspapers behind us. We don't have television behind us. There are so many distractions. In that respect, I felt frustrated and low at times because I wanted to do so much. We had such good intentions, and we wanted to believe, to see the potential of people realized. I wanted them to believe so that they could do it, too.

Notes

1. This introductory vignette was developed in collaboration with Victoria Pérez. The substance of this chapter comes from several interviews that occurred mainly in 1998 but continued through 2008.

2. The Methodist Episcopal Church founded Holding Institute in Laredo, Texas, in 1880. In 1983, it was closed due to finances but later reopened as a social-service agency. A. H. Sutherland and Joseph Norwood, two ministers, founded it for the education of Mexican children (McNeely, 2009).

3. Bishop Sheil was an auxiliary bishop, an anticommunist who was associated with popular labor causes and defense of ethnic groups, including Jews.

4. The Day of the Revolution is celebrated on November 20 in Mexico to commemorate the Mexican Revolution of 1910–20.

5. General Robert Elkington Wood had been a military officer involved in the Cuban and Philippines campaigns and was later vice president and chairman of Sears.

6. This is Victoria's version of what she heard and is probably, "¿Que dia é ele?" (What day is it?).

7. Victoria's aunt later testified in front of a Congressional committee about the events of that day.

8. The Fifth of May, a Mexican national holiday, celebrates the Mexican defeat of the French occupying troops.

9. Veracruz is a central eastern Mexican state.

10. *Milagros* (miracles) is a popular name for restaurants and other Mexican business establishments.

A Proud Daughter
of a Mexican Worker

MAGDA RAMÍREZ-CASTAÑEDA

The War on the Streets

Around 1969, Father Colleran invited me to a small gathering of workers, mostly parishioners from Saint Vitus in the Pilsen community.[1] The pastor helped get the group together. Pablo Torres was the main organizer. He later became president. His wife attended, but most of the people in the circle were men.

Father Colleran was always promoting me. He arranged for me to be the speaker at several Catholic high-school-commencement ceremonies because he thought I was a good role model for young Mexican women. He believed I could inspire more of them to get involved. Father Colleran thought it made sense for me to be at those meetings because of my interest in labor justice and my position with the Fair Employment Practices Commission.

Although I was a woman, I was well received because I was a student. Mexicans place a high value on education. At the time, they saw college students as people acquiring a great deal of knowledge who in the future might be teachers or other types of professionals. In Mexico, *licenciados* (persons who have a formal degree) are accorded a great deal of respect.

In the early 1970s, we began to discuss discriminatory hiring at places like the post office and the CTA.[2] APO sent letters and made phone calls requesting meetings with CTA officials but received little response. We wanted CTA to hire Mexican workers across all job classifications. The CTA was receiving millions of dollars in federal funds and was supposed to have a racially balanced work force, but they refused to be held accountable.

The first community demonstration APO sponsored around the CTA issue was small. There were twelve people arrested, mostly nuns and priests. The second demonstration was larger. However, the third demonstration was attended by well over five hundred people.[3]

We formed a picket line at 18th and Ashland, a major bus route that ran through the community. Police insisted that we stay on the sidewalk and not block traffic. They harassed the demonstrators, prodding and pushing folks even though we marshals were trying our best to keep everyone moving and not obstruct traffic. It was the cops that incited the crowd with their rudeness and aggressive behavior.

Police began to arrest people for not moving fast enough. A cop grabbed my arm to take me away, but a group of people pulled me back. I bit another cop when he attempted to grab me, but with the help of the crowd, I was able to escape. Others were not so fortunate, and those arrested were treated brutally. We marched down 18th Street to Loomis and Blue Island, where the three streets meet. It is the major Pilsen intersection and a place where several bus lines come together.

We sat down in the middle of the intersection. Our plan was not to disrupt traffic on Ashland, but we had planned to sit down and block traffic on Blue Island. People chanted, "¿Qué queremos? ¡Trabajo! ¿Cuándo? ¡Ahora!" (What do we want? Jobs! When? Now!). Other people took over buses. We asked riders to please get off because we were not going to allow the CTA to come through the community if it was not going to hire Mexicans.

The cops attacked the demonstration violently. They began beating people, wading into the crowd, swinging their clubs wildly, trying to move people sitting in the street *a macanazos* (with nightsticks). I saw Felipe Aguirre standing in the middle of the crowd blocking the intersection. He stood like a flag, his raised fist waving in the air. The cops beat him viciously with their batons, all over his body. They wouldn't stop, and he just stood there like a standard, refusing to be brought down by their billy clubs. Those in the demonstration were singing, "Estamos unidos, no nos moverán" (We are united, we shall not be moved!). Many people were hurt. Blood ran down faces. More arrests were made. At some point, young people began to throw rocks, cans, even eggs at the cops, anything they could get their hands on. Missiles were flying through the air from every direction.

We marched back down 18th Street to Harrison Park. People chanted, "¡Alto! ¡Alto! ¡Alto! . . . ¡Alto a la Discriminación!" (Stop! Stop! Stop! Stop discrimination!). By this time, those all along the avenue were infuriated. As we moved down the street, more things were thrown at the cops. Two sergeants got hit with rocks and bottles, and they were taken away. The riot squad arrived. People were ordered to get off the street and go into their homes. A general curfew was placed on Pilsen.

I spent much of the evening helping to raise bail money for the thirty-two people that were sent to jail. When I got home, it was after four in the morning. My grandmother was visiting from Mexico. I was twenty years old, a single woman, and was getting in the house in the wee hours of the morning. My father was quite upset. We argued, and a lot of things were said.

"¡Prefiero morir de pie, que vivir de rodillas!" (I prefer to die on my feet than live on my knees), I shouted, quoting Zapata.[4]

Finally, I told him that with all the horrible things I had seen, I was going to be a communist. He was quiet after that. He didn't say anything more. Not long after, APO held a benefit dance at Providence of God to raise money for Rutila Mendoza, who was accidentally hit in the head by a hurling bottle at the demonstration. She needed an operation. It was there that I met my future husband.

Home, Family, and School

I always tell people two things. You don't choose the family you're born into, and you don't choose the color of your skin. If I could have chosen, I would have been born in the south of Mexico, but instead, I was born in the north, in Nueva Rosita, Coahuila (a northern Mexican state), in my maternal grandmother's house. The house is still standing. A midwife brought me into the world. My mother was nineteen at the time. But as she tells the story—and my father before he died—I was the firstborn, no miscarriages, no other children before me.

I was a big baby. The midwife got very scared because at the point of coming through the birth canal, I was crisscrossed, not exactly breech but crisscrossed, a few centimeters away from the actual canal. The midwife could not really help my mom. She said, "We're either going to lose you or your baby." My father didn't know what to do. All he could think of was to go for the doctor in the next town, which probably saved my life.

My mom tells me she remembers the pain. The doctor didn't use any forceps. He just put his hands into the area where the babies come from and pulled me through the birth canal. Whenever I'd misbehave, my mother would say, "Oh, I think that doctor pushed you too hard." But that's how I came to be. I want to think of it as a miracle. I was a miracle baby. Anything could have happened, but I waited patiently inside my mother's womb, and the doctor came, and whoosh . . . I was born.

I was born in a dramatic way. The circumstances of my birth were especially dramatic because my father was agnostic. He never labeled himself, but as I grew older, I realized that this is what he was. My mother made him promise to go to La Virgen de Los Lagos (Virgin of the Lakes) to express his gratitude.[5] My father would said, "Okay, okay, okay." But I think he never completed that promise, so maybe that's why my life has been dramatic. My dad at that time *era un taxista* (was a cabdriver). He worked the coal mines, but at that time he was a *taxista*. But that's the story of my birth. I wasn't a baby for too long.

CHILD OF SOCIAL JUSTICE

My mom has a picture of me in a dress when I was about six months old. A photographer took it. It's the kind of baby picture taken of little girls in new filly dresses so that everyone can ooh and aah. Whenever my mother sees that picture, she sighs deeply and apologizes. She feels badly because the clothes I was wearing were made from remnants of one of my grandmother's dresses. The money that should have been used for a fancy dress went to the strike. In the 1950s, my dad was an organizer, and so my mother did without because the strike was so important to what was happening then. At that time, Nueva Rosita, Coahuila, was the fourth-largest coal-mining area in the world. But my grandfather was a white-shirt guy, and my dad was a worker, he was union. They were on different sides. My dad joined the strike and marched all the way to Mexico City. The demonstration became known as the Death March.

My sister was born two years after me in 1952 in a home my parents rented. My father being Mexicano wanted a boy, but each time there was a girl, then another, then another, until there were three of us, Magda, Margarita, and Norma Guadalupe. We all came to be called by our terms of endearment . . . Magdita, Tita, and Pinita.[6] We all grew to be very close.

In Mexico, my mom was a housewife, even though before meeting my dad, her dream was to become a teacher. She was going to *la escuela normal* (normal school) when she met him.[7] My dad didn't want her going to school. But my mom thought that education was very important, primarily reading. In Mexico during the *siestas* (short nap taken in the early afternoon), my mother would take the opportunity to read to us. By this time, she would have cooked and cleaned her house and done her baby chores. The floors were *mosaico* (tile). After my mother washed them, you could smell the cleanliness. I'd lie in front of the two doors that opened out to the patio. I can still see the curtains swaying, feel the afternoon breeze cooling the house, and hear my mother reading to us. Even when Pinita was an infant, Tita and I would fight to be near my mom.

She read books with pictures, *historiales* (historically based stories) like *La Cabaña de Tío Tom, Uncle Tom's Cabin*. I don't want to sound patronizing, but I got to understand the plight of Black people through *Uncle Tom's Cabin* as told by Harriet Beecher Stowe. I know there is a lot of controversy today about having African American children read that book, but it opened my eyes to slavery in a very dramatic way. My mother also read *cuentos* (short stories) and *novellas* (novels) about Sor Juana Inés.[8] But the one that stays in my mind was *Uncle Tom's Cabin*. I think in many ways that story prepared me for the bond that I developed later with Third World people in this country.

WE CAME HERE AS AN ADVENTURE

My father was kind of a rebel. He had the opportunity to study. He was sent to Monterrey to be a civil engineer. His family had the means, but my father did not see that as his goal. He played around with the guys, bullfighters and gamblers mostly. Although he knew a lot, studying wasn't his thing. My grandfather said, "Well, if you're not going to study, then I am not going to pay for your expenses."

My father asked if he could build a house in Nueva Rosita on the same land as my grandparents' house. It was a large plot, but my grandfather said no. That was the turning point. My father said, "Well, then I'm going to the United States." He wanted to prove that he could make it without his father. I learned a lot about this history on visits to my aunt in Mexico. My grandmother spoiled my father. Anything he wanted my grandmother gave him. She forked over the money to get the papers together and for whatever we needed. My father set out in 1956. The family followed and arrived in the United States in 1957.

Our family history in the United States goes back as far as the First World War. My grandmother's cousins served. At least three of them died. They received posthumous honors. They were all from Texas: San Antonio, Brownsville, and Eagle Pass. We had family in Texas, but we also had a distant cousin who lived up north. My father traveled along with a friend to Chicago. He and his wife later became my godparents for communion. We came by Greyhound and stayed with my "uncle," my father's cousin and his family.

In Mexico, everybody was excited for us. "Ah, you're going to speak English." We never heard anything negative about the United States. Everything was good, nothing about prejudice or racism. We didn't hear that the streets were paved with gold, either. We knew you had to work hard. We didn't believe the myths that people say immigrants believe. We saw it as an adventure. "Wow, this is going to be so different." Our cousins on our mother's side said, "You're so lucky you're going to Chicago." My father had drilled us in English. He was interested in learning English himself. We knew words like *pencil, window, door,* and those basic kinds of things.

When we finally got to Chicago, we thought it was so ugly. We lived in the vicinity where the University of Illinois (UICC) is today. My aunt lived on Halsted, close to Roosevelt Road. When we arrived, everything seemed tar-ish and dark. There were no trees or grass. We played on the roofs. It was so ugly we wanted to go back, but it was too late.

My father and mother were able to eventually save money. They found a place on the fourth floor of a building. Later, my mother discovered she had phlebitis. After the birth of my sister, Margarita, one leg got extremely huge; the circulation wasn't good. "En español le dicen pierna de leche" (milk leg). Her leg got kind of white, and she needed a lot of rest. But my mom was always working. She developed it again and had to go to the hospital to have one of the veins in her foot removed.

My dad, no matter how tired, would sit and tell us stories about the events of the day. My mother says my dad treated us all the same, but I felt I had a special bond with him. My father was agnostic, but he didn't want us going to a public school. He felt public school was not a good place. There were all kinds of boys there. He wanted us to go to a proper school, where they had discipline and where we could learn. We went to Saint Francis of Assisi on the Near West Side.

There was a Boys Club right across the street from where we lived on Newberry. The area was mostly Mexican. We could walk to school. We were just a hop, skip, and a jump from *La Garra* (the rag, Rag Town).[9] Since my birthday comes in February and because of the time I spent waiting in Monterrey for papers, I entered first grade a year behind. I entered together with my sister, so we were always in the same grade. We entered school and made our communion at Saint Francis.

My mother was very fearful because she was Catholic and my father wasn't. When we registered for school, they wanted to know my name. My mother changed it so that it would sound more religious. My whole identity changed from Magda to Magdalene. Learning English was exciting for us. My first-grade teacher was not a nun. She was from Argentina, Miss Hernandez. She had reddish hair and was a light-skinned woman, tall and slim. She took all the children that did not know English. This was bilingual education without the label. She would take us and teach us in our language. Many of us in the school didn't know English. But we loved school. We knew how to read in Spanish by the time we went to school. That's why the teacher was able to teach us in Spanish. We learned English at school, and my mother would teach us how to read in Spanish at home.

SATURATED WITH HISTORY

I don't know if my dad lacked friends who shared his interests or if I was the one that took an interest. But my father used to read *la revista Siempre* (the magazine *Always*).[10] It was a huge *revista,* and they had full-color picture inserts. My father also listened to the radio from Havana, Cuba. He talked about Castro like Castro was "the end" (the ultimate). He admired Castro a lot because "¡Le dio los gringos en la madre!" (He screwed the gringos). He would call me over and show me the big pictures. I don't know why my dad showed me those photos. I wasn't traumatized, but he would tell me, "Mira, Batista es un dictador" (Look, Batista is a dictator).[11]

"¿Qué es un dictador?" (What is a dictator?). I need to find out, I thought.

"Él es un hombre que no más le interesa los ricos. Y hay una Guerra" (He is a man who is only concerned with the wealthy. And there is a war). He talked about the revolution, "And this is what he does to the people who are *con* (with) Fidel!" You would see guys with their ears cut off. That was the first time I heard of people being tortured by having their nails completely torn off. My father would talk to me about injustices, and he would blame the United States. He would say, "Es la culpa de los Estados Unidos. Que esta la gente de Cuba así" (It is the United State's fault that the Cuban people are like this). He would say, "They want to do what they want to do with the sugar, and Cuba isn't going to go for it. They have been exploiting the Cubans for so many years. Y ya es tiempo" (And now it is time). It wasn't like I could dialogue with him.

When company came over, we were not even allowed to hang out with the older people. My father would give us a look, and if we didn't get it, we would feel my mother's pinch. If our guests had little kids, we had to bring them to our room. But I would overhear things. I don't know if my father's interest in unions and things like that had an impact on me. Once he got to the United States, he didn't join groups. But he told a lot of stories about Mexico. By the third or fourth grade, I was really saturated with a lot of history. Certain nuns would say things about Mexico, and I remember I would raise my hand and offer a comment that was totally contrary to what they were saying. I guess that part of my life stays with me more than dolls, although religion and dolls played a very important part of my life as well.

My father didn't want us baptized. He had not been baptized, and my mother was worried because my father was a real heathen. We were finally baptized and confirmed at the same time in Monterrey, right before we left for the United States. But religion played a role once we came to the United States. We had toys and took all our dolls and baptized them. We had a pretty good childhood. In spite of the fact that we never lived in the suburbs, I never felt I lacked anything. We lived in that house on the fourth floor for two years, for first and second grade.

My father got a new job that paid more. He was a welder. He wanted to live close by so he could come home for lunch. He found another apartment. It was around Grand Avenue and Aberdeen. We used to walk almost seven blocks to the Catholic school. We didn't know we were the first Latinos within two miles of that neighborhood. We had Carpenter School across the street. But my father—God rest his soul—he was such a good guy. He thought Carpenter was not a very good school for us.

We would probably not have done as well had we attended there. Instead, he sent us to Santa María Addolorata. There, either you spoke Italian or you spoke English. It was very Italian. The kids were kind of mean, and they used to call us apes or monkeys. They would spit at us. We lived in a French apartment. That's what they called apartments when they were close to the first floor.

We finally got used to being there, and the kids got used to being close to us. The people that owned the building were from Sicily. They became like grandparents to us. They would come, collect the rent, and always bring us fruit. In 1959, when my mother lost the baby, they watched over us when my father went to the hospital. When she came back, they brought her wine and fruit. They were very warm people. That's how I got to know the good side of Italian people. We really feasted on the food. My father would always bring different things to the house for us to try. He would say, "Aprueben esto" (Taste this).

There were only three Latino kids in the whole school. My father wanted us to learn English. He would say, "¡No me importa pero ustedes van a saber inglés y mejor que los gringos!" (I don't care but you are going to learn English and better than the gringos!). He would say, "En esta casa se habla español. Fuera, allá, el inglés, pero quiero que sepan español" (In this house we speak Spanish. Outside, over there, English, but I want you to speak Spanish). We went from a first- to a fourth-grade reader in less than a year. No matter where we were, my mother always managed to find a library. We'd take a shopping bag and bring back books for the house.

My grandfather was a big lodge man. He was a member of the *Masones* (Masons). My grandmother was a Baptist. Mamarita was my grandmother's aunt. She founded a school in Brownsville. I don't know if the school still exists. But my father's family came from a lineage of teachers and not necessarily

Catholics. They left their mark "en la religion Pentecostal" (in the Pentecostal religion). They're all hallelujah people. My grandmother as her mother before was very staunch. They read the Bible. Because of my grandfather, my father was never baptized. The 1930s was also a time in Mexico when people were literally baptized underground because of the division between the church and the state.[12]

But religion played a big part in our family. My mom never wanted to tell people my father was agnostic. She feared they would kick us out of school. We never let people know our father was a heathen. It was hard. I saw my father as so kind, and I associated kindness with being Catholic, not even Christian, Catholic. I was confused about my father. "My father sees injustices, and yet he doesn't believe in God! So, maybe there is no God or maybe God doesn't have to make you good. You're good because you see what's out there. If my father can see what is good and what is bad . . . well, I can see it, too, and I don't need God."

My mom wanted her own place. She wanted a house. They started looking on the North Side. My dad did not care for the South Side, maybe because he saw Newberry as a dead end. He saw that we couldn't go outside. We couldn't enjoy the air. Every weekend, my parents would take us to Lincoln Park. They wanted to see green, trees, and flowers. My father also said, "No quiero vivir entre Mexicanos" (I don't want to live with Mexicans). Because, he said, they didn't appreciate what they have. "We want to live with other people." He wanted diversity but not necessarily in terms of African Americans. "Quiero que viven entre gente que hablan más inglés, que conozcan otras culturas" (I want to live among people who speak English so you can know other cultures).

We moved to Orchard. Orchard had many trees. The Italian landlords immediately took a liking to my dad. They made a deal right then and there. There were two buildings. One was in the front and one in the back, which we rented because there was a yard. My father did not want us playing and hanging around with the riffraff. We could play by ourselves during the day, but we could not stay out at night. So for him, it was really nice because there was a backyard. Today, they call the area Lincoln Park. I went back recently and couldn't recognize it. It is very upscale. We attended Saint Michael's. That's where I met Cristina.

TOUCHED BY THE LORD

My fifth-grade teacher was Sister Mary Vincentine. Our school was by Eugenie and North Avenue. We walked the five blocks to the school. If I didn't make it home on time, I would get punished. But I would talk to everybody on the way. We lived in that place from 1960 until my sister and I graduated from high school in 1969. That's when they started calling me the Holy Roller. I was kind of weird. I used to preach. Our teacher wanted all the girls to become nuns, and she wanted all the boys to become priests. She brainwashed us and told us if we joined the order, our parents would immediately go to heaven. I really believed it all. Whenever I would enter the church, I would stare at the statues until they seemed to move.

Sister Mary Vincentine was crazy. Every day at school, all the kids had to make room for their guardian angel. Those little desks with little inkwells didn't have much space. I was a little tubby, and I had to make room for my guardian angel. I was always almost falling off the edge of my chair. I put a play together one year, "The One God Chose." It was about a woman named María Crespo, a Puerto Rican girl. Sister Mary Vincentine lent me her habit. I dressed up as a nun, and from then on, I was touched by the Lord. More than anything, I wanted my father, the heathen, to go to heaven. Probably in my subconscious, I wanted so badly for him to be baptized. All the orders would come to try to convince the boys to become priests. They would come and talk to the class. They'd ask, "Who wants to become a priest?" I said, "What the heck? Why can't I?" Sister Mary Verola, another nun who eventually was sent to the nut house, took me under her wing. I guess because I was so much a loner, and she was very sweet. She was crazy, but she was sweet. She spoke Spanish.

My mother wanted us to become Hijas de María, Daughters of Mary. The Puerto Ricans had that organization. We were not Puerto Rican, of course, but my mother used to go see Father Kathrine, who droned in a deep, robotic voice and did the Spanish Mass. "Ay vengan los Viernes para las juntas de las Hijas de María" (Come Fridays for the meetings of the Daughters of Mary). I went with my mom and wanted to go once again. If religion was calling me, I wanted to know. I still have my ribbon. It's a blue, glossy ribbon with a big medal of the Virgin Mary attached. My other sisters didn't go, just me. I was always a volunteer for everything.

Then I developed a crush on someone from the school. He directed the choir, and I liked to sing. The Germans used to have their feast. He asked a couple of the girls if they wanted to wear their uniforms and serve people. That's how I got to know German people. It was very cultural, very ethnic. I was also a member through Saint Francis of Juventud Obrera Católica (young Catholic worker). Somehow or other, religion always played a part of my life. There's a spiritual thing there. I can't get away from religion. It's there. I hate to admit this, but I think I've always been an attention seeker.

There must be a reason. But I don't know what it is. I don't know if there's a sense of theatrics in all of this. I was introduced to theatrics at an early age.

In Nueva Rosita, the theater was like a circus, *teatro de carpa* (tent theater), traveling shows, Al Jolson types, but Mexican. I was about six or five years old when I remember seeing a very young, a very good actress. She made a lasting impression on me. I wanted to be like her. I wanted to be in theater. So that's the other part of me. There is the religious part, the ethnic, cultural, historical person, and then comes the person that's theatrical, the part that I guess adds the spirit that makes me move, that motivates me, that says, "Go for it."

Even though we had crazy nuns, I kind of liked it. Maybe other kids didn't. Sometimes I look back and think Cristina's right. We didn't learn anything. But I was somebody's favorite. Somebody liked me for whatever reason. The way I look at it that's a very good thing for a Latina who wasn't brought up in a little theater, whose parents couldn't help her develop the way she should have.

Getting Involved

TRYING TO LOSE MY RELIGION

Actually, my changes began in high school with one of my teachers. There was the 1968 Chicago riot. I saw police brutality. My father would also come home and tell stories of injustices at his job. At night, my mother and he would talk. I could hear them. I would say to myself, "Something is wrong here." My father was passed over for a certain job. I would think, "¡injusticias!" (injustices).

But I think what brought on the changes was my teacher. Paul Barrett was one of the people that brought history to life. He talked about economics. I think I fell in love with his intellectualism. I felt I could understand because of the way he explained things. He also talked about my people. He talked about history and what the United States did to Mexico. He had respect for our culture, and that made a big impression. I began to stay after school. I said, "You know this material, but a lot of this information you didn't get from our textbook." He began to recommend other books. One of them was the *Communist Manifesto*. I remember when he brought it out of his briefcase, he told me, "Please don't tell anybody about this."

After school, he would smoke a pipe and talk about politics. I just sat there and listened. I learned a lot from him. I learned about economics, not the depths, because I picked up more of that at the university. But he got my feet wet. I fell in love with this man. I did nothing but think of him. I was young and vulnerable, but he was a gentleman. I learned more about my culture through him. I learned from my dad and mom, but he brought it all together. I could understand from a different perspective, not from religious one, but from a political and economic point of view.

I wrote poems in 1968 about Daley and the pigs during the brutality at the 1968 Democratic Convention.[13] I couldn't sleep thinking about some of these things that were happening in the city. I think I owe Paul a lot because he continued what my father had begun. I'm just sorry to say that it was a man that developed my consciousness. Feminists might say, "What do you mean a male brought you to reality?" You don't want to tell that to people, but, actually, that's the truth.

I wrote a letter and apologized for having fallen in love with him. We went to Lincoln Park, and we sat and had a picnic. I brought a tablecloth. We laid the blanket down by the pond by the Children's Zoo. That's where he explained to me why he could not love me. Why he could not return my affections. He said, "I'm you're teacher. You know I'm very flattered that you like me, that you have a special feeling for me." He was very shy. "But I do have . . . I live with a woman. I live with somebody." I told him I didn't care. Besides, I was graduating.

Here I am, coming on to him, and he says, "I find you very attractive. That's not even the point. But I am committed to somebody, but we can still continue being friends." I thought it was the biggest rejection of my life. It hurt me so much because I felt I had found my significant other, the man of my dreams. I use the word *soul mate* now. But at that time, I just thought that he was meant for me because I was enthralled with the fact I could learn from him. So I had a date with this teacher, and I always kept it in my heart. I haven't seen him in over six years. The last I heard he was teaching at a local university.[14]

There were other important instructors that made an impression on me. Another teacher brought in poetry. I got into it. I used to go and walk through Lincoln Park. It was during the Vietnam War, and he introduced us to poets like Thoreau. I remember he talked about the Mexican War and how Thoreau refused to go to war. Instead, he went to jail. These historical figures for me were very positive. I enjoyed Thoreau's famous poem to a prostitute. In many ways, we were very fortunate. They were the right elements for the time. They fit perfectly. I think if you wanted to get an education, you really could have been enriched. But it had to be off to the side because of pressures from the administration to abide by the curriculum.

When I was in high school, I visited the hippies in Lincoln Park, but I did not join in any of the activities. I didn't really get active until my first year of college when I entered Circle Campus. I go back to injustices. I read about César Chávez and the plight of the farmworkers in high school. I figured I could fit in with the UFW because there was a question of justice and Jesus and La Virgen de Guadalupe kind of thing . . . that was one offering.[15] When I went into the university, another offering was calling me. It was a political one. It was then that I stopped going to church.

I spent my first year trying to drop the religious aspect of myself. The Newman Center was where the Jesus people hung out. They kept coming after me. But in the student union, there were a number of organizations. I would stop at almost every table, pick up newspapers, and try to saturate myself with knowledge. I thought, "Oh God, this is what it's about! This is what my history teacher was talking about." I knew I had to make a decision. I couldn't go on being a Christian and be into this. It would be like living two lives. The first semester, I hid from one and then the other group. Finally, I said, "No, this is a game. I know what I want. I want changes in this society."

With my cousin, Nora Villarreal's help, I entered UICC. Sister Mary Verola was also very instrumental in getting me involved with the League of United Latin American Citizens, an organization that gave out scholarships to students.[16] I knew my parents would not be able to afford to have two kids going to college. My sister was going, also. They chose five Latinos and gave us a scholarship and a banquet. It was a big hoopla. I remember my mother was sick, so Nora went. A person whom I later knew as an activist had a sister who received a scholarship. A kid that went to school with me at Saint Francis of Assisi also got one. That's how I entered U of I. I was fortunate as a Latina to go through the front doors of the university. Almost all the Latinos would start out at junior college. You could renew the LULAC scholarship if you kept a B average. But the first year, I did not focus.

I began going to OLAS meetings. Later on, I joined them. OLAS was founded at Loop College. My cousin Nora took me to a party where I met a number of people. She was the cofounder of OLAS. It was through her that I got to know about the organization. Nora was my bridge. So that's how I got involved.

Nora's a marvelous person. I always wanted to thank her for all that she meant to me. She impressed me. She is now a specialist in the area of immigration. But she had always done this on her own. She took me to people's houses, and I saw what she was able to do for them. People would always come to her. People found out about her by word of mouth. She's older than I am, but she looks young for her age. She was born with a heart ailment. She loves children, but she could never have any. She tried having a child and almost died. So she adopted. She's a very good mother.[17]

I WAS A SELLOUT

Then in 1969, came *La Cruzada* (the crusade, reference to the Crusade for Justice). We went to Colorado to a conference sponsored by Corky Gonzáles. That's how Yenelli and I crossed paths. We hadn't met. We had only seen each other. But I was in my own world. I wanted to know everything. I went with a group through Nora. There were three buses that I can recall. We labeled them the street-people bus, the little gangbanger bus, and the student and professional's bus. I went with the students. There was a group of us mostly from Loop, including Chuy Negrete and some people who later on would come back and form Teatro de La Raza (at Loop Junior College). These people were all at Loop. So naturally, I hooked up with them. Focusing on *La Cruzada* made a very big impression on me. I could tap into my ethnicity, my political strengths, and organizational skills that I wanted to develop further.

But I was dating a White Anglo Saxon Protestant. I thought I was so hip, "Hey, I got an Anglo for a boyfriend" kind of thing. Then when I went to Colorado, I participated in all these different workshops and saw teatro. Some of the acts spoke about the *Gabachos* (White foreigners).[18] *La palabra Gabacho* (the word *Gabacho*) was a new word for me. Then, I thought, "Well, I'm a sellout. I'm dating an Anglo. God, I'm like committing a sin. I shouldn't be doing this. I'm not going to tell anybody."

I was a freshman, and he was a senior. I met him at Circle. Kenneth was his name. His parents were liberal types. They were the last White family on the West Side.[19] He was apolitical, but he came from parents that were Methodists. He dated Blacks. He didn't stay within his own people. In the end, he married a Japanese girl. His family lived in this beautiful house. I would hang out with them. I would go golfing and do different things. He would come to my house and have *tamales*. My parents and he thought that it was pretty serious. I guess I was the one that wasn't serious about the relationship, especially after having gone to Colorado.

When I came back, Ken was waiting for me to come off the bus. I hid between the seats until he was gone. I said to myself, "He has to go." I ended up taking a cab to my house after he finally left. I was embarrassed to be dating a Gabacho. Later, he called my house. He was very mild. He was totally the opposite of me. He said calmly, "Well, you know, Magda, I went to pick you up. What happened?" I said, "Oh, that's right, you said you would. Well, somebody offered me a ride, and I just took it. I'm so sorry we missed each other."

I wasn't being very honest. Our friendship began to sour. I began to look for any reason to break up with him. One day, my mother was watching some soap opera. Even today, you look at Mexican or Latino soap operas, and you find that the ones that are *mestizo*-looking (looking like a mix blood) are playing the parts of maids and chauffeurs. The real light-skinned, blue-eyed people are playing the major roles. I was sitting in the living room with my mom and Kenneth watching the *novela* (soap opera). Then he said, "Oh wow, look at these women! They're so attractive. They almost look White." When he said that, I thought, "That does it. This is my reason. He was dating me all that time, and he really didn't think I was attractive. Now these girls look beautiful because they look White?" I just severed it. I wish I had that kind of determination in my life now.

I began to play a role in the nationalist Movimiento Estudiantil Chicano (Chicano Student Movement). I severed my relationships with others. I became very nationalistic. It wasn't like I always felt I could unite with all Third World peoples and understood class divisions.[20] It was necessary to really look into my roots, not so much as a Mexicana but now as a Chicana. Even though I was not born here, I thought of myself as a Chicana. That's when I began to get more involved in OLAS.

I was very much involved with some brothers who ran a newspaper. They had filmed the Los Angeles antiwar rally that turned into a riot in August of 1970 when police attacked it.[21] They lent me the film, which I was able to show at an OLAS meeting. It was a silent film, no narrative to it. But you saw the action. You saw the Chicanas very close up, wearing the heavy makeup. You saw them marching and shouting, "Chicano!" You could read their lips. "Power!" You didn't need words.

At that time, a beautiful woman from OLAS was elected queen of the Mexican Day Parade. I'm not going to say she was not political at all. She was with OLAS. But she had a bad habit of saying she had a fatal disease in order to get sympathy and attention from men. As queen, she was expected to speak at the Grant Park band shell.[22] OLAS wanted to make an impact at that rally. Every year, we struggled with *El Grito*.[23] Why go? It's a bunch of crap. The stores use Mexican holidays to promote their sales.[24] Yet, thousands of people would be there screaming "¡Viva Mexico!" but nothing ever changed. The OLAS queen that year was the first one that gave a different kind of a speech. She gave a rip-roaring speech that I wrote.

Ironically, it was the year OLAS received a flag from the Mexican president, and we were going to be at the Grito to protest the 1968 massacre in Mexico, the continuous violation of human rights, and the presence of the man who gave the order to shoot protestors.[25] A lot of people were in Grant Park that night. The cops came and tried to disrupt the protest. They came into the crowd and ripped the banners and broke the poles. We were standing right there. We were peacefully protesting, but they blatantly violated our civil rights.

The queen questioned the significance of El Grito. She was coming out as a Chicana and asked what it meant to truly be liberated. She made it clear that we were not liberated. "No estamos liberados porque estamos en otro país que nos maltrata" (We are not free because we are in a country that treats us badly). I still have that speech somewhere. I gave it to her at a meeting. I wasn't sure what she was going to do with it. Anything could have happened up there. She could have gotten scared and decided not to read it. But the speech was well received. The OLAS queen later married an Anglo cop.

A STORY IN A CUBBYHOLE

Yenelli once told me, "Magda, you have youth. You have the power to do almost anything if you really put your mind to it and really get empowered or empower communities. But instead you choose to go where the current takes you." But I was at the right place for the Movimiento, to contribute to making change. I have been pretty good at that. I may not be a long-range planner, but I pretty much have a handle on what kind of politics I have. Mine really began to take shape when I went to Colorado. That's when I came back saturated with Chicano/Chicana politics.

Although Yenelli and I have had a close relationship, it was Cristina who was in OLAS with me. Cristina tends to be very quiet, but she is a strong person. I have seen the wisdom of silence. Sometimes, it is wise to keep quiet. There were some things that happened in OLAS that made me think about what being a Chicana meant. In Colorado, I found Chicanas were better off on their backs. This is what was being said, including by people in the Black Panther Party.

Some things happen when they are not planned. Cardiss Collins's husband died. He was a representative from the Seventh Congressional District. We in the Partido de La Raza Unida had the idea of running Angel Moreno as a candidate.[26] This was back in 1973. Angel was kind of a jolly, chubby kind of guy. You could be friendly with him, but at the same time, he had another side. I saw him as sneaky. I didn't quite trust him. He was a flirt. That's okay as long as you keep your politics. You can flirt, but you keep your head on the goal.

We had a makeshift office on 26th Street. That's when we met the young people from high school. There was a teacher at one of the city high schools who was there. She brought in youth to help us work in the office. Some became knowledgeable about politics. She brought in Rudy Lozano and others. There was a group of about eight.

OLAS used to have meetings on Sundays. We had them at El Centro de la Causa, our headquarters. Sometimes, we would have food, and the women would cook at meetings. This time, we were going to have a discussion about the election. We wanted to support someone from the community in opposition to the Daley machine. The president of OLAS would open meetings. This was the special topic. Cristina and I were both there. He said, "The girls," I think he called us "the girls." "The girls are going to go and prepare something while we discuss this political question." Today, he says he doesn't remember this incident. But Cristina is a witness. I was single. I didn't even cook. I used to go to every restaurant on 18th Street. Why the heck was I going to cook for some guys?

Cristina and I didn't budge. We stayed, and everybody else went. It was this camaraderie with Cristina that led us to have this bond. In high school, we were not friends. She was a friend of my sister. I felt like Cristina, a feminist. So we were in a room full of *machistas* (chauvinists), Chicano machistas. The president's wife and four or five other women left the room. We stayed. He was looking directly at us. His friends and others who always supported him were looking at us, too. We did not move. I think Cristina spoke up first. Like I said, there is a power in silence, but, sometimes, you have to speak, and you have to know when that time is.

Cristina said, "Well, you know, we're just as interested as you are in what's going to happen here politically." It was something we didn't have to talk about. It was a connection we shared. This womanhood, Chicanas interested in politics, no longer willing to just take a back seat in the Movimiento, Latinas in the back and *los hombres* (the men) in the front. We stuck around, and we stuck to our point. The rumor thereafter was that Cristina and I were lovers. That was the first attack. Then, they started saying that our problem was that we weren't heavy chested and that made us more masculine. Someone involved in culture claimed, "Women who are flat chested are more intellectual." I guess I'll take the compliment. This had a great impact on me. I'm glad it happened. It was just like a story in a little cubbyhole. No one really knew about it. But it made a big difference. Everyone has a chance to make history. That was our opportunity.

From then on, whenever we went to Iowa for conferences, we raised issues about not having any workshops related to Chicanas. There were no workshops for women, and we'd complain, "Hey, we have to discuss women's issues. There isn't anything here that addresses our concerns." Cristina wrote a paper where she argued that Chicanos should not exploit Chicanas, because they should have learned to appreciate the true meaning of exploitation at the hands of the White man. I recall a lot of young Chicanas at that conference. There were some older women who had their daughters attending the University of Iowa.[27]

One of the issues we discussed was the bond between mothers and daughters and issues related to real love and sex. Health was another topic along with sisterhood and how we saw ourselves in the Movimiento, what roles we should be able to play, and the fact that we were being stepped on by our own brothers. I recall that there were often tears. It was really moving as women opened up about many issues. I think when you have a workshop where people can open up, that's a good workshop.

BECOMING A SOCIALIST

While I was at UICC, I became associated with the YSA because of the Cuban question. What I enjoyed about the university and YSA was that I met some terrific people. I learned a lot from two Mexican brothers. I had a very close relationship with one of them. Here I was, this Mexican woman who didn't feel very attractive, but I felt like I had some knowledge to offer. I was very moved to see this tall Mexicano. To me, he was another Che Guevara. So I gravitated to him . . . in terms of learning. A Puerto Rican woman who became a physician was enthralled by him, as was Yenelli. We were like his little groupies. He had an impressive awareness of Mexican politics. He was in his last year at the university. People said, "He's such a dummy. He can't graduate." He keeps going, but I saw that a lot of people never wanted to leave that university life because it filled your spirit. It fulfilled your intellectualism. He gave us the information that we needed.

A Mexican official with the Chicago Consulate's office at that time was a drunkard. People saw him as associated with the government that carried out the Tlatelolco Massacre. There was a weedy lot just south of the UICC campus. It was rumored that in the center of that empty lot, meetings took place. I didn't know very much about it other than the fact that I heard that there was a plan to kidnap this politician and exchange him for political prisoners in Mexico. This idea might sound crazy today, but it was motivated by the revolutionary spirit of Chicanos, our frustration with the system, and the knowledge that our brothers and sisters in Mexico were in jail, many of whom were being tortured for fighting for freedom. This encouraged people to act.

Anyway, I mention this story to recall the times and to understand that people that became involved were very serious. This man from the YSA was a revolutionary that we all looked up to. I don't know where I acquired the ability to be able to speak extemporaneously. Sometimes with only three words in my head, I could make a speech. I began to get really good at it. He began to put me forward, maybe thinking they had this Latina sound box.

We didn't have a Latino group like OLAS at the university, so this YSAer and myself sat down one day in the cafeteria and started talking about what we could do. "Look at all these great ideas we have. Look at the people that are joining us. We could really be big. But we don't have a Latino group." So we founded the Latin American Student Union. We drew up the papers, had our first meeting, and the chancellor invited us to one of his student receptions, a little tea. This YSA leader joined the group, but he was like the leader on the outside, like a consultant. I would go to different universities like Rosary College to speak against the war.[28] That was an issue that was really on the minds of Chicanos. A lot of the materials that were useful for us were written by Bert Corona, the labor organizer.[29] I studied his writings and speeches when I went on speaking tours.

I was able to travel to Indiana, Michigan, and speak at some of the surrounding colleges. I spoke on issues like abortion. To my knowledge, I was one of the first Chicanas to speak out and be prochoice. It was just a beginning. It was not until 1973, when the new law went into effect, that abortion became legal. Being a Catholic and coming to this point of view I could see my own political development going even further.

I had just gotten a position with the state. I was an interviewer for the Fair Employment Practices Commission. I also had just gotten my paperwork to become a citizen. One day I came home very paranoid. We had this old piano, and I was about to move it in front of the door. Cristina said, "What's the matter with you?" There was somebody following me. Someone had called my job and left a message, an Agent Murphy. He was from the Federal Bureau of Investigation. I was trembling, but I thought I had to return the call. When I called, they said, "Which Murphy? There are ten Murphys here." I told them to put a note somewhere that I called. The guy called my mother's house and identified himself as FBI. They spoke to my sister. He said he was looking for me. She told him, "If you're the FBI, you should know where she is." That's what I mean about women like Cristina and my sister—when they speak, it makes a lot of sense. They don't say much, but when they do, they make a good point.

The guy eventually got a hold of me, and he introduced himself. He asked, "Have you heard of the Attorney General's list?"

Suddenly I was very nervous. I said, "Well, kind of . . ."

"There is no 'kind of' . . . The group that you're running with . . ."

I said, "What group is that?"

"You know what I'm talking about." Then he said, "We have you at this meeting and that one," and he gave dates. "You know exactly what I'm talking about."

I said, "No. I don't know what you're talking about."

"They're on the Attorney General's list, and they're being investigated, and if you are involved in subversive activities, you could be jailed." Then he went into this explanation of what was going to happen. I really was angry, but I was scared at the same time. That whole week, I was really paranoid. I got off the subway on my way home really petrified and constantly looking over my shoulder, thinking they were following me. They really do a good job on you. Later, the organization found an informant in the group. He was a jerk. Anyway, that was one part of my life where I felt like, "Oh my God, the *federales* (government troops) are going to get me."[30] I thought, "Where can I go? Can I go back to Mexico?" I even thought this was happening to me because I had fallen away from God. I guess I wasn't as scared as I should have been, because I didn't stop what I was doing. I never admitted that I was a member of the organization. I wasn't. But the YSA supported what I believed in. They were the ones that drove me to places where I was going to speak.

I was at the university for two full years. I dropped out just before beginning my third year. I met some good people there, including a professor of Spanish literature. I loved her. Ruth El Saffar was a fantastic professor. I was in her Spanish class, and the majority of people there were *Cubanos,* the *gusanos* (worms).[31] I decided to do my paper on César Chávez. I gave a class presentation on him. Immediately, the gusanos jumped on me. According to them, César Chávez was a *comunista* (communist). The discussion got really heated, and my professor came to my rescue. I will always be grateful to her.

We started LASU (Latin American Student Union), but we didn't have a Latino studies program. We needed one. We wanted it, and we were going to get it. We took over one of the buildings. We organized a successful demonstration with gays and Black students. But when we took over one of the buildings, someone set one of the floors on fire. Then we were told that we had to get out. Looking back, I have to say this may have been a trick played by the university. There were no flames, just smoke. It may have just been the excuse they used to evacuate us.

LASU was also involved in organizing the strike after the killings at Kent State.[32] We had a rally, and as we marched, we went into different halls and pulled students out, "Hell, no!" Later, on the news, you saw all the walkways between the buildings filled with lines of students coming out of their classes. We were part of the university contingent. We addressed issues related to the war, the question of abortion, and the need for a Latin American Studies Department. We sponsored many discussions on campus. We met with the chancellor about some of these issues. I actually think he had respect for us.

There was no OLAS there then. OLAS continued in whatever they were doing. In a way, I split with them, although not openly. They seemed to be going nowhere. We weren't doing anything. My new home base was the university. I think I was attending school primarily to raise the level of consciousness. Basically, what I did was to help the movement in every possible way that I could. Almost immediately after I left the university, Cuadro formed. They also fought for Latin American Studies and were able to get it. The students were able to bring Otto Pikaza to campus. He began to develop the Latin American Studies program. The past president of OLAS was one of the major leaders of Cuadro. So there was an OLAS connection.

My sister was on campus with me, but she was in the Teacher Corps.[33] One of the Teacher Corps members later went on to become a politician. I wish I had taped him on television after he was appointed and he looked at the mayor and said, "I won't let you down, Mayor." He didn't look at the people or the cameras. He didn't say to the people, "I won't let you down." Instead, he made that commitment to the mayor. What a *stúpido* (fool)! I always wanted to tell him that to his face.

THE THREADS THAT LED TO PILSEN

Yenelli and I hooked up after Colorado. I remember thinking this woman is very attractive, but she looked a mess because of her long hair and she's *chaparita* (short). She later told me that I made an impact on her. Yenelli was not married, and neither was I at the time. She was a kindergarten teacher and lived within the vicinity of the university. Her then-fiancé was a member of SDS. One night I was with a street musician who was in and out of politics. We lost track of time and stayed out too late. I didn't dare go home. Then I thought about Yenelli. I had her phone number. We headed to her place in the early hours of the morning. I rang the bell, and the door opens, and this Lady Godiva is standing there. I wasn't high. I had a glass or two of wine. That was it.

From that day forward, we became friends. We talked a lot about politics. Yenelli is this tiny woman who just knew a lot. I felt that by being around her I was going to gain more knowledge, to be able to dialogue more, to be able to look at things from a more free-spirited perspective. She was like a hippy but a radical hippy. Through Yenelli, I met Isaura and others, and that was one of the links that brought me to the Pilsen community.

I also still had ties to the church. I was very much involved along with Maximo in APO. Maximo had also been in OLAS, working with the community group that met at Centro. APO began like a lot of community organizations working around an issue. The issue was jobs and discrimination against Mexicanos and Puertorriqueños. It was cofounded by several people. One of the major forces was Pablo Torres.[34] Raul Medina, a Puerto Rican guy who lived on 18th Street, was also important. They worked closely with Jim Colleran, a priest.

Of course, I was a supporter of the UFW. One Saturday, there was a huge rally in front of the Jewel on Cermak.[35] Jim was on the picket line. I saw this very handsome man, well, a priest, but I didn't know that at the time. He was not wearing a collar. He spoke Spanish almost like a Mexicano. We were picketing, and I was new to the group, so Jim walked over to me and said, "Hi, where are you from?" I told him I was a student at the university. Then some little boy came running over, shouting out to him, "Father! Father!" The little boy looked very Chicano—*un niño muy bonito* (a very cute child). I asked if that was his son . . . hoping, but he said, "I'm a priest."

"Oh," I said barely audibly. At that moment, I thought of my recent rejection of the church. Here was this priest who seemed totally different. He was involved. I said to myself, "What the heck." We talked as we moved along the picket line. Afterwards, we went to get coffee and became friends. He was part of a group from El Comité Latino. The committee was part of the archdiocese, which at that time dealt with a lot of workers' issues. It was under the Cardinal's Committee for the Spanish Speaking. Many of the big unionists were involved with it, like Jose Ovalle from the United Auto Workers, who was a good planner and thinker. I began going to those meetings. Puerto Ricans and Mexicans worked together in a unified way. Jim knew I worked with the State of Illinois. By this time, I had already moved on my own. I had him over, and he played his banjo. Then we watched the basketball game.

Well, we began to talk a lot about *el trabajador Mexicano* (the Mexican worker) and the issues he faced. He knew I worked for the FEPC. I became a resource for him. All the cases that arrived at APO, he sent to me. I was also a translator, so I would go with the group to Springfield.

At that time, this Republican politician headed a commission. He approached me, maybe because I could translate or because I was perky and quick, but he saw something in me. He asked, "How would you like to do something very special? We need a new chair for the Young Republicans."

Republican? Me? My God, what is this? I thought, "Where has he seen me? What's he thinking?" I was in shock. All this time, I've been in left politics . . .

this has been my love, my life, everything. But he made an offer. I didn't have to do anything. He would just place me there as a token. He asked me three times, once at a major social gathering, "Well, have you made up your mind?"

On one occasion, I was translating. I had my legs crossed. He put his hand on my knee. I thought, "This son of a bitch." I didn't want any part of it. Politically, what was it going to do for me? It's nothing that I believe in. It just didn't fit. So that's another part of my life. But, anyway, that's how I became involved with APO. I continued being involved with them throughout those years. Maximo and I tried to convert them to our greater cause.

Father Jim played a very important role in my life. He supported the feminist in me. He made sure I was a speaker at graduations for young Latinas. For somebody who is not Latino, I thought, he's trying to do something. He played a very good role in the Mexicano Movimiento on 18th Street. He helped a lot of people. Margarito Resendo Padilla was one of them. He was shot by the *migra* (immigration authorities).[36] We held a march in protest of his treatment. They said he was eating in a restaurant and had a knife and that he was going to attack the immigration official, and that's why they shot him.

He was taken to the University of Chicago Hospital, which we initially thought, "How benevolent of them to operate for free." But they were experimenting on him, simple as that.[37] APO held meetings at the Saint Vitus rectory. Margarito would sometimes come out in his stocking feet, because he was staying with Father Jim. Ultimately, Margarito died from complications due to the shooting.

I admired Jim. Here was a man who had a master's degree and yet worked in a gas station to make his own money to travel to Mexico. He didn't use the money of the people. He worked. He helped and gave shelter to undocumented people. He lent money to them while they were looking for work. He was arrested three or four times when we were seeking jobs from the CTA and from the United States Postal Service. His involvement was not just from someone who is a staunch Catholic but from someone who is to the left. There was always that passion, that feeling that he had to make change. It couldn't just be the status quo. One had to keep applying pressure, and if the government needed to be defied, then so be it. He defied Cardinal Cody. Cody was the most racist, close-minded person that ever lived. Father Jim disagreed with him. Cody wanted to close down Saint Vitus. Jim fought many times to keep the church open.[38]

Jim and three or four nuns were the first few people arrested during the CTA struggle. We stopped the buses on the Blue Island line. This was done to stop the traffic. We were on the ground, and I remember thinking, "I don't know how far we can go." My picture came out with me in a miniskirt with a *portavoz* (bullhorn) in my hand. My mother and my father both said, "¡Aii! You just got a job. You're going to lose it!" Here I am working for the state. I was hoping nobody would see that picture. If you know me, you know, but I had on a *boina* (beret). I'm standing in the middle of all the people lying on the ground. Thirty-two people were arrested in the third demonstration. It was building up, and there was increasing violence. You see Felipe in the *Sun Times,* putting up his hands and the billy club hitting him on the knees. I get goose bumps thinking about it. But I saw changes. You look around, and you can see some change. But if we had not fought, things wouldn't be where they are today.

The church wanted to get Jim out of the community. They offered him several parishes. He had a choice, but he wanted to stay working with Latinos. He was given a beautiful church on the North Side, where he became the pastor. This was before he decided to leave to Mexico. Jim invited me to leave Chicago, "Go organize where it really counts, Magda!"

"Yeah," I said. "It's easy for you to say. You don't have a family." He was assigned to a small church in Guerrero.[39] There was no phone, only an address where one could write to him.

I ran into Jim again when I had gotten an influential job working with an important historical figure in Chicago, the late Al Raby. Sometimes, things happen for a reason. I met Al Raby through a man I knew who worked for the Board of Education. I was going through a depression. I had just had my second child. She was about a year and a half. I needed to go back to work. I'd been offered a job that I wasn't interested in. My brother-in-law told me that someone had called asking about me. I had supported this person in some struggle. He was a supporter of César Chávez, too. We had been involved in that cause, and he knew Father Jim. He knew what kind of a person I was. He told my brother-in-law that he wanted to see me. I said, "I hope this is an interview." He said, "Magda, Al Raby needs an assistant. Raby needs a bilingual assistant." I said, "Oh, I'm supposed to be the token?" He said, "No, no, Magda, this is a real job." He explained that they had pressures to only hire Blacks but that Raby wanted to give a Latino a chance.

I hate competition. I'm not very good at it. The day of the interview, people came with leather portfolios. They had master's degrees. But Al Raby had a political reason to hire someone. He wanted an organizer, something out of the usual for a city job. At the second interview, he said, "What I like about you . . . because I already had a little history on you . . . was that you had a question back for me. You didn't ask the typical questions. You asked about my relations with the Latino community and how I felt about the fact that we had so few Latino representatives. I was impressed by that."

We built a good relationship. I wanted to know everything about the Chicago Commission on Human Relations. Raby would say, "I have a mission. Don't fuck with my mission. You can do whatever you want, but when I ask for a certain report, you have it." Every time a Latino group came to see him, he would ask for me.

I didn't like UNO (United Neighborhood Organization). They were a group that was not with the people. They were opportunists. One time, they invited several directors from different departments of the city to a meeting. I liked the way Al Raby operated. I also wanted a good relationship with him because I wanted the Latino community to be more involved. I was the only Latina there, one Asian and one Latina. Everybody else was Black or White. So, I wanted to keep some good political relationships. That evening, he sent me to the meeting.

They were asking for all the directors to come up to the podium. To come up to the little stage at a church on the South Side. I announced who I was representing. I knew what they were going to do. They were going to use the meeting as a platform to criticize the different department heads. They were going to scare the crap out of them. I didn't care for them, and I didn't respect them. I knew it was just about getting favors for themselves, not addressing the needs of the community. When Al got there, he asked, "What's going on?" I told him, "If I were you, I wouldn't go up there. It's just a bunch of crap." I said, "If this were a good organization, it would be different. But it's up to you," and I left.

The following day, he called me into his office. He said, "That was a wise move, Ramírez. I want to thank you. I owe you." That was all that was said. He was always very fatherly to me. Later, he asked me to recommend a Latino for one of the Humanitarian Awards that the commission gives each year. I was in the room when she was called. She was very excited. These are some of the good things that have happened to me. Al Raby died almost a year after Harold Washington.

End of a Collective Vision

When I look at the news today, I have flashbacks of the past. Back then, there were abuses against immigrant workers by the United States Immigration and Nationalization Service, and they continue today under, the United States Department of Homeland Security. Whatever the name of the bureaucracy, the same kind of injustice is being meted out to undocumented Latino workers. These are poor, honest, hard-working people driven to cross borders in search of employment because of economic policies that profit elites on both sides of the border, policies that derail healthy economic development in Mexico and other Latin American countries. Back then we had the Vietnam War, and today we have the war in Iraq and Afghanistan. "Bring our troops home now!" was what we demanded when we protested. Today, we march against the war and get told to go screw ourselves by the same government, which is only interested in making the rich even richer, even if it means more young people coming home in coffins or returning to their families permanently damaged, physically and psychologically.

Now, it is the responsibility of young people to take up the struggle against racism, war, and the exploitation of workers. Apathy is the greatest killer, the greatest disease, and the greatest enemy that stands in the way of social progress. Sometimes, I think we wait hoping that someone else will do it for us. I was always attracted to strong, intellectual men who saw something in me. I guess I looked to them for leadership. Ironically, I had to become the leader I had been looking for if I wanted to see change.

There were so many who impressed me. Yenelli impressed me. I was enthralled with some of her friends who were at the university. One of them was this intelligent young man that I perceived had a lot of knowledge. The way he spoke was very impressive. Then, Jonell Smith started coming around, and she was also progressive. These were youth who were thirsty for knowledge. They wanted to be part of the Movimiento for whatever reason, maybe something they learned about in college, or whatever, but they had an interest. They were coming from the university, and I didn't talk to them a lot because I was involved with the workers' group.

When I met some of these young people through Yenelli, I thought, "This is great." People like me who are a little older believed that when you got the youth, you got something here. I had this impression that a new set of people were becoming involved. I had the idea to take whatever experience I had, whatever knowledge I possessed, and put it back into the community and then let the youth come and build it, give it new blood.

Today, we are living in a very anti-Mexican, anti-immigrant, racist period. Despite this, my daughter Julissa courageously decided to name her child Che Emiliano. This legacy of rebelliousness, of opposition to oppression, is what I want to leave to my own children, the next generation. But back then . . . it was our time.

Notes

1. This introductory vignette was developed in collaboration with Magda Ramírez-Castañeda. The substance of this chapter comes from several interviews that occurred mainly in 1998 but continued through 2008.

2. A document distributed by APO charged that Latinos made up only 1.9 percent of CTA employees while Whites and Blacks each were 49 percent of the work force ("Latinos versus CTA," 1972).

3. One estimate places the crowd at closer to one thousand people, according to some people who were present.

4. Emiliano Zapata was an agrarian hero of the Mexican Revolution of 1910.

5. It is a common practice among Catholics to promise to pray at a shrine (in this case, the Virgin of the Lakes) for a certain length of time or fulfill another promise in exchange for a favor or to give thanks.

6. Magda, Margarita, and Norma Guadalupe are the names of the three girls referred to here. The diminutives are of first or middle names.

7. Normal schools are teacher-preparation programs integrated into secondary-level education, typically providing a few extra years' training beyond high school.

8. Sor Juana Inez de La Cruz was a seventeenth-century Mexican author and intellectual eventually silenced by the church for her nonconformity. Sor Juana championed the right of women to an education, and today is often referred to as the first feminist of the Americas.

9. Rag Town was a popular name for the Roosevelt Road merchant district where mostly working-class and poor people shopped. La Garra was known for its blues musicians, discount prices, and the sale of stolen goods.

10. *Siempre* was a Mexican magazine, its name perhaps alluding to the consistently problematic nature of political and social affairs.

11. Fulgencio Batista was thrown out of office by the 26 of July Movement led by Fidel Castro.

12. Anti-Catholicism and anticlericalism were characteristic of various revolutionary factions and governments, perhaps due to the church's traditional association with the old landed elite and the perceived overrepresentation of foreigners in the clergy, particularly Spaniards. Under the Mexican President Plutarco Elias Calles, these tensions came to a head. A Catholic-inspired rebellion was launched under the banner of "Long Live Christ the King." The Cristero Rebellion was waged from about 1926 to 1929.

13. Daley is Richard J. Daley, Chicago mayor. *Pigs* is a derisive term for police, used especially after the 1968 Democratic convention.

14. Paul Barrett taught at the Illinois Institute of Technology, among other colleges. He passed away in October 2004.

15. The Virgin of Guadalupe and other Mexican religious and cultural symbols were

used by the UFW and César Chávez to mobilize and unite the community in support of social justice for agricultural workers (Castillo & Garcia, 1995; Etulain, 2002).

16. LULAC active since 1929 is one of the oldest Mexican civic organizations in the United States. It has made many contributions to Mexican and Latino civil rights. However, it has also been criticized by many, particularly militants of the Chicano Movement, for being "assimilationist" and easily pacified. Contemporary Chicano assessments of LULAC have tended to be more generous out of respect for its impressive track record of advocacy, although there remains a sense among some activists that the organization is often too moderate and less relevant today.

17. In December 2003, Nora Villarreal, Magda's cousin and mentor, passed away. Other OLAS trailblazers include Carlos Heredia, Mina Heredia, Ada López, Omar López, Jesus "Chuy" Negrete, and Eleazar Mascorro. According to Carlos Heredia (personal conversation, May 28, 2009), "The first heads of OLAS were . . . Omar [López] and myself. Around 1970, there were two OLAS groups at then Loop College, one for day students and a second one for evening students. My wife, Mina, was president of the evening one. We also established another branch at Saint Mary's High School, on the west side, around Damen and Taylor. I can't recall the president's name. We also set up a base in the community, in Pilsen, at Saint Joseph's, a former parochial school, at 17th Place and Halsted. So we were in operation simultaneously at several locations. On Sunday mornings, we would conduct a general meeting for all the members to review progress, discuss issues, coordinate activities, and make plans for future actions."

18. *Gabacho* is often used pejoratively in the United States.

19. West of Chicago generally refers to the Black West Side area.

20. Magda would later advocate for a broad-based, multicultural alliance that united people based on their racial as well as class oppression.

21. Magda is referring to the 1970 Chicano Moratorium against the Vietnam War.

22. The Petrillo Band Shell was for many years the main outdoor, downtown performance venue in Chicago.

23. El Grito is Mexico's historic libratory proclamation that gave birth to the struggle against the Spanish crown and that eventually led to independence.

24. Magda is critiquing the commercialization and minimizing of the true character of Mexican patriotic holidays, which often commemorate the country's resistance to foreign intervention, including the United States.

25. The 1968 Tlatelolco Massacre was the culmination of a series of demonstrations opposing the authoritarianism of the Mexican government. Estimates of the dead ranged from the hundreds to the thousands. The Chicago protest was aimed at the presence of Luis Echeverria Alvarez, who many believe as interior secretary gave the order to carry out the October 2, 1968, killings. Echeverria subsequently became president of Mexico from 1970 to 1976.

26. Magda was elected Illinois chairperson of the Raza Unida Party and attended its first national convention as a delegate. Of the eighteen official Illinois delegates,

only a few were women, including Magda Castañeda and Cristina Vital. The presence of these women as leaders in this political process is testament to their determination. Others that attended the conference include Felipe Aguirre, Dora Martinez, Alberto Mendoza, Angel Moreno, Santos Rivera, Carlos Salazar, Eleazar Mascorro, Ruth "Rhea" Mojica-Hammer, Jose Valdivia, and Arturo Vasquez.

27. In the Midwest, the University of Iowa, through its Chicano and Native American Center, became a site of Midwestern Chicano activism, including through its student conferences. Nancy "Rusty" Barcelo was among the organizers of this annual event.

28. In 1997, Rosary College became Dominican University.

29. For more information on the life of one of the major Mexican leaders in the United States, see Garcia & Montgomery (1994).

30. The term *federales* is often used in reference to the government forces during the Mexican Revolution that fought the popular armies.

31. *Gusanos* (worms) is a derogatory term used to describe those who defected to the United States.

32. The shootings of antiwar protestors at Kent State University on May 4, 1970, led to demonstrations on college campuses across the country. On May 14 and 15, 1970, two students were killed at Jackson State University in a similar incident.

33. The Teacher Corps was a federally funded program to train teachers. The program had a unique curriculum and used a cohort model to prepare students to enter urban school systems.

34. Pablo Torres, a labor and community organizer in Pilsen, was seriously ill at the time of this interview.

35. Today, Jewel-Osco is a national food-store chain. It was the object of a Chicano boycott in the 1960s and 1970s because of its sales of nonunion produce.

36. *Migra* is often used derisively by Latinos and is short for immigration authorities, Immigration and Naturalization Service (INS), now U.S. Immigration and Customs Enforcement (ICE).

37. Magda is referring to the suspicion among community activists at that time that university hospitals sometimes admitted poor and limited English-proficient patients because the hospital could more easily obtain these patients' "consent" to participate in experiments. Concerns related to the abuse of poor and marginalized groups were given credence by the 1972 exposé of the Tuskegee Study. For more on the Tuskegee syphilis case, see J. H. Jones (1993).

38. Cardinal John Cody headed the Chicago Catholic Church from the middle 1960s to the early 1980s. He was aligned to Chicago's Democratic machine headed until 1976 by Richard J. Daley. Cody was accused of ruling with an iron hand, punishing priests who questioned his authority. There were rumors of corruption, but Cody would not voluntarily resign. He died in 1982.

39. Guerrero, a Mexican southern state, includes the coastal tourist haven of Acapulco. It has also been the site of armed uprisings, including one associated with the revolutionary Mexican icon, Lucio Cabañas Barrientos, who died in 1974.

Social Action

LEONARD G. RAMÍREZ

Foundational Sources of Opposition

Why do people become involved in social movements? There are many dimensions to this question that do not lead to simple generalizations. The vast majority of Mexicans in the 1960s and 1970s did not join the Movimiento. They did not realign priorities, uproot their families, or change the balance of their personal, social, and professional existence to make change the driving force in their lives. While there are no formulaic equations that can predict political involvement, the biographical fragments of these women help us to understand some of the elements and processes that allowed them to challenge generally accepted "truths" and refine their own interpretive lenses that encouraged social action.

As these women became alienated from prevalent ways of thinking, they came to reject what they believed to be the pervasiveness of false consciousness, what Patti Lather (1986/2004) views as rooted in "the denial of how our commonsense ways of looking at the world are permeated with meanings that sustain our disempowerment." The women felt compelled to make sense of society and their place in it by examining the nature of the system in light of its professed values, philosophical beliefs, and the approved practices of the day.[1] It was difficult for these women to ignore the contradictions they encountered. When social life and daily experiences fell far short of the "official story," each of them was driven to confront these incongruities. Segregation, relegation to low-wage jobs, discrimination at work and in public establishments, and lower expectations for women all acted to form deep crevices in the ideological and political edifice that claimed equality and fairness as its fundamental features.

Alienation from the narrative mainstream or the common stories that people construct to give meaning to their lives led the women to compose counternarratives, alternative framings of reality reflective of their own experiences. These developing narrative syntheses incorporated rudimentary analytical frameworks to which they had been exposed: family stories, their understanding of history, and the issues in their own lives to "tell" a different story. Their developing worldviews were aided by their positionality as working-class Mexicanas/Chicanas connected to immigrant communities. Their ambitions and paths diverged from a narrowly individualistic vision of personal mobility aimed at securing some semblance of the American Dream.[2] Instead, the women adopted a collective stance focused on social justice that was buttressed by the belief that struggle is endemic to every aspect of human existence. This facilitated a commitment to making fundamental change the central goal of their lives. The growing realization that the problems of brown-skinned, working-class people were patterned and structural, not exceptional or defined primarily by interpersonal conflict shaped their budding radical consciousnesses.

THE SOCIAL GOSPEL

Religion constituted an important moral system and font of meaning that motivated resistance. Faith-based perspectives have given rise to at least two broad socioreligious traditions. The first typically relies on scripture and prayer as venues to communicate with God. This more inwardly focused and pious perspective is often removed from the secular and the state of worldly affairs. It generally deemphasizes progress based on human intervention in favor of salvation linked to personal revelation and/or allegiance to biblical observance or some other call to religious orthodoxy. This tradition typically prioritizes the hereafter or personal salvation as the major focal point of the religious journey. Salvation is the consequence of behavior aligned to scripture, rooted in devotion or the outcome of a predestined mandate from God.

The other religious tradition often referred to as the social gospel is distinguished by a commitment to the improvement of life in the here and now. It requires the faithful to be concerned with the physical, economic, and emotional well-being of humanity. The social gospel is rooted in a religious mission that urges its followers to be invested in improving social conditions as a demonstration of one's faith and as a vehicle to foster personal and collective redemption. The social gospel offers a path leading to a good and ethical life. Even those not formally attached to a religion or who at some point disconnected from the church may nonetheless have been guided by the assumptions of the social gospel.

Religious beliefs sometimes motivated the search for truth and supported participation. It kindled compassionate concern and urged some of the women forward. In some cases, it "obligated" them to act in the face of oppression. Politics for Isaura was not simply a choice or a simple reaction to oppression but a compulsion to align her life to a greater purpose: "I think it was my fate to be active and to respond to this calling."

Religion and politics share many characteristics. Both are sites of passion and devotion. They are performative spaces, platforms where the rituals and the drama of life are enacted. Mexicana/Chicana activists of the 1960s and 1970s who eventually rejected the conservative messages of Rome and much of the Catholic hierarchy attempted to maintain a spiritual dimension in their lives. They looked to indigenous forms of faith or adopted other systems of belief. Still others returned to the church, rejecting what they saw as problematic, salvaging only what they believed meaningful for them.[3]

Clergy members involved in community activism served to bridge the revolutionary politics of *La Raza*. Their public example of involvement often served to validate the righteousness of resistance. The presence of religious leaders in social-justice campaigns, such as in support of the rights of farmworkers, evoked the human transformative message that activists believed religion originally once contained.[4] This bond between the oppressed and the clergy was renewed or reinforced with the emergence of liberation theology and Christian socialism in Latin America and other parts of the world in the 1960s and 1970s.[5]

RADICAL LEGACIES

Women such as Yenelli Flores benefited from a tradition of radical resistance and a more elaborated critical lens with which to comprehend life.[6] "I always had this consciousness in my mind . . . this consciousness about justice and being for the oppressed," she said. Her parents were antifascists and early supporters of the Cuban Revolution. A small but important core group of those who entered the ranks of the Mexicano/Chicano movement were introduced at a young age to earlier attempts to bring justice to the fields, even before César Chávez and Delores Huerta began to organize the UFW (Vargas, 2005).[7]

More socially conscious Mexicans looked toward their history highlighting, for example, the popular strands of the 1910 Mexican Revolution that spoke to the economic and political needs of disenfranchised populations. They identified not with the elites that eventually managed to harness the revolution but with the popular aspects of the rebellion. The revolt of *Los de Abajo,* the popular explosion that propelled the revolution forward, was for many Mexicans the most meaningful aspect of that upheaval.[8] The stories relayed by adults about the revolution provided youth with the rudiments of an analytical framework to interpret social reality. It also identified a primary dynamic in the lives of "those from below" and consequently in their own, the historical necessity of struggle.

A few women had personal connections to significant historical mobilizations in Mexico and in the United States. Magda Ramírez-Castañeda's father, despite his own father's wishes, had for a time been a union activist in the north of the country. He participated in the Death March of miners to Mexico City. Victoria Pérez's aunt Guadalupe Pérez Marshall Gallardo was invited by Ellen Gates Starr, one of the founders of Chicago's Hull-House, to attend a demonstration of striking steelworkers. She bore witness to the atrocity that would later become known as the 1937 Republic Steel Massacre. In the 1950s, Guadalupe Marshall was denied reentry to the United States because of her communist affiliations. Politics were, therefore, not far removed from some of these women's lives. However, class politics was but only one political tradition.

THE NATIONALIST LEGACY

While Mexicans and Chicanos often suffered from a profound sense of inferiority, the product of life in a racist society, many others possessed a deep and passionate love of their folklore and culture. The parents and grandparents of some of the women who crossed the border into the States often held the expectation that they would one day return to their beloved country of birth. Older family members shared stories of life in their homeland, and children were taught to respect, honor, and promote Mexican culture.[9] Public celebrations were celebrated by athletic and civic organizations. Even in such extremely racially tense areas as Texas (Mirandé, 1987), Mexicans dared to celebrate their cultural traditions and patriotic holidays.

In Chicago, young Mexicans enthusiastically participated in the social and cultural activities of the Mexican community. In the 1940s, Mexican cultural and patriotic festivities occurred in various places including the Centro Social Mexicano (Mexican social center).[10] Those with training in the arts, such as the Rico family, promoted cultural initiatives that played an important role in connecting youth to Mexican life.[11] The folkloric dance troupe that the Ricos founded was especially important in passing on culture to the young and actively engaging them in promoting *lo Mexicano,* or all that was uniquely Mexican to those who now lived in the diaspora.

Mexican cultural nationalism came via parents and family members. Those educated in the postrevolutionary Mexican educational system were more likely to be exposed to a curriculum that had been developed during a period of intense patriotism. Radical educators, including ardent nationalists and socialists associated with the Cardenist wing of the national party, created an educational curriculum that highlighted Mexican resistance to foreign intervention.[12] Ironically, this sentiment was eloquently voiced by the Mexican dictator Porfirio Diaz, who opened the door widely to foreign interests yet lamented, "Pobre Mexico tan lejos de dios y tan cerca a los Estados Unidos" (Poor Mexico, so far from God and so close to the United States). The annexation of Texas and the conquest of the Mexican northwest constituted a gapping wound, an unhealed lesion that defined relations between Mexico and its powerful neighbor to the north.[13] The cultural and folkloric components of Mexican nationalism blended with the political messages elaborated during the period of the Mexican Revolution and inflected nationalism with a revolutionary character that constituted a mixed legacy whose components could variously be integrated into the consciousness of later generations.

Mexican nationalists such as Victoria Pérez's father found themselves at odds with the more moderate wing of the Mexican American political generation. This group of leaders sought to secure full citizenship by demonstrating their loyalty to the United States through military service (Oropeza, 2005).[14] The moderates articulated a strategy of acculturation. They urged Mexicans to become more directed to the United States in order to gain rights and be treated as first-class citizens (M. García, 1989).

Socialist and nationalist political perspectives did not always comfortably coexist. How much nationalism and how much socialism one blended into one's politics often defined the political character of Mexicano/Chicano activists. Although Victoria's father rebuffed the "politics of loyalty," he did not always possess a radical class orientation or support socialist political agendas.[15] He shared an ethnic pride and desire for labor rights with the left, but he preferred nationalist analyses and interpretations over the class-based politics that for his sister led to a socialist alternative. Victoria's father's indecisiveness with respect to Guadalupe's more left-leaning ideals might have been influenced by his own professional aspirations. The often conflicting and competing political nature of nationalist and radical outlooks resulted in an ambivalent legacy that influenced the thinking of young activists as they entered the ideologically turbulent waters of the 1960s and 1970s. The divide among various forms of nationalisms (e.g., cultural, reformist, and revolutionary) and competing socialist visions became major points of contention that surfaced within the Mexicano/Chicano Movement and eventually contributed to its demise. Still, Mexicana/Chicana youth "saturated with history" felt compelled to become involved.

HISTORICAL LOCATION

The placement of oneself in history could increase the possibility of active resistance. It had the potential to link youth to a complex geographical and cultural identity. Placing oneself in a particular context of conflict facilitated a narrative logic from which to elaborate a vision of social change. It also served to connect concerned youth to radical activist traditions and provide those physically distant from Mexico with a sense of identity and pride. History had the power to address the inquietude of the young and ignite within them a sense of personal relevance and greater social purpose. It had the potential to reverse marginalization by repositioning Mexicanas/Chicanas as historical actors.

Those who did not come from passionate nationalist or socialist families may still have been affected. Isaura's family was not especially political. But when asked what her parents thought about the Vietnam War, she wryly responds, "What war? My parents were still fighting the war between Mexico and the United States." Framing her past on the historical border between combatant nations helped shape Isaura's politics. Her attachment to the symbolic lineage traced through the Mexican American War contributed to her understanding of the world. Her historical location encouraged her to interpret the events of the day against the backdrop of a contentious past. Chicano activists did not readily accept the elevated rationales that were used by the United States to justify military and political intervention and the eventual appropriation of Mexican land.[16] Historical parallels were easily drawn between Vietnam and Mexico, and the similarities were used to reinforce antiwar sentiment in the Mexican community.

Personal Sources of Opposition

IDENTITY

Adolescents and youth by definition are embedded in a transitional process. This is typically a period of self-definition and exploration of perspectives from which to interpret and engage the world around them. However, the social unrest of the 1960s is often simply dismissed as a product of youthful rebellion and generational conflict. This has allowed conservative observers to view the 1960s as a fleeting and less-meaningful phenomena, a youthful right of passage with little substantive message. This perspective ignores the critical issues that are involved for Mexican youth.[17] For subordinate groups at the bottom of the social hierarchy, the acceptance of societal assumptions is often the critical step in their internalization of personal and collective inferiority. If the democratic system is assumed to provide avenues for effective participation, equal access to opportunity, and economic mobility for all, then what can be deduced from differentiated social outcomes across racial/ethnic groups? Without a critical analysis, the educational and economic indicators that are commonly used to measure racial and ethnic progress can easily be read as signs of group failure.[18]

The ideological and social pressures for Mexican youth to succumb to the demeaning messages of cultural and racial inferiority prompted some to instead reject the master narrative and seek solace in their Mexican roots. It prepared those less connected to Mexico to consider alternate ways of framing their racial and political identities. New ideas emanating from the Southwest introduced innovative, complex, and radical outlooks that constructed a new Chicano identity. A hybridized notion of culture and race that affirmed working-class identity, and adopted a militant ethos, if not a revolutionary vision, constituted the powerful Chicano message. Chicanismo became a source of inspiration and a trigger for activism for many alienated Mexican youth.[19]

OPPRESSION

Linked to the search for a comprehensive identity, inclusive of both Mexican and United States experiences, was the need for Chicanos to define themselves along the axes of race, class, and gender. The hidden and not-so-hidden curriculum of schools implied that Mexicans had no history and made no significant contributions.[20] Their absence from textbooks spoke to their marginal status that was also made manifest in lowered expectations. Mexican children were "worth less," which helped to explain and perhaps even justify inferior schooling and their eventual placement further down the class hierarchy. Families who could not afford even a modest Catholic school education were relegated to the Chicago Public Schools that María Gamboa saw as providing poor quality schooling, which condemned community youth to a modest existence. Disconnected teachers, uninspired curriculum, and the assumption that Mexicans were in route to factories defined what public education meant for working-class youth. For many Chicanos, the message was clear: to be Mexican was to be inferior.[21]

Mexican youth were encouraged to either accept class oppression and the poverty that they often lived as the result of serendipity, personal, family, and group deficits or consider the possibility that inequality was a consequence of systemic dysfunction.[22] However, without a connection to radical nationalist or socialist oppositional frameworks or powerful religious values, it was difficult for youth to deflect corrosive social assumptions. Absent strong countervailing influences that could repel the omnipresent and powerful messages that on a daily basis reinforced damaging "truths," young Mexicans were often left with intense feelings of inadequacy and powerlessness. Fortunately, the motivation to reject inferiority was capable of coming from one's direct experience with oppression and discrimination, either observed or lived.

María Gamboa realized, "A lot of things that were happening to us were unfair." Circumstances in their own lives and the injustice that they observed around them made conformity unacceptable. "It was oppression that got me involved," she said. María's declaration suggests the stark reality that may have set some Chicanas on a journey distinct from their contemporaries. These women possessed a heightened sensitivity to differential treatment in neighborhoods and in schools. They felt themselves to be personally and profoundly affected by the racist assumptions and social structures of the day. Although at the onset they may not have had a developed ideological perspective from which to understand the nature of injustice, they nevertheless began to question the local logics that justified their continued subordination. They eventually set out in search of an interpretive filter with which to understand their position in society.

Racial and class oppression were sometimes accompanied by a sharp awareness of gender inequalities. Women were also "worth less." In some schools, this was reflected in a differentiated curriculum. Those fortunate to live among the White working class were privileged by a slightly more advantageous placement along the educational hierarchy. Yet, the opportunities for White women, relatively privileged by race, were still limited. A typical pathway was from schools to work; for many, it meant secretarial employment. Cristina Vital initially believed that higher education was available for only a few "smart" women. For the rest, raising families was the ultimate gender duty, obtaining a profession was the exception.

Middle-class women, Cristina Vital discovered, were allowed to aspire to careers and delay marriage. They were more likely to be encouraged to enroll in college-preparatory classes along with males. "There has got to be something more" expresses not only the 1960s' generational search for relevance but also the desire of women, provided with a narrowed view of the future, to make life more meaningful and personally fulfilling. Gender subordination constituted an increasing source of dissatisfaction that led some women to question the social arrangements to which they were expected to adhere.

Gender oppression was not solely embedded in institutional structures. It was experienced at many levels, socially as well as within communities and families. Sexism permeated institutional life, such as, in schools, but it also appeared in ethnic and personal spaces as well. Movement women came to identify their oppression and see it tied to the assumptions of patriarchy and capitalism. "The personal is political" is a slogan that emerged from within the White women's movement. However, long before this "truth" was widely popularized, many Latinas understood the impact of gender in their own lives. For some, sexism and inequality promoted involvement in social change. It gave María Gamboa a purpose and the desire to focus her political work on "recognizing [and promoting] women's leadership."

Contextual Factors

THE 1960S AND 1970S

The six activists of the Comité understood that their involvement was reinforced or deeply driven by the times in which they lived. These women are from the Vietnam generation. On a daily basis, they watched images of terrified children, napalm-scorched landscapes, battle-weary faces, and body-bag sacrifices offered in defense of a succession of dictators and Cold War generals, each one arguably more ruthless than the last. They also witnessed the tolerance of federal authorities to Jim Crow racism and Bull Connor justice, the repercussions of which were dramatically conveyed across television screens. This included Black protestors shaken by volleys from water cannons, beaten by club-wielding sheriffs, and intimidated by lunging police dogs.[23] The realization that what awaited Chicanas was absorption into a hierarchical system that assumed their subordination further deteriorated the legitimacy of the "official story." There is both an empathetic and highly personal component to the political commitment of these women. Even when they did not believe themselves to be personally affected by the worst of social prejudices, they felt the impact on the broader community with which they identified and were thus driven to action.

In the 1960s, Latin America joined the rising tide of nationalist armed resistance to foreign domination. Widespread opposition was fueled by rejection of economic models that favored developed countries. Resistance was also a reaction to the growing authoritarian nature of governments linked to foreign economic and political interests.[24] Seeing the control over their own populations deteriorating, elites responded with increasing repression. Countries once lauded for their respect for the democratic process produced massacres of horrific magnitude. Emblematic of these was the 1968 killing of unarmed students and workers in Mexico City and the 1973 coup in Chile (Poniatowska, 1975; Petras & Morley, 1974). In the face of popular revolt, the most conservative sectors of the Latin American ruling classes promoted limited democracy or out-and-out dictatorship. With the deterioration of civil society, armed guerilla struggles aimed at toppling repressive regimes appeared throughout the region.

The Cuban Revolution rekindled nationalist feelings across the continent. Many Latin Americans took special pride in Cuba's refusal to back down from the threats of the United States. Fidel Castro's bold disregard of North American authority suggested that the giant to the north was not invincible. Fidel became the champion of underdog nations, and Che Guevara the symbol of a new political morality and revolutionary popular resistance. In the United States, Magda's father "listened to the radio from Havana, Cuba. . . . He admired Castro a lot because '*Le dio los gringos en la madre*' (He screwed the gringos). My father would talk to me about injustices, and he would blame the United States." Antipathy to dictators allied to North American interests and identification with the poor and less-powerful nations recalled popular images of Mexican rebellion and contributed to the political development of Mexicano/Chicano youth.

It was by no means without consequence or sacrifice to be politically involved. However, for a time, there was growing social support for opposition among a small but increasing number of teachers, clergy, and certainly youth, particularly college students. Over time, Black civil rights, a blossoming antiwar movement, countercultural rebellion, and worldwide opposition to United States domination of Southeast Asia stirred massive opposition. Liberation struggles across the globe made social action if not acceptable, then at least not as completely isolating as it may have been for other activist generations. Pockets of resistance eventually entered public discourse. Political protest surfaced in somewhat unlikely quarters, such as within the military.[25]

Social unrest bred further resistance and inspired additional social movements, including those focused on women and gay liberation. As much as media pundits and public officials attempted to alienate progressive forces, left analysis and political militancy were becoming credible challenges to the political and economic system.[26] Cristina Vital felt that if not for the context of those times, she might never have become involved in social protest. Reflecting on the 1968 Democratic Convention with protestors camped in Lincoln Park just blocks away from her high school and the "whole world watching," she realized how much she was a product of the era. She saw herself as a more private individual. Yet, despite her retreating personality, she was overcome by a growing sense of responsibility and eventually joined the Movement. The windows of possibility had opened and change was in the air.

Anchoring Opposition

SOCIAL JUSTICE

The testimonies of these six Mexicana/Chicana activists in Chicago provide insights into the ways in which these particular women resisted and subverted the ideological forces around them. All of these women developed a keen sense of social justice. It was informed by a mixture of spiritual values, socialist and labor politics, nationalist and cultural loyalties, and a growing personal awareness of systemic, institutionalized oppression and injustice that was also present within local communities and even within families. The construction of oppositional narratives provided them with alternative ways to reflect and make sense of their lives. Their accounts highlight the elements that prevented their stories from being absorbed into the narrative mainstream. Their stories suggest how opposition can be sustained when linked to values that are anchored in one's location in history, specific legacies of resistance, spiritual inspiration, and cultural maintenance. They demonstrate the power of counterstories to inspire opposition when activated by memory and a search for truth beyond dominant ideological frameworks.[27]

Social justice often had a geographic location.[28] Nueva Rosita, Coahuila, is where Magda learned about racism through the stories told to her by her mother. It was also the site of her father's union involvement. Yenelli and Victoria associated social justice with the area around Chicago's Hull-House where many labor celebrations and worker's campaigns were initiated. Sometimes, the locations associated with resistance were local, such as, in neighborhood schools where inequalities were apparent or even within one's home where relationships of domination created cleavages and strained family bonds. Eventually, the new oppositional site for these women became the Pilsen community, which they saw as the location from which to participate in a national organizing effort aimed at radical change.

COLLECTIVE VISION

Social justice perspectives generally rest on a foundation of collective frameworks that tie individuals to communities. Speaking about the process of self-recovery, bell hooks (1989, 30–31) evokes "the way of knowing I learned from unschooled southern black folks. We learned that the self existed in relation, was dependent on its very being on the lives and experiences of everyone, the self not as signifier of one 'I' but the coming together of many 'Is,' the self as embodying collective reality, past and present, family and community."[29] The narrative voice of the six women follows along this same folk tradition. Even when using the first-person singular, "I," it is often meant to evoke the social "we."[30] While the women speak about their own personal experience, the broader reference is always to a larger community that is distinguished by a shared experience.[31]

The women's collective sense of identity fostered a them-against-us perspective. This was not characterized by exclusion but instead was used to make Mexicano/Chicanos aware of the necessity of unity for oppressed peoples. Mexicano/Chicano identity as an oppressed group was reinforced by international circumstances, since Chicanos saw similarities between Latinos and the Vietnamese. They also saw themselves reflected in the faces of the popular forces in Latin America waging armed struggle against their own national elites and imperialist allies (Oropeza, 2005; G. Mariscal, 2005).

The UFW worker's struggle was critical to the budding formation of activist consciousness. Witnessing the brutality used against defenseless strikers by sheriff's police and guards hired by California growers further helped to define Mexicanos/Chicanos as members of an oppressed group.[32] César Chávez, someone with an ambivalent relationship to the Chicano Movement, helped Chicanos to see themselves as part of a larger community (Muñoz, 1989). The UFW inadvertently played a role in radicalizing Chicano youth. It borrowed Mexican cultural and nationalist political symbols such as *La Virgen de Guadalupe,* the indigenous patron saint used by rebel armies during the Mexican Revolution, to promote *La Causa,* the cause. These cultural, historical, and revolutionary symbols beckoned Mexicans into the folds of a sacred community, and Chicanos interpreted them as a rallying call to political action.[33]

The 1965 grape boycott provided a practical means for Mexicans across the country to connect to a national political campaign. *La Causa* soon came to signify not only the fight in the fields but also the need for collective action to change the circumstances of Mexicans across the country. The union struggle provided early connective links to a "residual culture" on which the "protonationalism" of Chicanismo could be based.[34] Although the union boycott attracted a diverse following of clergy, liberal students, radical activists, people of all ages, and ethnic groups, Chicanos believed *La Causa* held a special meaning for them. The appearances of Chávez and Huerta on college campuses and community centers drew large numbers of Mexicanos/Chicanos. Even after El Teatro Campesino became independent of the UFW, it continued to disseminate the message of political awakening across the country, using symbols of cultural affirmation and class solidarity and projecting a message of revolutionary resistance.

THE IMPORTANCE OF STRUGGLE

The women identified with a powerful metaphor, struggle, which they saw as being a dynamic aspect in their lives. The concept of struggle was ubiquitous throughout their reflections. It was understood by them to be an elemental component of life. Struggle was described as almost a natural force embedded in the physics of the universe. Magda's account of her birth is indicative of this constant in the human life cycle. Her first breath was itself a struggle, and she was born into a life of struggle. María's defines her attempt to arrive at a healthy partnership with her husband as a struggle. She viewed this as a critical aspect of human relationships, especially given that the aim was equality. Yenelli warns that struggle is unavoidable: "One either struggles alone or chooses to struggle in a collective way." Each of the women sought to encourage people to struggle collectively because they believed it was the most powerful weapon that could be wielded by the oppressed against dominant social forces, especially to challenge institutional mechanisms of state control.

Chicanos also defined themselves as a hybrid people. This was not just a reference to their mixed Indian and European ancestry but also spoke to their various positionalities that provided them with a powerful vision, a third eye from which to experience and understand the world (Mora, 1993).[35] The development of a *mestizo* or border consciousness was an advantage that Chicanos possessed.[36] They were not limited to one or two optics that could be used to understand reality but were advantaged by a multiplicity of experiences and exposure to various and oftentimes conflicting narrative traditions, for example, those based on Mexican folklore, history and political realities as well as the national and local community influences formed across the border in the United States. Chicano social consciousness arose at the intersection of two national experiences, which facilitated the development in the 1960s, of an oppositional consciousness and a new legacy of resistance.

Chicanismo

The Chicano movement provided those with little direct connection to Mexico and those alienated from Mexican culture and history with an innovative framework to elaborate an identity. The assumptions of a society predicated on White supremacy motivated an internalized hatred and a weak sense of self for many Mexicans and Chicanos.[37] It fueled community divisions, especially among barrio youth. For those confused and in search of an acceptable identity, free of the negativity cast on *lo Mexicano,* Chicanismo carved out a definite cultural and physical space from which to elaborate a contemporary and dynamic identity. Somewhat ironically, Chicanismo had a boomerang effect, renewing for some their frayed connections to Mexico via the concept of Aztlán.

Chicanismo appropriated Mexican iconic symbols, borrowing freely from indigenous Mesoamerican cultures, especially the Aztec and Maya cultural traditions. It placed Chicanos on an epic journey. This history comprised multiple strands that began with the indigenous crossing of the Bering Straits, the Aztec migration to what would be become known as the Valley of Mexico, the Spanish Atlantic crossing to the Americas, and the eventual migration or, more aptly, the return of the indigenous and *mestizos* to the Southwest to join those who had never left.[38]

This historical weave tied Chicanos on both sides of the border to ancestral land. Chicanismo established a connection to a geographical location in the Southwest well before the arrival of Anglos to the continent and before they entered the Southwest as conquerors, thieves, and land robbers (Acuña, 1972). This borderlands cultural space, also known in Nahuatl as Nepantla, was not an ill-defined liminal territory, a neither-here-nor-there limbo. It was a definite geographic region, the product of specific historical forces.[39] For some, the Aztec space in the middle world was the American Southwest. The existence of Aztlán served as a beacon that summoned Chicanos to return and reclaim their lost lands.[40]

Chicanismo integrated the experience of Mexicans south and north of the border into a unitary narrative. It incorporated racially validating elements with cultural symbols that had roots in urban environments as well as in Mexico. This new alternative perspective provided a new historical synthesis, which acted to subvert stereotypical and racist social constructions.[41] An example of this reversal is evident in the elevation of the *bato loco* (crazy guy or dude).[42] The bato loco was refashioned as a quasi-political Robin Hood. Street youth were reconstructed as primitive rebels often responding with wit and insight to the injustices embedded in everyday life.[43] To some, this reframed *bato loco* became a role model and a source of inspiration.[44] Chicano opposition was evident in the *cholo* (marginal working-class Mexican) subculture of resistance that welcomed marginality from the mainstream. Allegiance to a community of alternative values reflected in a style of dress, language, *caló* (street argot of English, Spanish, and slang), and other aspects of street culture symbolized the oppositional conscience of Mexicano/Chicano youth.[45]

Organizations such as the Crusade for Justice encouraged the recruitment of bato locos into the Movimiento.[46] Community-outreach projects often sought to appeal to this segment through dropout-prevention, prison initiatives, and drug intervention programs. Some street youth and ex-offenders were attracted to the Movement and joined organizations such as the Brown Berets, a paramilitary Chicano nationalist organization that sponsored social programs and declared its willingness to use violence in defense of the community (Acuña, 2007; E. Chávez, 2002; and Muñoz, 1989).

Two of the Movimiento's most celebrated iconoclastic writers, Oscar Zeta Acosta and Ricardo Sanchez, admired certain attributes of the bato loco.[47] Both Acosta and Sanchez felt a special connection to their rebellious lifestyle and ethos. Sanchez had spent two terms in prison for armed robbery. Both had been born in poor Texas barrios and moved to California, where they maintained their connections to barrio street life (Acosta, 1972/1989 and 1973/1989; López, 2001; Stavans, 1996).

The new Chicano nationalism erupted with its own language, dress, emblems, history, and sacred icons that were informed by barrio images and aspects of immigrant Mexican culture. This new and more militant perspective inspired Chicanos to reject what they believed to be the Mexican American generation's emphasis on political accommodation, incremental reform, and assimilation.[48] Chicanos celebrated their mestizo identity, refusing to be blended into a false and humiliating White statistical category that might serve as a shield from discrimination (Valls, 1936/2000).

Chicano identity drew from Mexican history, particularly its revolutionary traditions, indigenous past, and mestizo cultural and racial heritage. It reconstituted cultural elements, straining them through a filter of community experience. This new identity integrated *rasquache* (coarse or vulgar) aesthetics and the bato loco outsider persona, which encouraged an attachment to *Los de Abajo*.[49] Chicanismo upheld the sacredness of community, cultural nationalism, and a vision of working-class popular resistance.

Chicanismo made it possible for youth to finally take pride in a newly reconstituted identity that operated to reverse the alienation that many Chicano youth felt toward *lo Mexicano*. Yet, ironically, it acted to bring them closer to their cultural roots. Chicanos hinged their identity on both a Mexican and a community axis that validated their own barrio experiences and provided them with a unique perch from which to understand and appreciate the culture of their parents.[50] For those with an already strong cultural identity, Chicanismo generally served to reinforce their Mexican cultural and historical traditions. For these Mexican-identified activists, Chicanismo's principal attraction was its political message, its rejection of the politics of accommodation and supplication (I. Garcia, 1997; Oropeza, 2005; G. Mariscal, 2005).

The Movement prioritized social justice. It established a new geography of resistance whether located in Aztlán or in local communities such as Pilsen where the fight was for community control, access to quality education, political inclusion, and working-class empowerment. Whether one accepted every aspect of Chicano culture or rejected the reinvention of Mexican identity, the focus on social justice was often enough to unite Chicago activists. For these six women, the goal was not only the reform of society but ultimately its ultimate transformation. Whether as nationalists or socialists, their vision was centered on the establishment of new values and social priorities and the creation of a racially just society.[51]

The first National Chicano Youth Liberation Conference sponsored by Rodolfo "Corky" Gonzales's Crusade for Justice was held in Denver, Colorado, in 1969. The conference drew participants from across the nation, the majority from California (Muñoz, 1989). The conference galvanized the Chicano struggle into a national movement. It also operated as a forum for Corky Gonzales, Luis Valdez from El Teatro Campesino, and Alberto Baltazar Urista (Alurista), a student activist and artist from California, to articulate the poetics of *Chicanismo*. The resolutions from the conference were incorporated into El Plan Espiritual de Aztlán, the Spiritual Plan of Aztlán, a document that connected liberation to a Mesoamerican cultural and political legacy.

Shortly thereafter, a second conference was called in California by the Coordinating Council on Higher Education (CCHE) as a follow-up to the Denver meeting. Primarily attended by student activists, the ideas raised at the California conference were compiled in the Plan de Santa Barbara, a document that signaled the official birthplace of a national Chicano student movement. Many local campus groups renamed their organizations MeChA. MeChistas sought to link the identity of Chicanos to the historic Aztec homeland, believed to have existed in the Southwestern portion of the United States (Menchaca, 2001; Muñoz, 1989).

Muñoz (1989) credits Valdez for initially linking Chicanos to an indigenous identity.[52] Valdez played a major role at the Denver conference. He "argued that there was only one identity appropriate to the oppressed Mexican American, and that identity was rooted in the non-White indigenous past and in the working-class history of the people. Valdez stressed the Native American roots of Mexican American experience and diminished the role of the Spanish, who were European and White" (quoted in Muñoz 1989, p. 63). Alurista in his "Epic Poem of Aztlán" articulated the specific connections between Chicanos as a "Bronze People" tied to a long history beginning with the migration of the "Chichimecs" from their ancient Aztlán homeland and the cultural flow that led back to the original Aztec lands located in the United States Southwest. The ethnic politics embedded in Alurista's poetics challenged the perception of Mexicans as a recent migration. His outline also provided a historical foundation for ethnic pride, a defense against continuous racism and ethnic disparagement that Chicanos experienced in *el norte* (the north).[53]

Complications

ETHNIC AND POLITICAL IDENTITY

Chicago's Movimiento displayed certain unique features. The Movement followed a slightly different timeline than the other major Movement centers in the Southwest, particularly California, Colorado, and Texas.[54] This may be due to the relative infancy of Mexicans in the Midwest as compared to regions where the presence of Mexicans predates that of Euroamericans. The extensive history of Mexicano/Chicano settlement in many areas of the Southwest facilitated the development of social and political networks and the formation of community. For much of the early part of the twentieth century, there was no predominantly Mexican community in Chicago, although there were several major areas of settlement. The establishment of Pilsen as a majority Mexican neighborhood did not occur until the 1960s, which perhaps not coincidentally parallels the development of the Movement in Chicago. As Yenelli and others state, it was upon the return of activists from the 1969 and 1970 National Chicano Liberation Conferences that a more fully developed consciousness of being part of a national Chicano movement occurred. However, by this time some of the more emblematic events of the national Chicano Movement had already taken place.

Chicago was also distinguished by its unique mix of Latino populations. The city had a spread of immigrants from across Latin American, which at that time was not common in other parts of the nation. While Mexicans constituted the majority, sizable populations of Puerto Ricans and Cubans existed and even predominated in certain areas of the city. The numbers of South Americans although initially small also increased over the decades, especially given the economic deterioration experienced by the popular classes and the heightened and continuous repression in Latin America. Although small in numbers, social activists escaping turmoil and repression in Latin America began to play a role in the broader Chicago Latino movement.

Most Mexicans in Chicago were immigrants or the direct descendants of immigrants. Families often had children born in Mexico and in the United States. In Chicago, there was no community where second- and third-generation Mexicans predominated. Activists were as likely to be born in Mexico as in the United States. Even if they had come as children, the constant inflow of Mexican immigrants diminished the cultural and political presence of the second generation and gave Chicago's growing Latino community an immigrant character.

Demographic realities lessened the presence of the second and third generations. Therefore, it was much more difficult for Chicano activists alone to define the character of the Movement in Chicago. Mexicans were often reluctant to accept the new Chicano identity. They suspected its motivations. To some, it appeared that Chicanismo was but a variant of "Mexican American" and double ethnic names were seen as colonized appellations, signs of an attempt to escape or dilute one's cultural identity. Debates regarding the use of the term *Chicano* occurred on college campuses and in the community. Eventually, Mexican activists began to identify with the political dimensions of the term while muting the cultural messages emanating from the Southwest. Some Mexicans saw the value of using the Chicano identity as an educational tool. They referred to themselves as Chicanas/os to highlight their political resistance. However, for some youth, the term had a profound cultural as well as political significance. The Chicago compromise was the commonly used Mexicano/Chicano expression that allowed for the coexistence and/or blend of the full range of ethnic identities without giving preference to any one.

BECOMING CHICANA FEMINISTS

In addition to regional, ethnic, and generational characteristics, the role of women and the elevation of gender issues in the Mexicano/Chicano agenda became major points of contention locally and nationally. Differences developed among Chicanas over their understanding and prioritization of gender oppression, the perceived obstacles that they encountered as women in the Movement and the manner in which to address the patriarchal attitudes of Mexicano/Chicano men. This divide has been characterized as a schism between "feminists" and "loyalists" (A. Garcia 1997, p. 7). Accordingly, Chicana feminists moved aggressively to include gender as a central component of the Chicano agenda while loyalists moderated or even silenced their gender critiques for the sake of Chicano unity.[55] Feminist politics in some instances led to the creation of Chicana caucuses or even independent organizations. On the other hand, loyalists attempted to address gender issues by cautiously maneuvering within male-dominated organizations or focused their efforts on other areas of oppression or simply succumbed to male dominance and accepted their limited role in the struggle. The experiences of these six women from the Comité suggest the need for a more complex framing since their relationship to feminism cannot so easily be situated within this polarity.

Women of the Comité came to understand and appreciate the importance of gender discrimination as a *political* issue at various times in their lives. María Gamboa, Cristina Vital, and Magda Ramírez saw gender as a primary component of their early political consciousness. Gender, race, and class became intertwined in a message of inequality that urged their growing commitment to social justice. These elements were not unchanging or always equally balanced. Awareness of gender and race were more pronounced early in life for some women, while the consciousness of class may have been understood only as they began to unravel the often intertwining and confusing nature of racial and class relationships in the United States.

Gender consciousness developed both within personal and social contexts. Daughters often experienced gender hierarchy within families. They witnessed its affect on the lives of their mothers, siblings, and themselves. Patriarchal control whether in the form of punitive or benevolent authoritarianism was often the norm. However, the subordinating messages of gender were also communicated through the media and other social institutions. The media supplied women with images of themselves as well as role models of what they could aspire to become. Women were largely portrayed as weak and in constant need of protection given their generally vulnerable natures. School curricula narrowly defined women's options. These differential expectations assumed that women would play limited roles in society because of their biological or psychological natures.

While all of these six women became leaders, they did not all elevate gender as a critical political priority. Three of the women saw class and race as the major community obstacles. Sometimes, it was a question of not seeing sexist practices for what they were, such as when parents placed greater importance on the professional futures of their male children or when a different standard of behavior was used for men. The lack of parental support or other debilitating family dynamics were sometimes seen as affecting all siblings equally and not a specific obstacle imposed solely on women. Since they did not perceive gender barriers as serious impediments in their own lives, they were more prone to prioritize other forms of oppression.

Interestingly, the greater resiliency and determination of these women sometimes led to their minimizing the affects of sexism. Initially, they may not have felt that their personal and professional advancement was seriously affected by family or societal attitudes and structures. Their personal strength and resourcefulness often led to individual resolutions to problems whenever they were encountered. Should a man stand in the way of a woman's progress, it was obvious that she should dismiss his objections and move forward. The barriers and issues that some of the women encountered could be understood as idiosyncratic aspects of individuals or something peculiar to a situation or accounted for in some other nonsystemic way. However, while some women did not feel particularly constrained by the assumptions or limitations of patriarchy, this does not deny that sexism and the conservative gender arrangements of society did not affect them or play a role in structuring their lives.

Comité members as a group began to appreciate the necessity of raising gender issues to the level of a political priority with greater exposure to Chicana feminist theory and as they began to understand how gender might be included as part of a political practice. Their consciousness of these concerns also increased as they began to appreciate the importance of sexism for the women around them and as they began to feel the impact of gender creep into their own lives. It was only as Yenelli grew older that the encroaching obligations of marriage, motherhood, and economic survival began to constitute a systemic vice limiting her ability to sustain the level of involvement characteristic of her early youth.

All of the six women rejected mainstream feminism or what they often labeled White feminism. Yet, some Comité women felt gender was very much a part of their political activity. The poor treatment of community women and their generally overburdened lives were apparent to all. Some even saw Mexicana/Chicana concerns and their empowerment as a priority of the Comité's work. However, although convinced in varying degrees of central aspects of White feminist critique, they collectively felt that the feminist movement primarily focused on greater upward mobility for already economically well-positioned women.[56] White feminism's emphasis seemed unduly concerned with professional glass ceilings and not on making life better for working-class women. In the eyes of these Mexicanas/Chicanas, mainstream feminist critique had a developed political practice and policy agenda for some segments of society but was insensitive or ignored the needs of others, perhaps even of those women with the greatest need.

The varying and ambivalent reaction of these women to feminism shifted as more information about the "woman question" became available and as an understanding developed of how these issues affected them on a personal as well as on a political level. However, in the early 1970s, a Mexicana/Chicana feminism had yet to be comprehensively elaborated and made available to these Mexicana/Chicana community activists. They as a group were generally unclear how to move from feminist critique to a Mexicana/Chicana feminist practice, specifically how to make use of a feminist perspective and integrate it into their daily organizing practice with mainly working-class, immigrant women and men.

Another critical aspect of these women's experience is that while they came together in coalition, their political practice was often in smaller units, as members of cultural groups or as community, labor, or student organizers. The six Comité women did not belong to a male-dominated political structure. They did not exist in an organization with a steep hierarchy.[57] Members were free to develop their own projects and had many opportunities to exercise leadership. These smaller collectives often solicited the cooperation of the network only when necessary, although they might rely on the Comité for political direction and resources. In addition, the six women were central to the network. They were among the leadership core. They were important organizers, and they contributed to determining the group's projects and general political direction. As a network of mobilizers, these women rejected White feminism; however, as individuals and participants in other groups, they were able to prioritize Mexicana/Chicana women's issues in their daily political work, and ultimately, this also informed their collective political practice in the broader network as well.

While the women criticized the sexist behavior of groups or individuals in and out of the Comité's orbit and struggled with issues of sexism in their own personal lives, gender discrimination was not seen by them as a major organizational obstacle.[58] Through their political involvement, the women developed a more thorough understanding of sexism and the importance of the "woman question" in the life of the community and in the Movement as a whole. However, despite their varied responses to gender issues and how gender was perceived as operating in their own lives at any given moment in time, these activists were all strong, independent women and valuable community leaders. They did not conform to the agendas of men or collapse in the face of male resistance to women's equal participation. They were often strong advocates for women in their respective spheres, sometimes without a full understanding of how their work was addressing the needs of community women. In many ways, each of these women was an archetypal example of a Mexicana/Chicana feminist.

MOVEMENT QUESTIONS

The Comité as an organizing center faced formidable challenges that impeded its progress.[59] The group's weaknesses generally reflected those of the 1960s antiwar left and social justice movements whose character had largely been forged on college campuses and at times was spiritually more connected to international revolutionary movements than the pulse of change in local communities. For much of its history, the Comité was fueled by the moral commitment and political fervor of the national Chicano liberation struggle and other similar movements within the United States as well as the antico-lonial and liberation struggles that erupted across the Third World.

REFORM OR REVOLUTION

Many political groups and individuals contributed to the Mexican com-munity's progress during the 1960s and 1970s. Civic organizations such as PNCC built largely on the Alinsky model initiated a number of important campaigns, such as, the fight for a new high school in Pilsen.[60] The partici-pation of traditional organizations such as LULAC was less evident but not unimportant. Latino liberal leaders, especially those associated with com-munity agencies, at times provided support and created an environment that generated enthusiasm and facilitated mobilization.[61] These organizations and individuals also provided a level of legitimacy since they were often already recognized by the political establishment and had greater access to resources. Political officials generally preferred to work with civic groups and established representatives because they were seen as "reasonable" commu-nity power brokers, more inclined to compromise and less likely to resort to militant tactics.[62]

In the 1970s, the Movement was a critically important engine for social change. El Movimiento in Chicago as in other cities included cultural na-tionalists, revolutionary Mexicano/Chicano nationalists, traditional Commu-nist Party members, and revolutionary socialists.[63] The latter included those influenced by the revolutionary wave emanating from Latin America and the New Left college-based politics of the United States. In the community, the left acted as a pressure on civic leaders and organizations to be diligent, honest, and responsive to local concerns or risk the loss of credibility in the community. Mass meetings, conventions, and cultural and political events created public forums where issues were debated and criticisms often aired.

Not all those pushing for social change shared similar visions or utilized the same strategies and tactics. Some groups and individuals were issue oriented. Others possessed a broader reform agenda. The majority of concerned community people probably never affiliated with any organization.[64] However, the two major Third World left tendencies played pivotal roles in Pilsen: CASA-HGT, a national grouping with a more formal organizational structure, and the Comité, an informal, activist network of small working groups. Both acted as mobilizing centers with allies across the community and within other organizations such as APO and Casa Aztlán. The Third World left supported specific issues and social reforms but believed that only through profound structural change would the fundamental inequalities of society improve the status of working-class Mexicans. The importance of the radical left cannot be overemphasized. Members of these two groups often provided the people, energy, and at times even gave strategic direction to major community campaigns.

A chief strength of the Comité was its involvement across a variety of contexts. The Comité attended most public meetings in the community. Wherever neighborhood people gathered to discuss problems and develop solutions, Comité representatives were present. The activities of the left put it into close contact with various segments of the community, including agency staff and administrators, civic leaders, artists, teachers, workers, small-business owners, students, immigrant families, and the spread of residents associated with churches. However, work among these sectors was never prioritized nor objectives clearly defined. Projects arose as a function of individual interest or as a response to a crisis. The character of the network was such that policy decisions were difficult to make and even harder to implement. The development of a common set of priorities and clear sense of mission that might serve to better direct the efforts of the group never materialized.

A broad range of political views was present in the community. Yet, there was little understanding of the necessity to focus less on differences than on commonalities. One of the major sources of tension occurred between reform-oriented individuals and groups and the left. The Comité had no consistent approach that identified friends and prospective allies. Basic issues such as deciding what relationships to develop into productive collaborations or alliances were not thoroughly discussed or decided. Some members worked well with members of the clergy, while others suspected at least some religious leaders as self-aggrandizing, manipulative leaders, quick to patronize and quick to impose their perspectives.

The slow pace of change often promoted by these liberal activists and their easy accommodation to city-hall politics was often misunderstood. Although some reformers were opportunistically focused on self-promotion and only wished to institutionalize their roles as community brokers, the purpose of others was to engage institutional elites and politicians in a dialogue in order to maneuver and win a demand. Reformists valued partnership with politicians and other influential stakeholders, while the left focused on community empowerment and integrating neighborhood residents into a process of radical change, which for the most part relied on permanent mobilization. How reformers and radicals implemented their objectives often led to suspicion and animosity. But there were few strategies proposed to address these practical concerns. Comité activists entered into each struggle without a plan that could be implemented and assessed across time. It had no method for accumulating wisdom on the challenges it confronted that might serve as a practical guide to the future.

Tensions within the left in Pilsen remained largely untheorized. For a time, Mexican leftists and activists groups on 18th Street worked together on specific issues for the good of the community. However, relationships among political groups in the competitive, left political environment of the 1970s became easily frayed. No consistent approach to conflict was formulated, and relationships were often discarded without formal reflection or intervention. This was true of the Mexicano/Chicano left in general that allowed national political tendencies and local coalition partners to unduly influence relationships within the Mexicano/Chicano community.

Collaborations with local activists resulted in some successful community actions. Building relationships with APO, Casa Aztlán, and other community groups had achieved positive results. The independent message of the network attracted artists and young people with Chicano-oriented politics. However, recruitment into a loose activist structure did not always result in consistent participation. It was often necessary to invest time and effort to convince affiliates and sympathizers to become involved in activities. Recruits often drifted across groups or remained affiliated but independent. This made it difficult to rely on their involvement.

Without a strategy, the Comité looked largely to the organized left outside of Pilsen with which to build long-term alliances and set a more permanent direction. A leadership group within the Comité attempted to switch to "a party building mode" that might address organizational questions and provide the Comité as a whole with a strategic direction.[65] The Comité invited various left groups to discuss their political positions as a first step in the development of a formal relationship. However, this approach, although broadening the circle of Comité allies, provided no long-term positive results, perhaps because the unraveling of the Comité may have already been irreversible.

ORGANIZING CHANGE

Two strengths of the Comité were its fluid structure and flat hierarchy. These created an environment that facilitated the rise of women to leadership. The Comité's flexible and open character also encouraged a range of activists to become affiliated. It welcomed Chicano revolutionary nationalists, some of whom eventually expanded their public agendas to include issues of class and gender. Yet, the fluid structure of the network also posed serious limitations. Its highly participatory nature and the organization's open democratic process operated inefficiently, involving members in long and exhausting meetings. Activists entered and exited the group easily. This added a degree of instability to the network. There was also only a vaguely defined agenda that activists shared, and launching a campaign could require that all those in the network be convinced of its importance before moving forward. This was time consuming and often demoralizing. The quality and consistency of cooperation made sustaining a major effort a complicated endeavor. This resulted in a few people shouldering an inordinate amount of responsibility, such as occurred around the management of the bookstore.

In order to improve their effectiveness, Marxist groups across the country adopted centralist organizational structures with developed cadre structures and defined leadership hierarchies. Ideally, centralist practices encouraged debate, but once discussion was completed, members were expected to support group decisions. It was a mechanism in part designed to balance democracy and effective action. However, this did not always produce the intended results.[66] The development of mass organizations was another option. However, this organizational form has also been met with criticism. Creating mass organizations in times of widespread mobilization, some argue, may actually work to minimize protest and reduce the possibilities of reform. Rather than operate as a useful tool to coordinate and institutionalize resistance, mass organizations may lead to demoralization and cooptation (Piven & Cloward, 1979).

Examples of innovative organizational forms that have been lauded for their ability to unify otherwise-competing constituent groups while providing a buffer of protection from external forces and preventing the drift toward oligarchy include leadership coalitions such as those used in the South to secure Black civil rights (Morris, 1984) and mass organizations with chapter or unit autonomy such as SDS in its earlier days (Breines, 1980). Yet, the Comité, which possessed aspects of each of these participatory forms, was not able to identify an effective organizational vehicle to meet the long-term particular needs of activists under the conditions that prevailed on 18th Street.[67]

DEFAULTING TO ACTIVISM

The Comité lacked a comprehensive analysis of conditions and a practical work plan capable of tying social reform to the goals of fundamental structural change. Social justice activists in Pilsen did not possess a realistic understanding of the dynamics of reform or the broader process of social change. Like much of the 1960s left, the Comité relied on international models of transformation that were never formalized into a meaningful vision of reform and transformation relevant to a local community constituency. Instead, the Comité operated mainly on an ad hoc basis, and important aspects of its work were never formally structured. The group rarely developed a unified response to major community issues or elaborated a comprehensive strategy or program to guide its efforts.

The Comité typically initiated projects as a reaction to events, for example, actions in support of local strikes, a new neighborhood high school, or in solidarity with national campaigns, such as UFW boycotts and international solidarity, including antiwar protests. However, the network did attempt to use multiple and creative mobilizing approaches. Street theater supported direct actions and operated as a popular education venue. Educators associated with the Comité encouraged parents to begin school-improvement projects. Comité leaders were at the head of efforts to create a Latino student cultural center at UICC. The Comité helped to provide valuable direct services such as those offered by Nuestro Continente bookstore for adult learners. The bookstore also served as an organizing resource, meeting place, and visible site of community resistance.

Yet, the ad hoc style of the network gave it a rather scattered character. Initiatives were often uncoordinated, and the Comité was handicapped because it did not incorporate projects into a unified plan with a larger scope of purpose. Members functioned without a sense of overall direction or knowledge of how one activity was logically connected to another. For the most part, there was no sense of where things were heading or how the various projects of the network fit into a comprehensive strategy for fundamental social change.

As happened across the country, the Mexicano/Chicano left helped to create greater opportunities for traditional political participation. However, the Comité never thoroughly discussed the possibility of entering into local political elections. Some members held an all-spaces-must-be-contested position; yet, others felt participating in the "electoral game" held few rewards. They feared it would drain resources or, even worse, reinforce the illusion that a corrupt and oppressive system was, in the long term, capable of meeting their needs.

As a group, the Comité took an agnostic position on elections; therefore, the potential benefits and drawbacks of voting were never thoroughly analyzed. As a consequence, an arena of participation that the Comité had indirectly helped to create was left for others to pursue. In effect, this ceded the field to those with a more limited sense of change or, still worse, to those with only personal gain as their primary motivation. The possibility of using elections as a mobilizing vehicle that could reach greater numbers of people was never seriously considered by the Comité.

CULTIVATING LEADERS

In order to make change a permanent feature of the community, the ongoing incorporation of new leaders was necessary. Some initiatives were put into place that provided an opportunity to outreach to members of the community. Political forums facilitated the identification of those with an interest in issues and the capacity for leadership. At every turn, Comité affiliates met people across many organizing contexts who expressed an interest in the group and community-mobilizing efforts. However, there was no structured mechanism to inspire, commit, train, and integrate prospective leaders.

Informal mechanisms predominated. New recruits could be invited to meetings or a social occasion or asked to fulfill some function at an event. Given the charged nature of the times and the proliferation of activities, prospective recruits were typically pressured to immediately take on major responsibilities. It was easy for the inexperienced to become intimidated and overwhelmed. Social movements in the past have been fortunate to have access to resources that played important roles in developing leaders. The Highlander Center in Tennessee, a leadership institute, served this function for the Black civil rights movement as it had previously for labor (Morris, 1984). The existence of such resources was not commonly known among 18th Street activists in the city, and nothing similar developed locally for the Mexicano/Chicano Movement.

THE PACE OF SOCIAL CHANGE

The left operated with an understanding that fundamental change was imminent.[68] Faith in the inevitability of revolutionary change for a time was able to buoy the spirits of 1960s activists. This was promoted by Third World revolutionary leaders and representatives of the left worldwide.[69] The Comité internalized the urgency and rhythm of antiwar student organizers working to halt the devastation of Vietnam, the suffering and loss of human life, the necessity to support revolution abroad, and to end racist practices at home. Over the long haul, this permanent state of crisis and mobilization dissipated resources and fostered an unrealistic view of social change. It also discouraged the development of an overall analysis of specific conditions nationally and locally that might function better as a guide. Activists commonly defaulted to the apparent "obviousness" of world revolution evidenced in the current events of the day rather than develop an analysis of local conditions.

Third World revolutionary activists often existed in two worlds.[70] They witnessed the revolts that were occurring internationally in the 1960s and 1970s, which confirmed their belief in the necessity and inevitability of revolutionary change. Yet, at any given time, activists could be involved in many low-intensity skirmishes, a fight for a stop sign, improved city services, or school repairs. The relevance of local struggles was not always apparent. Local issues often seemed disconnected and less relevant to the dramatic events unfolding across the globe. The gap was wide and often disillusioning. The Comité operated without a framework to establish short-, intermediate-, and long-term goals. Absent a comprehensive framework for social change, the chasm between local work and world revolution only widened.

Although a vibrant and exciting period, the intensity of the 1960s and the 1970s created unrealistic expectations. Organizations assumed that activists should be involved in every campaign, work to exhaustion, and make profound personal sacrifices (M. R. Chavez, 2000; Pulido, 2006). A more realistic approach would have integrated prospective recruits at a level and in a way that made sense to their own personal lives. Instead, the sometimes severe, activist morality of the times counterposed personal goals with a rigid understanding of collective purpose and an unrealistic standard of dedication. To be a leader was to uphold the collective interests of the community and to be self-sacrificing at all times and at all costs. The standard bearer was Ernesto "Che" Guevara. It was a formulation guaranteed to promote self-doubt and disaffection. Activists hardened to one another, and sometimes the spirit of solidarity and humanistic concern dissipated (Pulido, 2006).

Moreover, the creative energy and passion that had initially characterized the left were replaced with a mixture of abstract theory, academic conceptualizing, and often formulaic nostrums with pretenses to scientific authority. Activists forgot what had attracted them to the Movement. The "truths" that compelled them to be involved were ignited through systems of meaning that fueled their passions and created a vibrant vision of change. The magnet of mobilization was linked to powerful symbols, an inspiring iconography, and a transformative message of hope. One joined the ranks of the Movement out of concern but also because it had much to offer. Radicalism at its best was a counterculture, not merely a prescription to address societal disease. The inability to renew and project a compelling vision of change made it difficult to recruit new activists to a process of organized struggle.

Repression and infiltration took their tolls, and these also contributed to the unraveling of the movement. The deaths at Kent State and Jackson State Universities, the assassination of Fred Hampton, and the general repression against Third World groups, including the Black Panthers and the Crusade for Justice in the United States, all played a role in the unraveling of the 1960s left (Churchill & Vander Wall, 2002; Vigil, 1999). Since at least 1969, the left had been imploding in a splintering process, which resulted in a battle of competitive groups increasingly detached from a collective vision of change and alienated from their potential constituent bases of support. In addition to state-sponsored attempts to dismantle the left, cultural and political shifts were occurring across the country. Those threatened by the rise of an effective American left took advantage of the opportunity to play on the insecurities and fears of others who felt threatened by what they perceived to be the domination of minorities. The cultural wars of the 1980s that continue to this day constitute a prolonged backlash against the 1960s. The drift to the right and the dispersal of progressive forces created a leadership void, and the left has been incapable of mobilizing a response to the highly organized and well-funded conservative movement that culminated in the rise of Ronald Reagan and the Republican Party.

REGAINING THE VISION

Community activists worked tirelessly to improve the lives of working-class Mexicans. The efforts of the Pilsen left together with that of many others helped reshape a marginalized community and transform it into a visible constituency with increased capacity to attain resources and secure its rights. Comité militants were among those who pressured for reform, expanded opportunities, and improved the overall position of Mexicans and other Latinos in Chicago. In the end, however, it failed to establish a community-based organizational structure or institutionalize a process capable of promoting radical social change.

The Chicano Movement ignited the passions of Mexican activists around a collective vision of social justice. The Comité as part of the Third World left helped to bring various forces together and move a community forward. Pilsen ignited with an energy that produced significant change. Ordinary people stood up and made history. Mexicanas/Chicanas in Chicago were at the forefront. Without their contributions, little would have been accomplished. Although the vision of a united fighting community, *un pueblo en lucha,* fractured and then collapsed, each generation offers renewed hope that its youthful leaders will take up the struggle and build the unity that can make profound social change possible. Women will undoubtedly be among its leaders. When that moment arrives, the Chicanas of 18th Street will be present, marching alongside the new wave of social activists.

Notes

1. Wilkerson (2007) in her activist memoir refers to the "post World War II rhetoric of liberal Christianity, Judaism, and democracy" as an important motivating force in her personal sixties journey and eventual life as a member of the Weather Underground. There is often an assumption that only those from the upper-middle classes and intellectual elite are moved by social and philosophical contradictions. The stories of these women from Pilsen challenge such assumptions.

2. It is common to hear in the stories of immigrants and their children aspects if not fully developed versions of the American Dream. However, beneath the first layers of these stories often lie fragments or more-nuanced and variegated accounts that are perhaps richer in meaning.

3. For examples, see Anzaldúa (1999), Castillo (1995), and Mora (1993).

4. Priests in Pilsen played an important role in the Movement. They were associated with civic organizations or even left groups. However, they were at times criticized for imposing a Catholic-style authoritarianism on organizing efforts. However, many activists praised the sacrifices of priests and nuns. They admired the hard work of religious leaders and their willingness at times to go against the local conservative church leadership. They saw certain members of the clergy as important community allies or even prime movers in certain struggles.

5. See Cardenal & Walsh (1978) for an example of a religious community organized around principles of liberation theology.

6. Several names of nationally known Mexicanas/Chicanas surface as early radical participants in United States social-justice movements. Among these are María Varela, community organizer and photographer, and Elizabeth "Betita" Martinez, writer and activist. Muñoz (1989) mentions Varela and Martinez as early leaders of the Chicano Movement with past participation in SDS and the black civil rights movement. See a biography of Varela at http://www.takestockphotos.com/pages/varela.html.

7. The Chicano generation inspired research on Mexican participation in social activism and labor militancy. Two more recent examples are Varga's (2005) review of twentieth-century labor militancy that touches on agriculture and the essays collected by J. García and G. García (2005) that focus on immigration and agricultural labor in the Pacific Northwest.

8. The expression *Los de Abajo,* often translated as "the underdogs" or "those from below," is the name of a popular novel about the Mexican Revolution written by Maríano Azuela (1963).

9. Obviously, not all Mexicans remained attached to Mexico, since, as María Gamboa makes clear, government corruption and abuse of the poor encouraged some to turn away from their country of birth.

10. The Centro was located at Roosevelt Road and Western Avenue in Chicago.

11. The Rico family has a long musical tradition that includes preservation of Mexican culture in the United States. José and Angelina began the Chicago Fiesta Guild, a dance troupe that participated for many years in the Museum of Science and Industry's "Christmas around the World" holiday event. José and Angelina have four children, all of whom were involved in music. Elena Rico sang with the Chicago Symphony Orchestra Choir. For many years, George Rico, who taught at Lane Technical High School, organized a community *Messiah* production performed by volunteers. Angelo is a violinist and educator. Manuel is also involved in the various cultural projects organized by the Rico family.

12. Lázaro Cárdenas was Mexico's president from 1934 to 1940. For a discussion of the cultural legacy of the Mexican Revolution and case studies, see Vaughan (1997).

13. Anzaldúa (1999) refers to the border as an open wound.

14. The Mexican American generation is generally defined as the leadership group that was active between 1930 and 1960.

15. For a discussion of the politics of various political tendencies that can be incorporated under the umbrella of the Mexican American generation, see M. T. Garcia (1989).

16. Mexicans activists eventually accepted the complex nature of the colonial past, learning to appreciate the complaints of Native Americans, who reminded Chicanos of the rights of the indigenous to their land.

17. For a discussion of the role and importance of youth in the 1960s, see Muñoz (1989).

18. Ogbu's (1974, 1991) controversial theory addresses differences in the ways that immigrants as opposed to involuntary minorities understand schooling and social outcomes. See Valencia (1997) for a discussion of the prevalence and evolution of deficit models in the academy.

19. The debate around the fundamental character of the Chicano Movement continues. Muñoz (1989) argues that the Chicano Movement was a "counter-hegemonic struggle," while authors such as I. Garcia describe the Movement in more amorphous terms (e.g., radical ethos), perhaps emphasizing the more liberal or reformist nature of its political trajectory.

20. For an examination of school ideology and processes of disempowerment embedded in education, see Loewen (1995), Macedo et al. (2006), and Spring (2001).

21. Ogbu (1974, 1991) suggests an alternative framing for immigrants.

22. There were other alternatives. Ogbu (1991) mentions the often elaborate stories immigrant parents tell children to explain their current circumstances. This often involves a descent from a loftier social status or stories about individual family members that previoiusly achieved a high level of economic or professional success.

23. Bull Connor was a local law-enforcement official in Birmingham, Alabama, during the Black civil rights movement. His affiliation with the Ku Klux Klan became emblematic of a typical Southern faded-line structure of local control where police authority overlapped with racist vigilantism. The Jim Crow system of segregation was encoded in a series of laws that operated mainly in the South. The term *Jim Crow* was taken from a popular song that stereotyped Blacks.

24. Andre Gunder Frank's work (1969, 1970, and 1972) is central to the extensive critical literature on Latin American development and underdevelopment. Mexicano/Chicano activists along with other youth were impacted by Eduardo Galeano's popular *Open Veins of Latin America* (1973).

25. David Zeiger's film *Sir! No Sir* is a good documentary source for the GI movement.

26. Today's conservative media often reinterpret left analysis to mean any position to the left of the far right. Thus, a mildly liberal position or even a centrist perspective is often characterized as "left." The broad definition of the left used here describes those focused on social change and a more socially just society.

27. Galeano and Fried (1998) provide a more dynamic definition of memory: "When it's truly alive, memory doesn't contemplate history, it invites us to make it."

28. For a discussion of geography and resistance, see Valle and Torres (2000) and Villa (2000).

29. In her 1989 volume, hooks fears that this communal perspective may deteriorate with the passing of time.

30. Beverley (1989, Spring) speaks about the simultaneity of this dual-lens perspective.

31. Biographies of Mexicans living in the United States have been written across a continuum characterized by collective-oriented versus individually oriented frameworks. Two Mexican-immigrant narratives typify this spread of narrative perspectives: E. Galarza's *Barrio Boy* (1971) is representative of the collective voice that hooks refers to, while Luis Pérez (2000) exemplifies the more picaresque, individual voice. Interestingly, while Galarza committed his life to social justice, Pérez's only civic engagement may have been with the Republican Party.

32. For a moving Chicana autobiographical account that highlights the road to an oppositional consciousness as a response to personal oppression, see the story of María Elena Lucas (Buss, 1993).

33. See Anderson (1983) for a discussion of the development and role of socially constructed or "imagined communities."

34. E. Chavez (2002) uses Eric Hobsbawm to define protonationalism as "the consciousness of belonging to or having belonged to a lasting political entity." Raymond Williams is the source of his understanding of a residual culture, "experiences, meanings and values, which cannot be verified or cannot be expressed in terms of the dominant culture, [yet] are nevertheless lived and practiced on the basis of the residue—cultural as well as social—of some previous social formation" (p. 9).

35. The inclusion of Africans and other racial influences into Mexicano/Chicano lineage was slow to develop. But Chicanos accepted and promoted the concept of being a "cosmic race," a blend of peoples from all continents.

36. Anzaldúa (1999) later elaborated the idea of a border consciousness.

37. For classic political works centered on the psychological damage related to colonialism and White supremacy, see Memmi (1965) and Fanon (1952, 1963).

38. This Chicano historical vision is encapsulated in Rodolfo "Corky" Gonzales's epic poem "Yo Soy Joaquín" (I am Joaquin) (1972).

39. See Anzaldúa (1999) and Mora (1993).

40. Menchaca (2001) discusses the broad historical accuracy of Chicano conceptions of Aztlán.

41. The practice of reversing meanings as a means to challenge stereotypes forms part of the arsenal of resistance shared by other marginalized groups.

42. Bato loco is also spelled vato loco.

43. See Hobsbawm (1965) for a discussion of primitive rebels.

44. The uplifting of certain Mexican males as symbols of resistance while erasing Mexican females or ascribing to them traditional gendered identities is interrogated by Ramírez (2009). Mexicanas/Chicanas raised their concerns over the male-centered vision of Movement activists, arguing for the need to include women in the agenda for social change. The resistance to redefining women's roles in the Movement and incorporating feminist issues produced division and became another major fault line that led to the fragmentation and the eventual demise of the Movement.

45. Chicano theater was a common vehicle promoting indigenous community wisdom via the example of the bato loco through either negative example or enlightenment that came as the result of experience.

46. In a similar vein, the Black Panther Party urged the politicization and recruitment of street youth and gang members.

47. While Acosta's writings and passionate commitment to Chicanos was admired, many took issue with his rampant sexism. Patriarchal attitudes such as those of Acosta led to disillusionment on the part of some Chicanas and the eventual departure of some from Movement organizations.

48. Acuña (1972) and M. T. García (1989) are among those that have sought to correct this limited and in many ways inaccurate assessment of the Mexican American generation.

49. *Rasquache* is loosely translated as coarse or vulgar behavior, attitudes, or a sensibility, which Chicanos elevated to be meaningful and resistant.

50. This reinterpretation and blending of styles and categories have been associated with the concept of postmodernism.

51. There are many perspectives on the meaning and politics of Chicanismo. For different perspectives see I. García (1997), E. Chávez (2002), Gomez-Quiñones (1990 & 1994), and Muñoz (1989).

52. Treviño (2001) discusses his prolonged stay beginning in January 1974 with Valdez's teatro at their center in San Juan Bautista. Valdez had once been associated artistically with the radical San Francisco Mime Troup and politically with the Progressive Labor Party, a communist organization (Muñoz, 1989). At the time of Treviño's stay, Valdez espoused a "neo-Mayan philosophy" as the foundation for a Chicano libratory perspective that would replace liberal democratic principles and Marxist communism. Muñoz (1989) also mentions Valdez's much-later espousal of a form of assimilation.

53. Although Alurista's ideas were initially considered mythologized history, Menchaca (2001) supports the accuracy of aspects of this vision although she credits the reestablishment of historical ties to the period of the Spanish expansion into the north when Mexicans reentered the Southwest as a conquered people. See also Muñoz (1989) and Rendon (1971).

54. For a local history of the Movimiento, see Montejano (2010).

55. R. A. Gutiérrez (1993, March) suggests that narratives of the Chicano Movement understood exclusively through the lens of patriarchy or individualism have worked to obscure important issues of class.

56. Not all Comité members were aware of the various factions and politics represented in the organized Chicago women's movement.

57. While the women did not see sexism as a major barrier within the network, this does not mean it was nonexistent. They encountered sexism within the broader Movement, and even within specific groups within the network. However, the women always felt that by engaging in struggle, they were capable of changing attitudes and behavior. As leaders, they generally did not feel silenced or marginalized by others within network groups.

58. Issues did arise. For example, certain men tended to see themselves as the "theoreticians," but the involvement of the women in all areas of political work never allowed this kind of separation to materialize. In smaller units such as within the teatro, sexism and its assumptions did become points of contention as is evident in the accounts of both María and Victoria.

59. Block (2003) provides a specific set of leadership tasks in his review of "poor people's movements."

60. Valadez's (1985) dissertation provides an account of the prolonged effort to build Benito Juárez High School in the Pilsen community.

61. Padilla (1985) briefly discusses the importance of community agencies as a place where concerned people transformed into activists.

62. There was a significant degree of mobility across organizations and political

perspectives. Some civic leaders moved to the left. Others who began their careers on the left moved right. This was true not only of individuals but of organizations as well. Organizations that initially possessed a more Third World, left character drifted back to traditional Communist Party politics.

63. Another perspective on the nature of Mexicano/Chicano Liberation is in C. Mora (2007).

64. The Movement possessed a political ethos and was an attempt to unite around a common racial and ethnic identity; it was also a move to promote change, including revolutionary change. These all helped to define the Movimiento (I. Garcia, 1997; E. Chavez, 2002; Gomez-Quiñones, 1990, 1994; Muñoz, 1989).

65. For a discussion on how the 1960s left attempted to reorganize and build highly structured socialist leadership groups, see Elbaum (2006) on the party-building phase of the left.

66. Pulido (2006) discusses the limitations of centralism as an organizing principle with respect to the Los Angeles experience.

67. The definition of leadership and its role in social movements became major issues in the immigrant-rights Movement years later (L. Ramírez et. al, 2010).

68. Richmond (1973) emphasizes the need to develop a long view of social change.

69. Third World nations included those in Africa, Asia, and Latin America. A. G. Frank and others from the "dependency" school of analysis argue that these nations were distinguished not by their state of being in a process of development but by their being in a continuing state of underdevelopment, which largely benefited the major Western capitalist powers.

70. Pulido (2006) uses the term *Third World left* to describe 1960s and 1970s Marxist organizations of color. These groups typically looked to Africa, Asia, and Latin America for inspiration. They represented a blend of nationalism and socialism. The Black Panther Party was the most recognized Third World left organization of the period.

Women of 18th Street

Our Preliminary Assessment

YENELLI FLORES, MARÍA GAMBOA,
ISAURA GONZÁLEZ, VICTORIA PÉREZ,
MAGDA RAMÍREZ-CASTAÑEDA,
CRISTINA VITAL

> The Movement brought unity. . . . It brought
> us together for the same cause.
> —María Gamboa

What Was Gained

The Movimiento took steps to overcome some of the barriers that have tradi-
tionally divided Mexicans and deterred their formation into a strong political entity. Nationally, the Movement's response to racism and political and
economic disenfranchisement was community empowerment. In Chicago,
the Comité used popular education and direct action to fight for reforms
and recruit others to the process of social change. The long-term goal was
the creation of a unified and mobilized community that could join with
broader forces to offer an alternative to the economic and political system.

While activists of that period did not transform society or resolve the
problematic circumstances faced by the majority of Mexicans, some gains
were made. Families received health care. Immigrants were informed of
their rights. Workers attempting to unionize, secure a livable wage, and stop
workplace abuses received support. Pilsen activists also opened up employment opportunities that improved the lives of many families.

Nationwide, the pressures that the Movement exerted brought additional
resources into neighborhoods. Locally, this helped fund community cen-

ters and programs for children and adults. Activists helped stop the use of mobile trailer units to address school overcrowding and organized to fight for new schools and improve education. We joined the campaign to build a new library in Pilsen and pressured for bilingual programs so that children would not fall behind or lose their native language. Latino citywide coalitions pressured colleges to admit and support working-class and poor Latinos, not just at token levels but in greater numbers. University recruitment and support programs, cultural centers, and Latin American and Latino studies programs were founded to teach youth their history, develop self-awareness and pride, and prepare them for leadership.

The Comité also had a popular educational agenda. Grassroots education programs brought antiwar and alternative educational policy perspectives into the community. Through the Chicano bookstore and other ways, we made critical scholarship and journalism available to people who generally did not have access to alternative points of view. It was presumed that with greater exposure, working-class people would be more likely to contemplate issues that at first glance might seem unrelated to their lives. The left encouraged community residents to consider fundamental (radical) questions about racism and class inequalities. Militants affiliated with the network used the arts, including music and theater, to raise concerns about sexism and issues that came from the lived experience of ordinary people. The Comité sought to facilitate the critical capacity of Mexicano/Chicanos, who, equipped with a more accurate sense of their own interests, could develop a more profound understanding of policy and politics.

It often took the mobilization of many community sectors to produce results, but the Comité was in the thick of most of the important struggles of the day. The network was not always the leading force, but together as a group or as individuals with a dedication to *La Causa*, we were on the picket lines, passed out leaflets, organized events, marched down city streets, sat in, got arrested, or were involved in other forms of protest, direct action, and organization. Our objective was not to become Chicago-style politicians or in any other way be absorbed by the system. We were working-class Mexicanas/Chicanas that took responsibility for the empowerment of our community.

Fault Lines in the Struggle

In our attempts to be better organized and refine a process that could provide consistent and quality leadership for our community, we invested too much time and effort attempting to link up with groups that had already begun to lose touch with the realities of everyday people. This process ended up dissipating our energies and demoralizing our friends and allies. Competition among Pilsen-based left groups discouraged cooperation and sometimes made it next to impossible to work together to achieve important community goals. This eventually cast a gray cloud over the Movement and worked to depress enthusiasm for community organizing and progressive leadership.

Physical and emotional exhaustion followed years of intense organizing and political infighting. Infiltration by law-enforcement agencies seeking to destabilize the movement increased our paranoia. At the end of the era, there was no thorough discussion of the effectiveness of various strategies and tactics. Differences among groups were not clarified, and, therefore, many valuable lessons have yet to be gleaned from that period.

Opportunists from the right and even some with ties to the progressive movement filled the vacuum of electoral politics that the left had opened up. This is a development that has yet to be fully analyzed. While we have different notions about the value of electoral politics, we all agree that any set of tactics is bound to fail in the long run if social justice becomes secondary to electoral jockeying that typically defaults into casting votes for the lesser of evils, perhaps a necessary tactic but not a vehicle that can drive real change. There must be an alternative to the two-party dictatorship. However, if electoral initiatives are utilized, they must be anchored to a vision of social change that can benefit our communities, not self-promoting individuals and certainly not the narrow interests of political machines and economic elites.

Some of us were unrealistic about the sacrifices that each organizer was expected to make. As a consequence, there were times when families got neglected, personal goals were left unaccomplished, and some of those things that gave us great personal joy and satisfaction were ignored and put on a back burner until some indeterminate future. Luckily, many of us were able to rebound after years of personal neglect. Yet, none of us regret our involvement. Despite the errors and excesses of the time, it was the most exhilarating period of our lives, possibly the most productive. We still believe in collective struggle to achieve a more just society. The energy and enthusiasm of the 2006 immigrant-rights megamarches renews our optimism.

We Did What Needed to Be Done

It is difficult to find the words to describe what it is like to contribute to the making of history. It is a satisfaction that we will always cherish. We helped make the world a better place for those who followed, although we realize that nothing lasts forever, struggle is never over. It just takes new forms and responds to changing circumstances. The fight to secure social justice and create a new and more humane society is an ongoing process.

We all have had personally fulfilling moments as activists. The Movement enriched our lives in so many ways. It was a great way to meet extremely interesting and compassionate people. The Movement also laid the foundation for how we see the world and who we are today. The six of us gained many skills. Through the movement, we found our voice as activists and as women.

We believed in the potential of people, and we all saw what could be accomplished by a group with an ideology and purpose. It is time to reclaim what we are losing and take the fight beyond where it was left. All the raw materials are still available to us. We can reach back and mold it to respond to today's needs. When we were together in the struggle, we saw the Movimiento as being constantly renovated by new activists. We wanted people to share in a vision of a better future. We wanted them to understand that this would only come if we became an active fighting community, *un pueblo en lucha*. We all assumed that continuous waves of people would join the struggle. We wanted to take whatever experience we had, whatever knowledge we possessed, and put it back into the community and then let the youth come and build it, give it new blood. But back then . . . it was our time.

References

Acosta, O. Z. (1972/1989). *Autobiography of a brown buffalo* (Illus. ed.). San Francisco: Straight Arrow Books. (Reprinted from New York: Vintage Books).

Acosta, O. Z. (1973/1989). *The revolt of the cockroach people.* San Francisco: Straight Arrow Books. (Reprinted from New York: Vintage Books).

Acuña, R. (1972). *Occupied America: The Chicano's struggle toward liberation.* New York: Harper and Row.

Acuña, R. (2007). *Occupied America: A history of Chicanos* (6th ed.). New York: Pearson Longman.

Adelson, A. (1972). *SDS.* New York: Charles Scribner's Sons.

Alejo, B. (2008). *The Latino landscape: A metro Chicago guide and non-profit directory.* Notre Dame, IN: University of Notre Dame.

Alinksy, S. (1946/1969). *Reveille for radicals* (2nd ed.). New York: Vintage Books Paperbacks.

Alpert, J. (1981). *Growing up underground: The astonishing autobiography of a former radical fugitive—and the illumination of an American era.* New York: William Morrow.

Anderson, B. (1983). *Imagined communities: Reflections on the origin and spread of nationalism* (Rev. and extended ed.). London: Verso.

Anzaldúa, G. (1999). *Borderlands/La frontera: The new mestiza* (2nd ed.). San Francisco: Aunt Lute Books.

Arredondo, G. F. (2008a). Lived regionalities: Mujeridad in Chicago, 1920–1940. In V. L. Ruiz and J. R. Chavez (Eds.), *Memories and migrations: Mapping Boricua and Chicana histories* (pp. 93–120). Urbana: University of Illinois Press.

Arredondo, G. F. (2008b). *Mexican Chicago: Race identity and nation, 1916–1939.* Urbana: University of Illinois Press.

Avakian, B. (2005). *From Ike to Mao and beyond: My journey from mainstream America to revolutionary communist.* Chicago: Insight.

Ayers, W. (2001). *Fugitive days: A memoir.* New York: Penguin.

Azuela, M. (1963). *The underdogs.* New York: New American Library, Signet Classic.

Badillo, D. A. (2004). From *la Lucha* to Latino: Ethnic change, political identity, and civil rights in Chicago. In G. Cardenas (Ed.), *La causa: Civil rights, social justice, and the struggle for equality in the Midwest* (pp. 37–53). Houston: Arte Publico.

Banfield, E. C. (1970). *The unheavenly city: The nature and future of our urban crisis.* Boston: Little, Brown.

Berger, D. (2006). *Outlaws of America: The Weather Underground and the politics of solidarity.* Oakland, Calif.: AK.

Beuttler, F. W., Holli, M. G., & Remini, R. V. *The University of Illinois at Chicago: A pictorial history* (Illus. ed.). Charleston, S.C.: Arcadia.

Beverley, J. (1989, Spring). The margin at the center: On testimonio (testimonial narrative) [Special issue: Narratives of colonial resistance]. *Modern Fiction Studies (West Lafayette), 35,* 11–28.

Block, F. (2003). Organizing versus mobilizing: Poor people's movements after 25 years. Review of poor people's movements: Why they succeed, how they fail. *Perspectives on Politics, 1,* 733–735.

Breines, W. (1980). Community and organization: The new left and Michels' "Iron Law." *Social Problems, 4,* 419–429.

Brown, Elaine (1992). *A taste of power: A black woman's story* (1st ed.). New York: Pantheon.

Broyles-González, Y. (1994). *El Teatro Campesino: Theater in the Chicano movement* (Illus. ed.). Austin: University of Texas Press.

Buhle, M. J., Buhle, P., & Georgakas, D. (1991). *Encyclopedia of the American left.* Urbana: University of Illinois Press.

Buss, F. L. (1993) (Ed.). *Forged under the sun/forjada bajo el sol: The life of María Elena Lucas* (Illus. ed.). Ann Arbor: University of Michigan Press.

Cardenal, E. (1978). *The gospel in Solentiname* (Donald D. Walsh, Trans.). Maryknoll, N.Y.: Orbis.

Castillo, A. (1995). *Massacre of the dreamers: Essays on Xicanisma.* New York: Penguin.

Castillo, R. G., & Garcia, R. A. (1995). *César Chávez: A triumph of spirit* (Illus. ed.). Norman: University of Oklahoma Press.

Chávez, E. (2002). *¡Mi raza primero! (my race first): Nationalism, identity, and insurgency in the Mexican movement in Los Angeles, 1966–1978.* Berkeley: University of California Press.

Chavez, L. (1991). *Out of the barrio: Toward a new politics of Hispanic assimilation* (Illus. ed.). New York: Basic.

Chávez, M. R. (2000). "We lived and breathed and worked the movement": The contradictions and rewards of Chicana/Mexicana activism in El Centro de Acción

Social Autónomo. Los Angeles, 1975–1978." In Vicki L. Ruiz and Chon Noriega (Eds.), *Las Obreras: Chicana Politics of Work and Family* (pp. 83–105). Los Angeles: UCLA Chicano Studies Research.

Chungara, D. B., with Viezzer, M. (1978). *Let me speak! Testimony of Domitila, a woman of the Bolivian mines.* New York: Monthly Review.

Churchill, W., & Vander Wall, J. (2002). *The Cointelpro Papers: Documents from the FBI's secret wars against dissent in the United States.* Cambridge: South End.

Coyle, L., Hershatter, G., & Honig E. (1979). *Women at Farah: An unfinished story* [Brochure]. El Paso, Tex.: REFORMA.

Deutschmann, D. (Ed.). (1987). *Che Guevara and the Cuban revolution: Writings and speeches of Ernesto Che Guevara.* Sydney: Pathfinder/Pacific.

Dominquez, D. M. L. (n.d.). Recent history: Don Mariano Leyva Dominquez. *Nuestra Familia Unida.* [Recording]. http://nuestrafamiliaunida.com/podcast/recent_history.html#dm.

Dunbar-Ortiz, R. (2001). *Outlaw woman: A memoir of the war years, 1960–1975.* San Francisco: City Lights.

Eastwood, C. (2002). *Near west side stories: Struggles for community in Chicago's Maxwell Street neighborhood.* Chicago: Lake Claremont.

Elbaum, M. (2006). *Revolution in the air: Sixties radicals turn to Lenin, Mao, and Che* (Illus. ed.). London: Verso.

Elshtain, J. B. (2002). *The Jane Addams reader.* New York: Basic.

Etulain, R. W. (Ed.). (2002). *César Chávez: A brief biography with documents.* Albuquerque: University of New Mexico Press.

Fanon, F. (1952). *Black skin, white masks.* New York: Grove.

Fanon, F. (1963). *The wretched of the Earth.* New York: Grove.

Fernández, L. (2005). *Latina/o migration and community formation in postwar Chicago: Mexicans, Puerto Ricans, gender, and politics, 1945–1975.* Unpublished doctoral dissertation, University of California, San Diego.

Frank, A. G. (1969). *Capitalism and underdevelopment in Latin America.* New York: Monthly Review.

Frank, A. G. (1970). *Latin America: Underdevelopment or revolution.* New York: Monthly Review.

Frank, A. G. (1972). *Lumpenbourgeoisie and lumpendevelopment.* New York: Monthly Review.

Galarza, E. (1971). *Barrio boy.* Notre Dame: University of Notre Dame Press.

Galeano, E. (1973). *Open veins of Latin America: Five centuries of the pillage of a continent.* New York: Monthly Review.

Galeano, E., & Fried, M. (1998). *Upside down: A primer for the looking-glass world* (M. Fried, Trans.) (1st ed.). New York: Picador.

Ganz, C., & Strobel, M. (Eds.). (2004). *Pots of promise: Mexicans and pottery at Hull-House, 1920–40.* Urbana: University of Illinois Press.

García, A. (Ed.). (1997). *Chicana feminist thought: The basic historical writings* (Illus. ed.). New York: Routledge.

García, A. (2002, July–August). Toward a left without borders: The story of the Center for Autonomous Social Action—general brotherhood of workers. *Monthly Review, 54,* 69–78.

García, I. M. (1997). *Chicanismo: The forging of a militant ethos among Mexican Americans.* Tucson: University of Arizona Press.

García, J., & García, G. (2005). *Memory, community, and activism: Mexican immigration and labor in the Pacific Northwest.* East Lansing, Mich.: Julian Samora Research Institute.

García, J. R. (1996). *Mexicans in the Midwest, 1900–1932.* Tucson: University of Arizona Press.

García, M. T. (1989). *Mexican Americans: Leadership, ideology, and identity, 1930–1960.* New Haven: Yale University Press.

García, M. T., & Montgomery, D. (1994). *Memories of Chicano history: The life and narrative of Bert Corona* (Illus. ed.). Berkeley: University of California Press.

Gitlin, T. (1993). *The sixties: Years of hope, days of rage* (Rev. ed.). New York: Bantam.

Gómez-Quiñones, J. (1990). *Chicano politics: Reality and promise, 1940–1990.* Albuquerque: University of New Mexico Press.

Gómez-Quiñones, J. (1994). *Roots of Chicano politics, 1600–1940.* Albuquerque: University of New Mexico Press.

Gonzales, R. (1972). *Yo soy Joaquín: An epic poem.* New York: Bantam.

González, G. G., & Fernandez, R. A. (2003). *A century of Chicano history: Empire, nations, and migration.* New York: Routledge.

González, J. G. (2010). *Bringing Aztlán to Mexican Chicago: My life, my work, my art.* M. Zimmerman (Ed.). Urbana: University of Illinois Press.

Griswald-Del Castillo, R., & Garcia, R. A. (1995). *César Chávez: A triumph of spirit.* Norman: University of Oklahoma Press.

Gutiérrez, J. A. (1998). *The making of a Chicano militant: Lessons from Cristal* (Illus. ed.). Madison: University of Wisconsin Press.

Gutiérrez, R. A. (1993, March). Patriarchy and individualism: The politics of Chicano history and the dream of equality. *American Quarterly, 45,* 44–72.

Hillard, D., & Cole, L. (1993). *This side of glory: The autobiography of David Hilliard and the story of the Black Panther Party* (1st ed.). Boston: Little, Brown.

Hobsbawm, E. J. (1965). *Primitive rebels: Studies in archaic forms of social movements in the 19th and 20th centuries.* New York: Norton.

Honig, E. (1996, Summer). Women at Farah revisited: Political mobilization and its aftermath among Chicana workers in El Paso, Texas, 1972–1992. *Feminist Studies, 22,* 425–452.

hooks, b. (1989). *Talking back: Thinking feminist, thinking black.* Boston: South End.

Jacobs, H. (Ed.). (1970). *Weatherman.* Berkeley, Calif.: Ramparts.

Jacobs, R. (1997). *The way the wind blew: A history of the Weather Underground.* New York: Verso.

Jones, A. E. (1928). *Conditions surrounding Mexicans in Chicago.* Unpublished doctoral dissertation, University of Chicago.

Jones, J. H. (1993). *Bad blood: The Tuskegee syphilis experiment* (Rev., expanded, illus. ed.). New York: Simon & Schuster.

Kerr, L. A. N. (1975/2000). Chicano settlements in Chicago: A brief history. In M. G. Gonzales & C. M. Gonzales (Eds.), *En aquel entonces (in years gone by): Readings in Mexican American history* (pp. 109–116). [Reprinted from *Journal of Ethnic Studies, 2* (Winter 1975): 22–32]. Bloomington: Indiana University Press.

Kerr, L. A. N. (1976). *The Chicano experience in Chicago, 1929–1970.* Unpublished doctoral dissertation, University of Illinois, Chicago Circle Campus.

Landau, S. (1992). *Encyclopedia of the American left* (M. J. Buhle, P. Buhle, & D. Georgakas, Eds.) (Illini Books ed., pp. 172–174). Urbana: University of Illinois Press.

Lather, P. (2004/1986). Research as praxis. In R. A. Gaztambide-Fernandez, H. A. Harding, & T. Sorde-Marti (Eds.), *Harvard Educational Review Reprint Series, 38* (pp. 41–60). Cambridge: Harvard Educational Review.

"Latinos versus CTA." (1972). Working paper, APO.

Limón, J. E. (1994). *Dancing with the devil: Society and cultural poetics in Mexican-American South Texas* (Illus. ed.). Madison: University of Wisconsin Press.

Loewen, J. W. (1995). *Lies my teacher told me: Everything your American history textbook got wrong* (Illus. ed.). New York: Touchstone, Simon & Shuster.

López, M. R. (2001). *Chicano timespace: The poetry and politics of Ricardo Sanchez* (Illus. ed.). College Station: Texas A&M University Press.

Macedo, D., Freire, P., Kincheloe, J. L., McLaren, P., & Steinberg, S. (2006). *Literacies of power: What Americans are not allowed to know* (Rev., expanded ed.). Boulder, Col.: Westview.

Mariscal, G. (2005). *Brown-eyed children of the sun: Lessons from the Chicano movement, 1965–1975.* Albuquerque: University of New Mexico Press.

Mariscal, J. (2002, July–August). Left turns in the Chicano Movement, 1965–1975. *Monthly Review,* 59–69.

Martínez, E. (1998). De colores *means all of us: Latina views for a multi-colored century.* Boston: South End.

Mata, J. R. (2004). *Creating a critical Chicana narrative: Writing the Chicanas at Farah into labor history.* Unpublished dissertation, Washington State University, Pullman.

McCree-Bryan, M. L., & Davis, A. F. (1990). Introduction. In B. McCree, M. L. Davis, & A. F. Davis (Eds.), *100 years at Hull-House* (Rev. and expanded ed.). Bloomington: Indiana University Press.

McNeely, John H. (2009). "Holding Institute." "The Handbook of Texas Online." Texas State Historical Society. http://www.tshaonline.org/handbook/online/articles/kbh07

Memmi, A. (1965). *The colonizer and the colonized.* Phoenix: Orion.

Menchaca, M. (2001). *Recovering history, constructing race: The Indian, black, and white roots of Mexican Americans.* Austin: University of Texas Press.

Menchú, R. (1983). *I, Rigoberta Menchú: An Indian woman in Guatemala.* London: Verso.

Mirandé, A. (1987). *Gringo justice.* Notre Dame: University of Notre Dame.

Montejano, D. (2010). *Quixote's soldiers: A local history of the Chicano Movement, 1966–1981.* Austin: University of Texas Press.

Moore, R., Jr. (2001). *Weathermen.* San Jose, Calif.: Writers Club.

Mora, C. (2007). *Latinos in the West: The student movement and academic labor in Los Angeles.* Lanham, Md.: Rowman & Littlefield.

Mora, P. (1993). *Nepantla.* Albuquerque: University of New Mexico Press.

Moraga, C. (1993). *The last generation: Prose and poetry.* Boston: South End.

Morris, A. D. (1984). *The origins of the civil rights movement: Black communities organizing for change.* New York: Free Press.

Muñoz, C. (1989). *Youth, identity, and power: The Chicano movement.* London: Verso.

Navarro, A. (2000). *La Raza Unida: A Chicano challenge to the U.S. two-party dictatorship.* Philadelphia: Temple University Press.

Neumann, O. (2008). *Up against the wall motherf**ker: A memoir of the sixties with notes for next time.* New York: Seven Stories.

Ogbu, J. (1974). The next generation: Ethnography of education in an urban neighborhood. In E. Hammel (Ed.), *Studies in Anthropology* (p. 275). New York: Academic.

Ogbu, J. (1991). *Minority status and schooling: A comparative study of immigrant and involuntary minorities.* New York: Garland.

Oglesby, C. (2008). *Ravens in the storm: A personal history of the 1960s antiwar movement.* New York: Scribner.

O'Malley, S. G. (1992). *Encyclopedia of the American left* (M. J. Buhle, P. Buhle, & D. Georgakas, Eds.) (Illini Books ed.). Urbana: University of Illinois Press.

Oropeza, L. (2005). *¡Raza sí! ¡Guerra no!: Chicano protest and patriotism during the Viet Nam War era.* Berkeley: University of California Press.

Ovando, J. C. (1977). *Factors influencing high school Latino students' aspirations to go to college: The urban Midwest.* San Francisco: R and E Research Associates.

Padilla, F. (1985). *Latino ethnic consciousness: The case of Mexican Americans and Puerto Ricans in Chicago.* Notre Dame: University of Notre Dame Press.

Pardun, R. (2001). *Prairie radical: A journey through the sixties.* Los Gatos, Calif. Shire.

Parra, R. (2004). Latinos in the Midwest: Civil rights and community organization. In G. Cardenas (Ed.), *La causa: Civil rights, social justice and the struggle for equality in the Midwest* (pp. 1–18). Houston: Arte Publico.

Pathey-Chávez, G. (1993). High school as an arena for cultural conflict and acculturation for Latino Angelinos. *Anthropology and Education Quarterly, 24*(1), 33–60.

Pérez, L. (2000). *El coyote: The rebel.* Houston: Arte Publico.

Petras, J., & Morley, M. (1974). *How Allende fell: Study in United States–Chilean relations.* Nottingham, England: Spokesman.

Pilsen Neighbors Community Council. (n.d.). *Pilsen Neighbors Community Council.* http://pilsenneighbors.org/index.php?option=com_content&task=view&id=69&Itemid=108

Piven, F. S., & Cloward, R. A. (1979). *Poor people's movements: Why they succeed, how they fail.* New York: Vintage.

Poniatowska, E. (1975). *Massacre in Mexico.* New York: Viking.

Pulido, L. (2006). *Black, brown, yellow & left: Radical activism in Los Angeles.* Berkeley: University of California Press.

Ramírez, C. (2009). *The woman in the zoot suit: Gender nationalism and the cultural politics of memory.* Durham: Duke University Press.

Ramírez, L. G., Perales-Ramos, J., & Arellano, J. A. (2010). Marchando al futuro: Latino immigrant rights leadership in Chicago. In A. Pallares & N. Flores-Gonzalez (Eds.), *Marcha!: Latino Chicago and the immigrant rights movement* (pp. 123–145). Urbana: University of Illinois Press.

Rendon, A. B. (1971). *Chicano manifesto: The history and aspirations of the second largest minority in America.* New York: Collier.

Richmond, A. (1973). *A long view from the left: Memoirs of an American revolutionary.* Boston: Houghton Mifflin.

Rudd, M. (2009). *My life with SDS and the Weathermen.* New York: Morrow.

Rudy Lozano his life, his people. (n.d.). Chicago: Taller de Estudios Comunitarios.

Sale, K. (1973). *SDS.* New York: Vintage.

San Francisco Bay Area Farah Strike Support Committee. (1974). *Union drive in the Southwest: Chicanos strike at Farah* [Brochure]. San Francisco: United Front.

Sherman, S. (2007). *America's child: A woman's journey through the radical sixties.* (1st ed.). Willimantic, Conn.: Curbstone.

Spring, J. (2001). *Deculturalization and the struggle for equality: A brief history of the education of dominated cultures in the United States* (3rd ed.). Boston: McGraw-Hill.

Stavans, I. (1996). *Bandido: Oscar Zeta Acosta and the Chicano experience* (1st paperback ed.) New York: Icon.

Taylor, P. S. (1930a, October). Some aspects of Mexican immigration. *Journal of Political Economy, 38,* 609–615.

Taylor, P. S. (1930b). Employment of Mexicans in Chicago and the Calumet region. *Journal of the American Statistical Association 25,* 2006–2007.

Tijerina, L. (2000). *They called me "King Tiger": My struggle for the land and our rights* (J. A. Gutiérrez, Ed.). Houston: Arte Publico.

Treviño, J. S. (2001). *Eyewitness: A filmmaker's memoir of the Chicano movement.* Houston: Arte Publico.

Valadez, J. (1985). *Chicano political development: The role of political participation and agenda-building in expanding the biases of the polity, a case study.* Unpublished doctoral dissertation, University of Washington, Seattle.

Valdés, D. N. (1991). *Al Norte: Agricultural workers in the Great Lakes region, 1917–1970.* Austin: University of Texas Press.

Valdés, D. N. (2000). *Barrios Norteños: St. Paul and Midwestern Mexican communities in the twentieth century.* Austin: University of Texas Press.

Valencia, R. R. (1997). Conceptualizing the notion of deficit thinking. In R. R. Valencia (Ed.), *The evolution of deficit thinking: Educational thought and practice* (pp. 1–12). Stanford Series on Educational & Public Policy. London: Falmer.

Valle, V. M., & Torres, R. D. (2000). *Latino metropolis.* Minneapolis: University of Minnesota Press.

Valls, J. (1936/2000). A poignant defense of the whiteness of Mexicans. In F. A. Rosales (Ed.), *Testimonio: A documentary history of the Mexican-American struggle for civil rights* (p. 173) [Interview]. The Hispanic Civil Rights Series. Houston: Arte Publico.

Vargas, Z. (2005). *Labor rights are civil rights: Mexican American workers in twentieth-century America.* Princeton: Princeton University Press.

Varon, J. (2004). *Bringing the war home: The Weather Underground, the Red Army Faction, and revolutionary violence in the sixties and seventies.* Berkeley: University of California Press.

Vaughan, M. K. (1997). *Cultural politics in revolution: Teachers, peasants, and schools in Mexico, 1930–1940.* Tucson: University of Arizona Press.

Vigil, E. B. (1999). *The crusade for justice: Chicano militancy and the government's war on dissent.* Madison: University of Wisconsin Press.

Villa, R. H. (2000). *Barrio-logos: Space and place in urban Chicano literature and culture.* Austin: University of Texas Press.

Wilkerson, C. (2007). *Flying close to the sun.* New York: Seven Stories.

Zeiger, D. (Producer and director). (2006). *Sir! No sir!* [Film].

Contributors

Yenelli Flores

Yenelli selected for herself the pseudonym of an indigenous woman she met in her travels across Mexico. Yenelli followed in the footsteps of her activist parents, who fought for the rights of Mexican workers and immigrants. In the 1960s, Yenelli found a home among the community of international students and college activists at UICC. She became a member of SDS, organized around the rights of farmworkers, and opposed the national oppression of Blacks and Latinos in the United States as well as intervention in the political and economic affairs of developing nations, including Vietnam.

In the 1970s, Yenelli joined the ranks of student militants across the nation who left their campuses for factories and communities to establish new organizing sites, attempting to integrate working people in efforts to promote social change. Yenelli was known in the community as a fearless and tireless organizer, a vocal representative of the Comité, the left Mexicano/Chicano activist network in Chicago. Yenelli returned to Pilsen in 2004 and is active in antiwar, anti-intervention activities and campaigns for social justice. She maintains much of the same fervor from her days as a Movement leader.

María Gamboa

María was an actor and writer for Compañia Trucha. Teatro was not only a labor of love and a lifestyle but also a venue for expressing her political ideals. Trucha's plays were anchored in struggles of the Chicano Movement and those of the community. As a long-time Pilsen resident, she was very much aware of the hardships and inequality that poor women suffered. She incorporated these issues into her cultural and political work.

An ardent Chicana nationalist, María came to accept the necessity for a more encompassing, class-based analysis promoting social change. Through her involvement in the Comité and Casa Aztlán, the energy center of Chicano politics in Pilsen, María helped to construct a bridge between cultural nationalism and transformative politics. Her agenda has always been to overturn the social structures of domination as well as the oppressive relationships that operate within the family. María was associated with the 1980s Chicago school reform. She worked on staff and served on the board of Casa Aztlán for many years. In the 1990s, she resigned when the veteran Aztlán leadership was challenged by a Mexican nationalist current in the community. She is committed to educating younger generations of leaders, transferring to them the wisdom learned in the process of struggle.

Isaura González

Isaura was born on the Mexico-Texas border in 1944. Her family migrated to Illinois and settled in Chicago's skid-row district. They later relocated to a neighborhood on the city's Northwest Side. Growing up in multiracial, economically disadvantaged working-class communities contributed to her belief in the possibility of a class-based, interracial coalition supportive of social change.

In the early 1970s, Isaura was affiliated with the IRC caucus of WSA-SDS, UFAI, and various Latino student groups, including SELA. As a member of the Comité, Isaura worked to establish a Latino-student recruitment and academic-support program at UICC. She also was instrumental in the creation of the RCOCC. Her hope was that the Cultural Center would serve to broaden student knowledge and appreciation of Latino culture, including the legacy of struggle that is so much a part of working-class experience across borders.

Art, politics, and Mexican culture were central elements in her life. While still a teenager, Isaura enrolled in classes at the Art Institute of Chicago and later traveled to Mexico to study art. She earned an arts-education degree at UICC. After working in the Chicago Public Schools for many years, she returned to college and completed a second bachelor's degree in photography at Columbia College. She participated in art residency programs and worked with cultural groups in Chicago to make arts an integral part of Mexican community life. Isaura was born with congenital heart problems, which caused her doctors to predict she would not live beyond her teenage years. She lived life as if every day mattered. She passed away unexpectedly on February 24, 2010, at the age of sixty-six.

Victoria Pérez

Born in 1939 on Chicago's North Side, Victoria was active in the Mexican community around Hull-House, including the Centro Social Mexicano located on the western fringes of the Near West Side. She has long been involved in cultural activities. As a young girl, she began to perform with the Chicago Fiesta Guild, a Mexican culture and folkloric dance group. She celebrated the *fiestas patrias* as part of her community involvement but also, following the example of her family, sought to address racism and discrimination.

Victoria was influenced by her father's nationalist politics. Her own involvement was a product of her belief in the necessity of struggle to address concrete issues. She joined her sisters in support of the UFW and later became active in the Comité. In the early 1970s, Victoria moved to Pilsen in order to be part of the political and cultural renaissance taking place in that community.

Teatro was Victoria's political venue. This allowed her to combine her interest in culture with her commitment as a fighter for social justice. Victoria was active in the campaign to stop medical abuse at Rush Presbyterian Saint Luke's Hospital and the struggle to increase the representation of Latinos in the health care workforce. Victoria spent most of her working life in educational environments. At the age of forty, she returned to school and became a licensed practical nurse. She and her *compañero* of forty years reside in Chicago.

Leonard G. Ramírez

A college-student organizer in the 1970s, Leonard helped form the IRC caucus of WSA-SDS and later joined others to begin the UFAI. He was a founding member of SELA and served as the major spokesperson for the SELA-UPRS coalition that spearheaded the effort to establish a Latino cultural center at UICC. As a member of the Comité network, he assisted in building a Latino support program at UICC.

Leonard has a long history working in educational initiatives. He began teaching GED courses for the BASTA (Halt) drug-intervention program in association with Right to Read at El Centro de la Causa in the early 1970s. He taught ESL to immigrants and worked as an educational researcher. He was a member of the collective of young college students and graduates who established Latino Youth High School in the mid-1970s. In 1980, he returned to UICC and joined the staff of LARES and eventually assumed the responsibilities of director.

Leonard served on then Senator Miguel del Valle's Community Advisory Committee on Higher Education (CACHE). He currently sits on the board of the Illinois Latino Council on Higher Education (ILACHE) and is a member of the New Majority Coalition, an alliance of Black and Latino educators supporting college access for underrepresented students, staff, and faculty.

Magda Ramírez-Castañeda

Exposed to labor struggles and injustice early in life, the 1960s jettisoned Magda into campus student politics, women's issues, and the Mexicano/ Chicano Movement. Like the other women in the Comité, Magda was well known in activist circles as a strong, assertive, and independent Chicana. She became a highly visible spokesperson for Chicana/o causes and was perhaps the first Latina in Illinois to speak publicly in defense of reproductive rights.

Magda was a founding member of LASU, possibly the first Latino student organization at UICC. She became active in APO during its heyday and the CSFS. She attended the National Chicano Youth Liberation Conference in Denver and spearheaded the delegation that challenged the limitations placed on female activists at that meeting and in the Movement as a whole. She participated in the talks that led to the formation of La Raza Unida Party in Illinois and became its first state chairperson. She was elected to be an Illinois delegate at the Raza Unida's first national convention, held in El Paso, Texas.

For most of her professional life, she has held positions as a civil servant. She has always chosen to work with people of color and the disadvantaged. She remains active today in church initiatives and Mexican-state hometown associations that support education and municipal development projects. She is also a member of the Comité Anti-Militarización (Committee against the Militarization of Youth, CAMI/CAMY) based in Chicago's Pilsen community. It was Magda's initial idea to document the experiences of the Comité women.

Cristina Vital

As a young woman, Cristina found herself in the swirl of social change and soon decided to become a part of it. She participated in community as well as student politics. As an undergraduate at UICC, she was on the leadership committee of the Chicano/Boricua Student Union. As a Latina student leader, she penned a position paper arguing for the equality of women in the Movement.

Moving to Pilsen, an impoverished working-class neighborhood, introduced her to a face of oppression and inequality that she had previously not witnessed. She joined the Raza Unida Party and was selected to attend its first national convention as a delegate from Illinois. She participated in the initial discussions that led to the founding of Mujeres Latinas en Acción. She was cofounder of the only progressive Chicano bookstore in Chicago, Librería Nuestro Continente, and was involved in CSFS and other Comité campaigns. She was a regular Movement ghostwriter, drafting speeches for various community events and political programs.

Cristina began her education at Wright and Loop junior colleges. She completed her degree at UICC and later went on to earn a master's degree at the University of Michigan, Ann Arbor. Her professional life was spent working in Pilsen until her retirement in 2004 at the age of fifty-two. Being a member of a community of activists struggling toward common goals remains one of her fondest memories.

Index

LATINOS IN CHICAGO
AND THE MIDWEST

Pots of Promise: Mexicans and Pottery at Hull-House, 1920–40   *Edited by*
    Cheryl R. Ganz and Margaret Strobel
Moving Beyond Borders: Julian Samora and the Establishment of Latino Studies
    Edited by Alberto López Pulido, Barbara Driscoll de Alvarado, and Carmen Samora
¡Marcha! Latino Chicago and the Immigrant Rights Movement   *Edited by*
    Amalia Pallares and Nilda Flores-González
Bringing Aztlán to Chicago: My Life, My Work, My Art   *José Gamaliel González,*
    edited and with an Introduction by Marc Zimmerman
Latino Urban Ethnography and the Work of Elena Padilla   *Edited by Mérida M. Rúa*
Defending Their Own: U.S. Puerto Rican Literature, Art, and Film   *Marc Zimmerman*
Chicanas of 18th Street: Narratives of a Movement from Latino Chicago
    Leonard G. Ramírez with Yenelli Flores, María Gamboa, Isaura González,
    Victoria Pérez, Magda Ramírez-Castañeda, and Cristina Vital

The University of Illinois Press
is a founding member of the
Association of American University Presses.

———————————————

Composed in 10.5/13 Adobe Minion Pro
with Meta display
by Jim Proefrock
at the University of Illinois Press
Manufactured by Thomson-Shore, Inc.

University of Illinois Press
1325 South Oak Street
Champaign, IL 61820-6903
www.press.uillinois.edu